My Mother's Daughter

My Mother's Daughter

a memoir

RONA MAYNARD

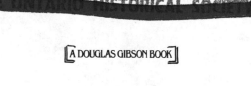

A DOUGLAS GIBSON BOOK

McCLELLAND & STEWART

Library and Archives Canada Cataloguing in Publication

Maynard, Rona

My mother's daughter : a memoir / Rona Maynard.

ISBN 978-0-7710-5701-4

1. Maynard, Rona. 2. Maynard, Fredelle Bruser. 3. Mothers and daughters.

4. Journalists–Canada–Biography. I. Title.

PN4913.M44A3 2007   070.4'8347092   C2007-900456-3

We acknowledge the financial support of the Government of Canada through the Book Publishing Industry Development Program and that of the Government of Ontario through the Ontario Media Development Corporation's Ontario Book Initiative. We further acknowledge the support of the Canada Council for the Arts and the Ontario Arts Council for our publishing program.

Typeset in Caslon by M&S, Toronto
Printed and bound in Canada

A Douglas Gibson Book

This book is printed on acid-free paper that is 100% recycled, ancient-forest friendly (100% post-consumer recycled).

McClelland & Stewart Ltd.
75 Sherbourne Street
Toronto, Ontario
M5A 2P9
www.mcclelland.com

1   2   3   4   5   11   10   09   08   07

In memory of Fredelle Bruser Maynard

July 9, 1922 – October 3, 1989

CONTENTS

PROLOGUE

My mother gave birth to me twice. The first time is a matter of record. The second, almost forty years later, took place at her deathbed.

She lay in her own room with the cathedral ceiling and the seaglass-green walls. Her red lipstick was freshly applied, her skin still sun-burnished from afternoon teas in the garden. I could have sworn she was only resting up for her next project – a speech, a book, a cocktail party for a hundred guests, with all the appetizers cooked from scratch. In fact, she had reached the final stages of brain cancer. Weeks had passed since she could move or speak. "Talk to her," the visiting nurse had said. "Hearing is the last sense to go."

All my life I had been talking with my mother, and most of the time she took the lead. No one else I knew could tell such stories, or declared opinions with such pungency. Now my turn had come to do the talking. I took my mother's hand, which the nurse had manicured to unnatural perfection. My mother should have had parsley under her fingernails, or a thin line of dirt from planting tulips. When no one was looking, she used to bite her nails to the quick. I stroked the soft place on her wrist where her watch had always been. "It's me," I said.

Did she know? Or had she already gone?

My mother's house had never been so quiet. What I said to her that day felt more like meditation than speech. One thought opened onto another like a series of doors swinging wide. Behind the last door I found a dream in which I won a job that took me to the top of my profession. I got there by doing what had always seemed too dangerous: competing against women of drive and talent. I became what I had never been before – a leader.

If my mother had been well, I would not have told her any of this. She would have engulfed me with reasons why I was the woman for the job and all the others mere pretenders. She would have prodded and advised. I needed to believe that this dream was mine, not hers, and fear of her torrential enthusiasm would have nailed my tongue to my mouth. I held her hand and spoke: "I'm feeling restless. I want a new challenge. I want to be the next editor of *Chatelaine*. What do you think?"

No point asking her that. It was a courtesy to her, or a salve to my own pain at seeing her immobile and silent. Then my mother squeezed my hand.

No moment in my life – not marrying my husband, bearing my son or eventually winning the job – has changed me like that moment. At my mother's deathbed, I crossed the threshold between the life I had led in her orbit, craving her attention yet wary of its blazing intensity, and the life I made without her as a more or less grown-up woman. All the tangled frustrations and desires of my first forty years point toward my mother's blessing. All the rewards I later found are rooted in her final affirmation that I could succeed on my own terms without her hovering, shaping, controlling hand.

I have never loved anyone more than my mother, Fredelle Maynard – my first love but also my first and most formidable competitor. To become myself, I had to challenge her vision of who I was and what a woman should be. I had to face the irrational yet haunting fear that living my way would negate hers, and cost me a portion of her love. This book is the story of that love – the price it exacted and the power it eventually unlocked.

The model for all my other loves, it has been by far the most conflicted of them all. I craved my mother's company while resenting her warnings and prohibitions. I wanted to know that she was always ready to console me, amuse me and bake me a pie on my birthday, yet I found her competence diminishing. She was always right, she was always wrong. I never stopped needing her reassurance, or finding fault with how she gave it. No matter what she did, she fell at least a tad short of what I wanted and expected: perfection.

As long as she lived, I felt a little smaller than life. I remember her planting euonymus in what passed for my garden, driving her spade into the rocky soil with her broad, size-nine foot because I didn't have the strength to the job myself. She made things grow; I killed them off (even euonymus, despite her brave predictions). At lunch dates, she wore Garbo hats and commanding jewellery that clinked when she walked; I dressed in slivers of unobtrusive black. She had a thriving career as a writer and broadcaster (four books, hundreds of articles, two TV series); I was just starting out. Her voice could fill a room with stories, liberally embellished for comic effect; I had a low, soft voice and learned early to be careful how I used it.

Mother, that's not the way it happened.
   Oh, relax! I tell a story the way it should have happened.

My mother's voice used to echo in my head, proclaiming her views on everything from misplaced modifiers (a crime against language) to baking with margarine (a crime against cookies). I couldn't pay full retail price for a winter coat without hearing her urge me to wait for the sale (which had to be at least fifty percent off; lesser reductions didn't count). Sometimes my husband would tell me, with a sigh of exasperation, "You sound just like your mother." I did. And I expressed my mother's opinions with a vehemence that I rarely mustered for my own.

I once phoned a bewildered freelance writer to tell her, in my mother's voice, why I was turning down her story idea. At the newsmagazine where I was then working, it was standard operating procedure to toss unwanted proposals without a word. But I just had to tear a strip off the upstart who had turned her not inconsiderable talents to a proposal like this. It concerned a then new medical procedure being offered to women with a family history of breast cancer: they could choose to have their healthy breasts removed now instead of risking cancer later. My mother had written crusading articles about unnecessary mastectomies. Knowing what she'd say about the proposal on my desk, I said it for her in a voice that shook with ferocity: "Do you have the foggiest notion how hard women have fought to prevent the needless mutilation of our bodies? What you're doing is worse than off the mark; it's downright dangerous. Surely a woman with your skills can find something else to write about!" The writer eventually convinced me to give her the assignment, but I did so with a stab of guilt.

At such moments I remembered Anne Sexton's famous line: "A woman *is* her mother. That's the main thing." It was my mother, of all people, who introduced me to Sexton's poetry. Every fold of my brain seemed to bear her stamp.

I had all the trappings of adulthood – job, mortgage, family – yet in her presence I was still a little girl who cringed at her anger and dreaded more than anything the loss of her love. I wanted to speak in my own voice, but the world didn't seem big enough to accommodate two narratives, hers and mine. I didn't admit this, even to myself, until I was past fifty. The very idea seemed humiliating.

Growing up with her was like being chiselled from a boulder. With every stroke, my mother aimed to prepare me for the dangers she believed I would face as a woman in a world controlled by men.

She was one of the women for whom Betty Friedan wrote *The Feminine Mystique*. Despite a Ph.D. from Radcliffe and a boxful of medals, she could never get a permanent academic post. Her subsequent career as a writer, despite its many satisfactions, remained in her mind an improvisation to replace the career she had earned, only to see it snatched away. She never stopped resenting the men who had exiled her from academia. The experience made her a feminist long before the word entered everyone's vocabulary. In the days of coffee klatches and *Father Knows Best*, she told me that a woman in our town, Anna Rivers, had put a bullet through her head. People were shaking their heads: *How could she? That lovely home, those darling little boys.* To my mother, who barely knew Anna Rivers, the suicide was no mystery. Mrs. Rivers, as everyone called her, was really Dr. Rivers, but she had never practised in our town because the male doctors wouldn't make room for a woman. The only work available to her was giving out polio vaccine in the school gym. According to my mother, she died of grief for her lost career.

The men who ran the workplace were not the only ones who aroused my mother's indignation. My father, a dashing professor and artist, turned out to be an alcoholic, another child in the house instead of a responsible parent. Her all-consuming project was concealing the truth about her husband – especially from her own mother, who had fought the marriage with tears, pleas and prophecies of doom. My maternal grandparents were Jewish immigrants; they remembered pogroms in the old country. Of all the men their Fredelle could have loved, she had the audacity to choose a gentile.

Despite her bold feminist streak, my mother was a woman of her time. She projected the unspoken belief that a woman has three defining duties: to gratify her mother, to be a good wife and to raise happy, confident children. If she has any energy left, she is free to invest it in herself. I watched these rules constrain her and I knew by adolescence that they were not for me. As a pampered daughter of the baby boom, I expected a better life than my mother's. She wanted to give it to me, but as she had defined it, and stripped of every thorn and crag that might impede my progress. Expecting gratitude for her efforts, she got none.

At fifteen, I once came home in a new string of multi-coloured beads from Mexico. "I wish I had a string of beads like that," my mother said. "Why don't you give it to me?" I explained why this proposition didn't seem fair. She had her own Mexican beads, a whole boxful of them. My mother wouldn't let the matter drop. After all she'd given things to me, it was about time I gave something to her. A trifle was all she asked. How could I refuse? I knew what I was in for if I kept the beads – icy looks, withering remarks. Sighing, I gave up my treasure. She threw it back at me: "Keep your precious beads! I wouldn't touch them now! They're *trayf*." Forbidden, unclean, unfit for human contact: that's what *trayf* means in Yiddish. I never wore the beads again.

My mother thought I withheld my love; I thought she lavished hers on me with too much force – and exacted too high a price for her devotion. And so, for a good many years, love itself appeared dangerous to me – a fatal, essential temptation. I was a melancholy child, then a chronically depressed young woman, weary with the effort of loving.

"My mother is my friend," I used to say toward the end of her life, after she had divorced my father and moved on with newfound zest. It wasn't a lie but didn't capture the truth. We looked and felt like friends, curled up on her couch while we talked until dusk about whatever entered our minds. Yet our bond was more mysterious than any friendship I have known. My friends are equals; in my mother's face I still saw glimmers of the authority figure who used to red-pencil my book reports before the teacher saw them. By this time, of course, she no longer saw herself that way. But every conversation between us held the faint echoes of all the other conversations that had mapped my world ever since I learned to speak.

I eventually found a way to be myself that encompassed her love and her legacy. But before I could complete this process, I had to lose her. Only then could I begin to see the woman she really was in all her confounding, magnificent complexity, and not the intermingled fears and illusions that had distorted my view.

I used to think I'd never known a more fearless woman. With her quick stride and robust voice, she seemed invincible. But in fact there was someone who inspired a primal fear in her, which was all the more powerful for its enveloping layers of devotion and awe. That person was her own mother. With a grade-six education and the will of a warrior queen, my grandmother steered her family through the Depression, when they never knew for sure where they'd be living next year, or on what. Two daughters competed for Grandma's love, and my mother was convinced she had won the battle early. Victory brought her no comfort. The more Grandma pampered and protected her favourite daughter, the more she expected in return. Words were my mother's medium, yet on the subject of the woman who formed her she was oddly tentative, a lost wanderer at the edge of a fairy-tale wood. She began but never finished a book about her mother. It was called *I Cannot Let You Go*.

⁓◦◦◦⁓

I did not set out to tell a story of mother love and its consequences. I was going to tell the story of a pessimist's journey toward hope and vitality. I liked to think my own choices had cleared the way – a good marriage, a rewarding career and close to twenty years of conscious effort to rise above the past. Living the advice that I would later share with *Chatelaine*'s readers, I invested in yoga classes, personal training and more than one course of therapy. I connected with women who inspired me and learned from their stories, while keeping my mother's example at arm's length. Even after her death, she seemed faintly threatening, as if to write more than briefly about her impact would be to place myself in her power.

And yet, looking back, I saw her everywhere. My successes are at least partly tributes to her. My missteps have been acts of impulsive rebellion against her rules (the Mr. Wrongs of my student days) or grudging compliance with them (the dress I wouldn't let myself buy at full price, even though it was the only one in my size and too beautiful to languish on the rack for someone else to find. I told myself that I could manage without her while secretly longing for some motherly assistance from the sidelines. It had to come from a trusted older woman who cared about my doubts and fears without overreacting, a surrogate mother who could guide me with offhand tenderness because she had never been charged with preparing me for life. I have found several surrogate mothers, and without their support I would be a less confident woman. But of course it was my mother – my flawed, human, dominating mother – who conditioned me to seek out these wise female mentors in the first place.

Growing up, I often heard her offer blithely bracing advice to younger female friends. "Your mother was my Auntie Mame," one of them later told me. "She never judged me. No one has ever accepted me the way Fredelle did." How I envied that woman! My mother was never so accepting of me. In everything I did or didn't do, she saw a reflection on the job she had done in raising me. She would compliment me on my latest magazine piece and then say, "I'm surprised you didn't catch the grammatical mistake in the second paragraph." She took me to task for wasting money on dinner at a famously posh New York restaurant called The Quilted Giraffe (when the place appeared on a list of America's most overrated restaurants, she phoned me, chortling, to share the news).

I learned to brush off most of her criticisms. *There she goes again*, I would think. But she made one judgment, repeatedly and forcefully, that never failed to wound me. She thought I cared too much about my career, and not nearly enough about raising my son. I was a neglectful mother, she said. In the hundreds of carbons she left of her letters to family and friends, there are comments that still make me wince. "Rona has not mothered

Benjamin, and his behaviour is worrying," she observes, as if every schoolyard fight and late science project were my fault. I want to demand an explanation for the blame she has callously heaped on me. Then I realize that she wasn't any harder on me than she had been on herself. In one of her letters, written when I was in my thirties, I find this: "With Rona, I very easily feel guilty. Is it *my* fault that Rona's self-esteem is so precarious?"

Perhaps she feared that my son's misdemeanours could ultimately be traced to some failing of hers. I'm guessing; we never discussed that subject. It was simply too painful for us both.

—⬥—

At my mother's side, I learned what it means to listen to a woman, not just her words but her silences. My mother's silences reflected her fear of speaking unacceptable truths about the roles she played as a daughter, wife and mother. Only in midlife did she find the courage to stop censoring herself, and even then there were some things she could not say. From her example, I too acquired the habit of self-censorship. Critical by nature, I grew up asking tough questions and then biting my tongue when my mother made it clear that I'd gone too far. The story of my life has been, in large part, a story about learning to speak the whole truth as I see it.

I learned to do this in the company of women. Many of those women were interview subjects who shared the true stories of their lives with me. Sometimes they would tell me, as I closed my journalist's notebook, that hardly anyone on earth had yet heard this story. It had seemed too alarming, too shameful to tell, although in fact there was nothing in the story that I hadn't heard from someone else, perhaps even my mother. Men who left – if not physically by running off with somebody else, then emotionally by retreating into addiction, as my father had done. Children whose daily care brought as much fatigue and frustration as delight. The allure of work and the competing tug of family. In counterpoint, I heard about women's life-changing discoveries: love that turned up like an unexpected guest, or a just-for-fun pursuit that revealed a great talent or opened up a new career. Over time these intimate stories enhanced one another like the layered background vocals in a soul song. And in the foreground, carrying the melody, I heard my mother. If not for my mother, I would never have become the editor of a magazine that stands or falls on its ability to bond with women and find the common thread in their experience.

⁓◦◦⁓

Some families produce actors – or doctors, or politicians, or chuckwagon racers. In my family the women tell stories. We do it in cafés, hot tubs and all the other places where stories are women's common language, but we don't stop there. We write memoirs. My mother wrote two books about her life: *Raisins and Almonds*, a lyrical evocation of her prairie childhood, and *The Tree of Life*, in which she wrote more frankly about sorrows and struggles while still biting her tongue on the subject of Grandma. In 1998 it was my younger sister Joyce's turn. Her memoir, *At Home in the World*, created an instant sensation with the chapters on her destructive adolescent love affair with the most famous recluse in modern letters – J. D. Salinger, author of *The Catcher in the Rye*. Yet the real subject of my sister's book is not sex and scandal; it's the Maynard family, and Fredelle in particular. Her relationship with Joyce had a seductive, overheated character that could not have been more different from her flinty treatment of me. A harrowing scene depicts our parents sending eighteen-year-old Joyce off to meet Salinger (and spend the weekend with him) in Mary Janes and an alphabet-print dress like the one she wore at age six. They don't ask why a fifty-three-year-old man is inviting their child to his lair. Worse, our mother has actually overseen the sewing of the dress, created especially for Salinger. I had left home; I didn't witness the scene. Had I been there, I might have protested, but perhaps I'm kidding myself. To challenge my mother's view of things was always risky, and she very much liked the idea of a celebrated writer in our family.

I was editing *Chatelaine* when Joyce sent me the printed proofs of her memoir. Reading it left me sick with shame for us all, but especially for our mother, whom I loved beyond measure in spite of everything. I didn't question Joyce's right to speak her truth, yet I wanted to shout to millions of people, "My mother was more than this. She was brave and brilliant and funny, and if you could have known her, she would have amazed you – unless she'd decided that you didn't deserve her attention, and then you'd discover what scorn could be." While the unspoken words resounded in my head, I longed to come from a different family. I didn't want to be my mother's daughter, much less write the whole truth about her impact on my life, as my sister had done.

I got on with a less threatening task, the redesign of *Chatelaine*. For ten years I was the smiling face atop my editor's column, "Woman to Woman." Readers would send me their children's drawings and anniversary photos, as if I were part of their family. Meanwhile my real family made fleeting appearances in "Woman to Woman." What I wrote there was in no way a lie, but didn't capture the truth. Only when I left my job – the blizzard of e-mails, the incessant meetings – did I have time to hear my own private thoughts. And what often came to mind was the first home I knew, my mother's house, where we all looked to her as the steadying hand of order. Her love represented nothing less than survival.

A family is supposed to be a refuge from the casual cruelty of the world, and at our best the Maynard family lived up to that ideal. But we were doubly wounded by my mother's anger and my father's alcoholism. I learned early that, if not for my mother, the bills would have gone unpaid while decaying leaves clogged the drainpipes and the car lurched off into the night with my drunken father at the wheel. It never crossed my mind that she might leave him. "He's a brilliant, original man," she always said in those days. Having scandalized her mother for his sake, she felt compelled to justify her choice. She never mentioned his drinking and brushed off its symptoms – the rages, the impenetrable despair – as the price of his extravagant gifts. I grew up terrified that she might die (it nearly happened once), leaving Joyce and me alone with the prince of darkness.

My mother always said that our family was special, blessed with talents denied to lesser mortals. In reality, we were typical of families where one parent cannot stop drinking. Someone had to make excuses (my mother). Someone had to create the illusion of cheer (my sister, the adorable sprite, the dancing clown). Someone else had to take the blame for the unspoken sorrow in our house (that became my role). My sister staged comedy routines in the living room; I was sent for therapy.

Long after our mother died, a friend of hers told me, "It must have been hard for you, knowing that Joyce was her favourite." The observation stopped me short. As a little girl competing with a prettier, bouncier sister, I would have been quick to agree. I no longer do. Our mother loved each of us in profoundly different ways, seeing Joyce as an extension of herself and me as a nettlesome adversary. While she often tried to subdue my complaints and change my doleful nature, she never expected to succeed. And despite my childhood fears, she never withdrew one iota of her love. She might have wanted to at times; she remembered every slight. But a mother cannot choose how much to love her children, any more than she can choose the tone and texture of her loving.

While my mother was alive, I saw her with a daughter's myopia, placing myself at the centre of her world. Imagining her before I came along was a challenge on a par with picturing my death. But of course she had known earlier passions, which included her first career as a professor of English literature. Later, with no classroom to teach in, she wove her favourite poems into everyday conversation wherever we happened to be, from the dinner table to the family car. She never explained these passages, trusting that their music would one day reveal the meaning. More often than not, she chose thoroughly adult poems about love and its imperfections. To me love was a fairytale state, gauzy and shimmering, but those mordant poets had other ideas. "Fair and foul are near of kin," my mother would say, quoting Yeats. I had no idea what she meant. Now I do. And I am grateful.

BETRAYAL

I thought my mother looked like Queen Elizabeth. The navy blue housedress she wore all day was just a passing disguise for the brilliance that I saw when she put on her gold brocade party dress and all the splendid trappings that went with it. Red lipstick, high heels, her black curls brushed until they gleamed. With an evening bag over her arm, she bent to kiss me goodnight. She was off to the "president's reception."

My mother at the White House! Soon generals and kings would be asking her to dance. I clapped my hands and she laughed. "No, Pussycat, not *that* president! The president of the university where Daddy teaches. He's having a party for Daddy and all the other professors."

I must have been four. What did I know? Only that my mother had such radiance and power, she could have stepped from a fairy tale. Rapunzel spun straw into gold; my mother transformed a cast-off curtain into the dress she wore that night, cut low to reveal her full bosom. She called me Pussycat after a nursery rhyme she liked to tell me: "Pussycat, pussycat, where have you been? I've been to London to look at the queen."

I didn't need to see the queen in London. I had her right here at home in Durham, New Hampshire, and she could do anything. Snap the head back onto my ballerina doll. Kiss my skinned knee better. Tend my cat while newborn kittens slipped from her hindquarters one by one, wet and wriggling. My mother explained the marvel of it all to me: "See how Chrissie knows just what to do for her babies. Look how she licks them clean." Up and down went Chrissie's rough pink tongue on the tiny flat-nosed faces. The kittens' ears looked round like monkeys' ears, but my mother assured me they would change soon enough. We watched as each blind, stumbling kitten sniffed out one of Chrissie's pink nipples, kneading her tummy with its paws. The smallest kitten kept losing his spot as the bigger ones pushed him aside. "Poor little duffer," my mother said. "He's not long for this world." The next time I checked my kittens, the smallest one was gone. My mother had known what was coming. She always did.

Every day while my father was busy at the university, she worked wonders in the kitchen with the ceramic mixing bowl that had once been her mother's. A lump of bread dough swelled fragrantly under its tea towel, springing to life when I poked it. Flour and butter became shortbread cookies with my choice of decoration: nuts, chocolate chips, coloured sprinkles.

Exactly what Daddy did, I wasn't sure. He drove our second-hand Buick with an air of cautious formality, his foot always poised above the brake and both hands rigid on the wheel. He wore a fedora and an English raincoat that had a sheen to it, like the multicoloured film of gasoline on a fresh puddle. Instead of practical tools like Mother's wooden spoon and sewing machine, he had a leather briefcase full of papers. Every day he collected more papers at the office, which intrigued me only for its view of the most beautiful building in town, the university library. It looked like a temple, with tall white columns and a promise carved in the stone pediment: "You shall know the truth and the truth shall make you free." Sometimes I would stand in Daddy's office window breathing in the mystery of those words, which he read to me because I couldn't yet read myself. What was this thing called truth and when would I be old enough to know it?

After work Daddy went to the basement, where he kept his easel. Mother never stopped working but Daddy had time to play with paints, the way I did in nursery school. On the wall he hung fine-art postcards: Cézanne, Modigliani, Rembrandt. I couldn't have identified a head of garlic, but I came to know the dead artists he loved.

He collected books about art and they were the ones he shared with me, not Mother Goose and A.A. Milne. My favourite was *The Last Flowering of the Middle Ages* by Baron Joseph van der Elst. We would sit on the couch together, studying jewel-like paintings by the Flemish masters until, through sheer repetition, I learned to tell the Memlings from the van Eycks. The women in these paintings looked like queens, with filigree crowns and flowing robes that pooled at their feet. Their velvet gowns were trimmed with glittering embroidery, so meticulously painted I could almost touch every golden thread. One held a pale, scrawny baby who looked as if he never laughed or cried. Around them was a landscape like no place I'd ever seen: flowers, castles, mountains wreathed in mist. It was called the Kingdom of Heaven, Daddy said.

Many pages on in the book, we arrived at a different place, where everything was dark or on fire. "Bosch!" I cried. My father jumped up. He called out to my mother, "My dear, did you hear what your daughter just said? She's just identified 'The Garden of Earthly Delights'! This child has the eye of an artist!" But, really, who else could paint a scene like the one we were looking at? No velvet robes for Hieronymus Bosch; his trademark was naked people who cowered and screamed as monsters unleashed their torments. Some of these creatures didn't even have bodies; they had dead trees for feet, a bird's beak where a face should be. Objects of beauty became instruments of torture, like the harp on which a man was strung up to die. My father looked sombre as he told me the place that Bosch had painted. A place called Hell.

My mother held the world together; my father unravelled it. She found things; he lost them. Car keys. Lecture notes. A Dacron shirt purchased at a specialty shop in Boston and abandoned on the bus to Durham. My father would career through the house, slamming doors and drawers in the search for whatever had just gone missing, as my mother trudged in his wake asking, "Now, dear, where was it when you last saw it?"

There was a hole somewhere in our house. Things fell into it, never to be seen again. My mother patched and tugged, but the hole could gape at any minute. Or Daddy would run out of cigarettes (this was before he quit smoking, and began to rail against other people's filthy addiction). Then he would crawl on his knees at the hearthside, poking through the ashes of last night's fire for a crumpled butt to smoke.

My parents were earth and air, flesh and soul. At four I already knew this. I put my trust in the secrets of earth and flesh. My mother held them in her hands. Strong hands, unadorned except for her gold wedding band, callused from pushing the trowel and the lawn mower yet soft from the milky Jergens lotion she applied night and day. The nails ragged from biting when Daddy had one of his moods. Sometimes he came home in a fury about mysterious conflicts in the English department. He would throw his briefcase on the kitchen table, shouting, "Second-raters, the lot of them!"

I used to dream about my parents. In one dream a huge black bird swooped down over our backyard and snatched my mother from her clothesline. Off it flew while she dangled from its crooked beak and waved goodbye to me, still holding a wooden clothespin. I shook my fists and screamed after her while the navy blue of her housedress got smaller and smaller until it disappeared from view. Now I was all alone with my father. Then what would become of me? I already knew; I'd seen that in another dream: Daddy at the wheel of a car, in the fedora he wore on every outing, with me in the back seat. Only it wasn't Daddy. It was his empty coat and the fedora, floating in mid-air. The car had no driver as it sped away with me, faster and faster.

In the beginning I had my mother to myself, tagging after her while she did the chores. I loved nothing more than the balm of her attention and I found that I could win it with words. One day I said something that so enchanted her, she called out to Daddy, "Your daughter has just composed a poem for me! Listen to this! What an ear she has!" Then she wrote my words down and saved them:

> I am a princess. You are a princess too.
> I could throw love to you.
> I could whirl you over my heart.

This was the way it should have been between my mother and me, not the way it really was. She was the queen, I was the princess. Without warning she could withdraw her attention. I remember the two of us sitting on the floor, where my dolls were having a tea party. The pink china pot slipped from her hand and her face glazed over. Why did she look so sad? Was my game really that boring to her?

My mother liked to say, "I'm a happy person." Most of the time she looked the part, with her room-filling laugh and her delight in singing, even though she couldn't carry a tune. Instead of signing letters with her name, she would draw a twirling dancer with a single exuberant line. So if she seemed troubled, I thought I must be to blame. And she did find fault with me; no doubt about that.

I liked the word *no*, the short, sharp finality of it. *No* made me feel bigger and taller, like a magic potion. I was stubborn, she said. Provoking. After one *no* too many, she did something she had never done before: she slapped my face. We glared at each other. "Didn't hurt," I said. Slap! "Didn't hurt!" Her weapon was the large commanding hand; mine was defiance. She must have hit me half a dozen times when I finally cried. She had a flailing, hesitant stroke that didn't hurt much; it was her fury that hurt. So I paid the tribute of tears.

One day she warned me that she kept a magic basket in the basement. If I continued to leave my toys on the dining room floor instead of putting them back where they belonged, she would drop them into the basket. The basket was the mouth of a bottomless pit where my toys would keep falling forever. "It's a laundry basket," I retorted. "You're pretending. You don't have a magic basket."

"That's what you think, silly! You can't see it because it's magic and I'm the only one who knows the spell." Now she had me. I'd better watch out for this basket of hers before it swallowed me up.

I couldn't be suspicious of my mother for long. She mattered too much. Her stories rooted me in the world. My father never said much about the past, but my mother shared the details of my history, going back to her longing for a little girl. Daughters were what women had in her family; she was one of two, her older sister had two. (If I had thought about this, I would have seen a rival in my future.) She named me Rona, for the woman she loved best – her mother. The name is derived from the Hebrew word for "joy." Her own name, Fredelle, had once been Freidele (which means "little joy" in Yiddish), until she gave it what seemed to her a jaunty modern flair. The three of us – Grandma, Mother and me – formed a hierarchy of joy, nested one inside the other like painted wooden dolls from Russia, where Grandma had lived when she was small.

My mother used to tell a story about the day we became a family. Daddy was driving her home from the maternity ward; I lay in my bassinet behind the front seat. For once Daddy's foot hovered over the gas pedal instead of the brake. The old Buick picked up speed on every hill in the undulating road until a police car loomed in the rear-view mirror. Next thing Daddy knew, a badge was flashing in his face: "In a bit of a hurry, aren't you, sir?"

"Good God, so I am!" exclaimed my father in his faintly British accent. "Terribly sorry, I don't go in for this sort of thing. But it's not every day that a man becomes a father. You see, I've just acquired a new daughter and the excitement must have run away with me."

My mother held her breath. Whatever the figure on the speeding ticket, we couldn't afford it on Daddy's salary. And she didn't like police officers. She thought they were uneducated yokels whose favourite pastime was intimidating their betters.

The officer peered into the bassinet. He didn't exclaim at my cuteness; I wasn't that kind of baby. But he chuckled at my father and waved us on with a warning. His last words were, "I'm a family man myself."

For more than twenty years my mother told the story this way. After she threw my father out, she told it differently. Daddy had been terrified that day, she said, a reluctant father yielding to my mother's ultimatum: no children, no marriage. So, at almost forty-six, he found himself a family man in desperate need of a drink. And another and another. "After you were born," my mother said, "he was drunk for a week."

⸺⟡⸺

I was born in October 1949: the Red Scare in high gear, an atom bomb just tested in the Soviet Union, the brand new People's Republic of China transfixing the free world. George Orwell had just published *1984*. At home in New Hampshire, my mother finally had her little Rona. But motherhood was never her only dream. She wanted a marriage of mind, soul and body; she wanted a career. On those two fronts all she had was disappointment.

That husband of hers! So handsome, with his broad, chiselled jaw and penetrating blue eyes. So original with a poem, a paint-brush or a microphone. When they met at the University of Manitoba, he had a radio program on the side, much admired by women (that voice!). He was a professor of English with a danger-ous reputation; she was the ferociously hard-working student assigned to help mark his papers. In the judgment of those on high, she would focus on the task and not on the roguish Max Maynard. The department head looked at my mother, a nineteen-year-old wunderkind in a homemade dress, and saw only the power of her legendary brain, which already contained a good chunk of the English canon, ready to be quoted in exam papers that scored unheard-of one hundred percents. My mother's memory was something of an embarrassment to her – a gift so freakish that it threatened to upstage her analytical powers. My father saw the full measure of her: the reach of intellect, the delicacy of perception, the gallant ambition of this Jewish girl from dirt-street towns who would be the first in her family to penetrate the citadel of learning. He saw her exotic looks, those eyes dark as dates, and pronounced her beautiful, his Fredelka. He wrote her love poems on napkins; he sang to her in that radio baritone: "Here am I, here am I / And I'll stay here 'til I die . . ."

She couldn't resist. She couldn't say nobody warned her.

So many times her parents warned her. They didn't even know about his drinking. What they saw was bad enough: a divorced man (not quite divorced – he still had a wife who wrote pleading letters), too old and, worst of all, not Jewish, a *goy* to the bone. The son of missionaries, Christian soldiers who believed there were two kinds of people in the world, the damned and the saved. Max might have broken with his parents' faith, but what kind of consolation was that? Can a man break with his *goyish* nature? Where my grandparents came from in the old country, the *goyim* looted Jewish stores, burned Jewish homes and raped Jewish women. Fredelle had been their great hope, "the clever one" of their two girls, indulged with elocution lessons and the twenty-volume *Book of Knowledge*. Grandma had asked her every day, "Have you accomplished?" and of course she always had, with rhyming couplets published in the Saskatoon paper and always the highest marks at school. After all their striving, they should lose Fredelle to the enemy? Grandpa warned, "He'll call you a dirty Jew." When that didn't work, he said, "Your mother can't take the shock. She'll have a heart attack. This will kill her."

My mother agonized. Break her mother's heart – literally?
No, no. Give up Max Maynard? Never. For six years she
dithered, earning her master's and then her doctorate with her
usual distinction while waiting for a Jewish suitor to arrive on
the scene and banish her dreams of Max. My father pursued and
cajoled: *Your parents will come around. It's time to grow up, to be the
woman you were meant to be.* With a Jewish friend of my
mother's, he listened to Yiddish records and asked for trans-
lations in the hope of breaking down the cultural barriers in his
path. Finally my mother relented. She followed Max to
Durham, New Hampshire, where he had found a job teaching
English at the state university. As she told it, UNH was then "a
glorified cow college," best known for its agriculture department.
But my father could not afford to be choosy. With only a bache-
lor's degree, he was lucky to find any academic job at all.

They married. Nobody died. It was my mother's hopes that
died. She found herself married to a man with a hidden stash of
empty bottles and a sudden, baffling squeamishness about sex.
Grandma had been right after all, not that my mother was about
to admit it. Rona the First, an immigrant with no formal education, knew something Fredelle didn't know with all her prizes
and degrees. And what had those degrees gotten her in New
Hampshire? An entry-level job in the English department, lost
when she became pregnant with me. They replaced her with a
man, "a nobody with an almost-M.A."

They had a new policy. It did not say anything so backward
or blunt as "No women allowed." What it said was that married
women could no longer teach in the same departments as their
husbands. No exceptions. Not even for a woman with a Phi
Beta Kappa key and a doctorate from one of the finest schools
in the country. Surely she could understand, a person of her

intelligence. Rules are rules. And besides, babies need their mothers.

She understood. It had all been for nothing. The highest mark ever given on the comprehensive exam in her master's program: nothing. Praise along the lines of "most brilliant student I ever had in my life": nothing. The forthcoming article in *Studies in Philology*, the year teaching at Wellesley, where bright young women revered her, the late nights memorizing *Silas Marner* from cover to cover (which shouldn't even have been possible, but was for a young woman with her fever to impress): all nothing. It was as if she'd been invited to a banquet and found on her gold-edged plate a heaping portion of sand.

What was she to do with herself? In Durham the faculty wives exchanged recipes for children's birthday parties. She longed for the "magic years" of the doctoral program at Radcliffe, when she hosted her smart, funny friends in a charmingly raffish apartment with a cracked bathtub where she made her own yogurt. The women had scattered, mostly to follow their professor husbands (none of them had academic jobs of their own, despite their doctorates). She wrote to her friend Phyllis:

> The people one meets as married women have
> already made so many commitments and shut so
> many doors that you never do know them
> wholly. You and I and Lillian met each other at
> the peak of a kind of intellectual flowering and
> emotional intensity. Almost the best thing I can
> say of life at a graduate school is that it provides
> an atmosphere in which you can say "This is my
> mind" without pretension and with perfect nat-
> uralness. Nowadays when I meet even intelligent

women I find that I frequently end up discussing recipes or anecdotes about the baby. . . . In the [Radcliffe] period I was so terribly spoiled. . . . I really thought I could do anything and have everything. I've come to see that my talents are really not very considerable; or at least that whatever talents I had were somehow hopelessly crippled by my mother's devotion to them.

At least she had me, a comfort in her sorrow and a peace offering to her mother. Among Jews it's considered bad luck to name babies after living people but the usual rules did not apply to my mother and her mother. You might as well try to regulate the tides.

In letter after letter to Grandma, my mother chronicled the details of my progress. But among the stories of my sweet daily doings, my lips puckered for a kiss and my impressive vocabulary ("She is the chirpingest canary"), there was something my mother didn't mention. I wasn't cuddly. I stiffened when she tried to pull me close. What was wrong? Shouldn't a daughter melt into her mother's arms, the way she had always done with the first Rona? If I really loved her, I would love her embrace.

One day we were lying on the bed together – me naked on a towel, still damp from the bath – when an impulse came over my mother. She needed to feel my talcum-powdered flesh on hers. She needed me to laugh at the pleasure of her touch. To my father, her touch was a soiled and suspect thing; he wanted a marriage of true minds. It had to find a target, this desire of hers for physical connection. Scooping me up, she tossed me in the air and pulled me into the refuge of her arms. I didn't laugh, so she tried harder, swinging me by the arm until she heard what seemed a thunderous crack. My arm hung at a crazy angle and my mother froze. *Oh, God, I've broken my baby's arm.* She rushed me to the doctor, who popped it back into place and told her not to worry so much.

But she did. She couldn't help it. She thought she knew the right way for a little girl to love her mother. The way I loved her was different. Still, I wouldn't be her only daughter.

Time passed. Her cheeks bloomed and a lightness came to her step, as if she had a secret too delicious to contain much longer. It would have been spring of my fourth year when she told me her news: "You're going to get a very special surprise. A little sister! She's growing in my tummy right now. Remember how your kittens grew in Chrissie's tummy? Well, a sister is a lot more fun than kittens." No mention of any little brother. That could never be. My mother would rule a house of hair ribbons, hand-made doll clothes and gilt-edged editions of the Brothers Grimm – a tide of daughterly paraphernalia to swamp Daddy's papers.

When it came to sibling rivalry, my mother was no innocent (she had an older sister, after all). But being an optimist by nature and a disciple of Dr. Spock, she figured she could make me a partner in welcoming little Daphne. That's the name I chose while she read me the Greek myth about Daphne, the spirited young nymph who sent every suitor packing, including the god Apollo. When he chased her, she called on her father, the river god, to preserve her independence. Apollo threw his arms around Daphne just in time to feel his beloved turn into a tree. My mother read aloud from Edith Hamilton: "Bark was enclos-ing her; leaves were sprouting forth." I asked for this story again and again. Daphne was my kind of heroine, a woman who knew the dangers of love and had the presence of mind to renounce them. Yes, my sister would be Daphne.

For months I awaited the little friend who would adore me and look up to me. I talked to her; I saved toys for her. I told my mother that when I got married, Daphne would share my new house with me. "You can keep Chrissie," I said.

Daphne arrived in November 1953, when the sky in New Hampshire turns the colour of metal. Again Daddy drove to the hospital, leaving me with Grandma, who had come from Winnipeg to help. (As predicted, she had grown to accept my mother's marriage.) When my parents burst through our front door, Grandma rushed to relieve them of the white bassinet. It seemed to fill the hall like an enormous white flower with a lethal, intoxicating fragrance. "Isn't she beautiful?" "Have you ever seen such eyes?" I crept through the thicket of legs and coats to steal a look at Daphne. As I reached out to lift a corner of her white crocheted blanket, Grandma pushed my hand away: "Leave her be! She'll catch cold."

I saw Daphne soon enough, and she was trouble, with eyes like pools of melted chocolate, skin the colour of cinnamon and little gumdrop fingernails. I wanted to bite off her little cookie head, but my parents couldn't get enough of her. She curled herself against my mother's breast as if she belonged there and would never leave. My mother was in love. Even against Daddy's chest, so bony under his cardboardy suit, Daphne found a place to fill with her tawny roundness. All day she beguiled and seduced. All night she screamed for attention. My parents wheeled the baby carriage into the kitchen so they could take turns pushing it back and forth to soothe her. It wasn't like Daddy to concern himself with child care, but this Daphne was a force field of need. My book of Greek myths lay forgotten, along with all the other books my mother had been reading to me. "Grandma can read to you," she said. I didn't want Grandma; she barrelled through a story as if it were a dirty house to be whipped into shape. My mother had a different voice for every character. I missed her.

After a few days of this, I made a decision. I couldn't get rid of my sister but I could take away her precious name. "She's not a Daphne," I said. "She needs another name." She already had one: her middle name, Joyce. And so my sister became the smallest of the nested wooden dolls.

I found a new heroine to replace Daphne. Why bother with a nymph who turns into a tree? A tree just stands there. But Joan of Arc – now there was a woman to light up my dreams. Joan spoke with an angel. Her armour flashed like a comet. She rallied men who drew courage from hers and together they set out to save their kingdom.

I had an antique picture book about her – in French, so my mother had to translate the story. My mother snorted when the book arrived in the mail, an unlikely gift from a family friend with no children. So depressing! Such clumsy, old-fashioned prose! But I was enraptured. How splendid Joan looked on her charger, with her spear raised in triumph and the banners rippling overhead, stamped with the fleur-de-lys. In the end her own people sold her out. They gave Joan up to the English, who burned her at the stake. I liked to study the picture of Joan in her death smock, facing the flames with steely composure. I knew what she was thinking: *Do your worst. You think you're so strong, you fools, but you'll never destroy me. I'm the strong one and I'll make you pay for this.*

At the breakfast table, I made an announcement: "My name isn't Rona anymore. It's Joan." Why not? I had already changed my sister's name.

Daddy cleared his throat. He smiled indulgently. Then he asked, "Now, why would you want a name like Joan? There's no music in it. It's common. But Rona . . . that's a name you can almost sing. A name with presence."

My mother laughed. "Dear, you know how carried away she gets. She thinks she's the next Joan of Arc. Your timid little daughter has been picturing herself in shining armour."

I was timid, all right. At nursery school, I hung back while other children coasted down the slide on their stomachs. The teacher finally coaxed me up the ladder where I just sat, clutching the rails. This wasn't my only deficiency as a warrior. I also refused to wear pants. Only dresses would do, preferably ruffled ones with smocking and embroidered flowers. Now I wanted armour. What an idea! I claimed I was going to be "a fighter like Joan," but if a bigger child pushed me I'd run weeping to the teacher.

All day I refused to answer to Rona. Next day and the next, the same story: "I'm Joan. I'm going to be a fighter." My mother began to purse her lips. This wasn't funny anymore. She had given me the loveliest name she knew, her mother's name, and I was rejecting it. At last she took her stand: "Well, Rona, I think the police will have something to say about this. You can't change your name just like that. It's against the law."

She picked up the phone and dialled with baleful solemnity. The dial whirred and spat. "Hello, is this the police chief? . . . This is Mrs. Maynard on Faculty Road. I have a naughty little girl here who won't answer to her name. She seems to think she can change it. . . . Oh, really? . . . Hmmm, that's very serious. . . . No, she wouldn't like that at all. . . . Yes, I'll be sure to let her know." Down went the receiver. My mother looked stricken. "The police chief has a message for you, Rona. Laws are laws and you have to obey them. If you don't stop this Joan business, he's going to come with his paddy wagon and lock you in jail and give you nothing to eat except bread and water."

My mother, my mother. My amazing, all-knowing, necessary mother. The paddy wagon must be like the black bird who stole her from me in my dream. I could live on bread and water. I couldn't live without my mother. From that moment on, I was Rona.

DREAM HOUSE

M y mother was pushing her cart at the supermarket when Cindy Crandall's mother tapped her on the shoulder: "I hear you've just bought the Scudder place. Does it still smell of dog pee?"

My mother wheeled away with a regal smile, calling over her shoulder, "It's the Maynard place now."

True, old Mrs. Scudder used to keep rambunctious dogs that lifted their legs as the spirit moved them, but what an eye she had for proportion. Ample rooms, nearly square, opened onto hallways bigger than a good many kitchens. The Scudders had commissioned the house around the time of the First World War, and with the deed came a yellowed envelope of photographic negatives on glass in which the empty, newly built rooms awaited the right appointments like eccentric and particular ghosts. But the distinction of our house was lost on the likes of Mrs. Crandall. "She probably thinks the last word in home design is a boxy prefab bungalow with matching maple furniture and wall-to-wall broadloom the colour of a sparrow!" my mother said. "Dog pee, indeed! Has that woman never heard of elbow grease?" Maybe Cindy's mom was just jealous. There were plenty of bungalows in Durham but only one house like Maynard Hall, my mother's not entirely jocular name for the house that was finally ours. It stood behind the only picket fence in the town, like a castle behind its moat.

My mother was in love again, so smitten with the house that she broke her own budgetary rules to have it. A child of the Depression, she would drive out of her way to save a few cents on canned tuna, but she just had to live in the white colonial with its broad, panelled door and oversize brass knocker, even though she and Daddy couldn't really afford the place.

A less determined woman would have swallowed her hopes for a dream house and settled for a bungalow, but my mother was an ace at stretching a dollar. She would save Green Stamps from the supermarket; she would sell an extra article or two to *My Baby*, signing herself "Fredelle Maynard, Ph.D." (Let them think she'd earned her doctorate in child psychology – it was about time her credentials cut some ice in the world.) She would cook fewer roasts and more ground-beef casseroles. Besides, the house was a project she and Daddy could share. Big enough to accommodate a studio for his painting, it embodied what my parents called "style" (not to be confused with the passing parade of fripperies known as fashion). With no cornice mouldings or coffered ceilings, the house was not showy. Yet it had a sense of lavishness – not one set of double doors but three, and oversize windows throughout, with sixteen panes in every one. All winter long heat escaped from those windows while the aged furnace clattered and wheezed.

⁘

Who but my parents would buy such a house? They weren't even Americans; other kids said they "talked funny." Once a year they had to fill out "alien registration forms," a term suggesting bug-eyed creatures from outer space. In fact, my parents did seem to think of themselves as a higher life form whose country hadn't seen any witch hunts for Reds, or any angry crowds trying to keep kids like me from the neighbourhood school just because they happened to be "Negroes." Our town didn't have any Negroes, although a rumour went around that my mother, with her dark skin and wiry black curls, couldn't possibly be white.

Most isolating of all, my parents had no church. On the first day of school the teacher asked us all to tell the class what kind of Christian we were. Round the room went the chorus of belonging: *I'm Catholic, I'm Presbyterian, I'm Congregationalist.* There was one Baptist, Jeffrey Barlow, a farm kid who mucked out stalls before breakfast, wore a homemade flannel shirt and rode the bus into town to school. Jeffrey had questionable status at Oyster River School, but he was still ahead of me. When my turn came I looked at the floor and said, "I'm nothing."

My mother vetoed my pleas for Sunday school: "I'm Jewish, I don't want my daughter singing 'Jesus Loves Me.' Besides, church is where people go to worship God. Daddy and I don't go there because we don't know if God exists." It seemed to me that we were on the wrong team, the outsiders who couldn't make up their minds. "Agnostics," we were called, with no spire or stained-glass window to mark our place in the world. The other kids had things to believe in; I had things to question and reject. But I was moving into the loveliest house in town. They could keep their musty old churches.

~⚬⚬⚬~

In a flurry of preparations, we took possession of the house just after my seventh birthday. My mother collected abandoned

furniture to strip and repaint for two little-girl bedrooms –
white for mine, moss green for Joyce's. She turned remnants of
blue and green linen into squishy sofa pillows that cried out for
a pillow fight, not that we were allowed to have one (we might
get finger marks on my mother's hard work). I was so proud of
those pillows. The ones on other people's couches looked
about as inviting as military uniforms, all knife-edge pleats
and stiff buttons.

My mother never used the word *decorating*. To her it smacked
of fuss-budget rules laid down by matrons in prim pastel suits and
flowered hats like the queen mother's. Still, it's not as if she had no
decorating rules of her own. When Daddy made a pitch for a
La-Z-Boy, she overruled him on aesthetic grounds. Naugahyde
in her living room? Surely not.

With the money she'd saved at flea markets and fabric mills,
she treated herself to a teak table for the dining room. You
couldn't find teak in New Hampshire then, so our table came all
the way from Denmark, only to arrive with an impossibly
flamboyant grain. Back it went, replaced months later by the
perfect Danish-modern table – no mere resting place for dishes
and cutlery, but a statement of identity, our answer to King
Arthur's Round Table. I had read the Arthurian legends; I knew
the kingdom fell to ruin in the end. But Arthur kept on striving
to create what could never be, a harmony too fine for this world.

Our day as a family began and ended at the table. No
matter how early I came down in the morning, I always found
Daddy at the head with his bowl of oatmeal and his lecture
notes on eighteenth-century poetry. He kept watch at the
boundary between night and day: if anyone slept past seven,
he'd stride through the bedrooms, snapping blinds and exhort-
ing us to action.

Every evening at the stroke of six we gathered at the teak table for a dinner that revolved more on talk than on the meal that had occupied hours of my mother's day. Daddy held forth about art, ideas and the decline of Western civilization. He was the doleful cello; my mother was the flute, transforming her day into anecdotes that sparkled with sly wit and gleeful exaggeration. A trip to the grand opening sale of the latest discount store became a mock-heroic quest in which she fended off a horde of sharp-elbowed shoppers to seize the one treasure hidden in a pile of misshapen Orlon sweaters. Next, she had to do battle with the inept cashier who tried to overcharge her, and steer our gallant little humpbacked car through a phalanx of giant finned vehicles with radiators like dragon's teeth, each one driven by a glowering bully. All for a $3.98 gingham pinafore that you could swear had been made for Joyce. As usual she concluded her tale with one of the Shakespearian quotations that played in her head like a full orchestra:

> If you have writ your annals true, 'tis there
> That, like an eagle in a dovecote, I
> Flutter'd your Volscians in Corioli:
> Alone I did it.

Just like my mother to make a whimsical comparison between a shopping trip and a Roman triumph on the battlefield. My father smiled wanly. He answered her Shakespeare with a barb from Wordsworth: "Getting and spending, we lay waste our powers." In his view, my mother hadn't conquered any barbarians; she'd sold out to the worst of them all, the god of money. "Mammon marches on!" he sighed.

Late at night our house revealed its hidden self. While the rest of us slept, my father put his oatmeal on to simmer in the double boiler, the only kitchen utensil he had mastered. Then he filled his glass and put Beethoven on the record player. As the music began to crash and roar, he would stumble upstairs to wake me up, not that he needed to. I already knew what was coming, another sermon downstairs at the teak table.

He sat in his customary spot, his white hair wild. I sat at the foot in my nightgown, rubbing my eyes. I was in for it now, a peroration of anguish that wouldn't end until he pitched forward on his arms, asleep. "The soul is a pilgrim, Rona," he began. "I recognize the soul that you've been blessed with. Actually, cursed is the better word. You will be an artist. You have all the stigmata."

It couldn't be true, it mustn't be true. I had seen stigmata in centuries-old paintings of saints dripping blood from the places on their torn, exhausted bodies where Jesus had bled on the cross. Daddy's talk of recognition sounded equally disturbing. So he and I were supposed to be two of a kind? Yes. He had seen the temptations I would face. They had led him astray, he told me. I would have to be vigilant, or I would end up like him. No mention of Joyce in all this. Would the Adorable One be dancing and singing on a stage somewhere while I bled?

I thought I could keep a watchful silence and wait for release (no point waiting for my mother to end this madness; she could sleep through anything). But I wasn't getting off so lightly. My father had a question for me: "What is the purpose of life?"

The sooner we got this over with, the sooner I'd be back in bed, asleep. I said the first thing that came to mind. "The purpose of life is to have a good time while you're alive."

Daddy groaned as if my answer were a knife in his flesh. "Oh, Rona, Rona! You have listened too closely to your mother. A formidably clever woman, a remarkable woman in her way, but not one of our kind. She will complicate matters for you, Rona. There are more things in heaven and earth than she will ever know." He paused to make sure he had my attention, then pounded the table with his fist. "The purpose of life is to *save your soul!*"

I remembered the painting of Hell that he had shown me long ago, Bosch's pain-drunk demons and writhing sinners. Daddy's parents had believed that such a place really existed, and that he would go there for leaving their faith. But perhaps he had never really left. To look at him was to see that Hell could be a state of mind, and that my father was condemned to burn there forever. Hunched and sighing, he quoted from the Bible: "As the hart panteth after the water brooks, so panteth my soul after thee, O God." There was no God to hear him. That I knew for sure.

⁓◦⊚◦⁓

Our house was more than a place to live. It was a museum devoted to my father's work, which hung on every wall instead of the family photos and Picasso prints that other people displayed.

Max Maynard was an artist prized by no one but ourselves. Before he became a professor, he had been an up-and-coming painter in a distant Canadian city I'd never seen, a place he called "beautiful Victoria," as if the beauty of southern New Hampshire could not possibly compare to the lost homeland. In Victoria he went sketching with Emily Carr and sold his work to collectors. In New Hampshire nobody had heard of Emily Carr, and the local art association tucked Daddy's work in the most neglected corner of its annual show. Nobody bought Daddy's stripped-down, sculptural renditions of rocks and Douglas firs, but there were plenty of takers for pastel seascapes and dewy-eyed kittens with balls of yarn.

My mother used to say, "Your father could have been a famous painter but he gave it up to support his family." Sometimes she would add, quoting one of the famous dead whose works she had memorized in her student days, "He that hath wife and children hath given hostages to fortune." So it was all our fault that Daddy's art wasn't hanging in museums or reproduced in coffee-table books? He seemed to think so. Sometimes at night he would tear through the house shouting, "I could have been the most famous painter in Canada!" He would snatch a painting from the wall in a fit of disappointment and carry it away to his studio in the attic. A painting could die there during one of Daddy's spells, buried under swaths of black and grey. Then, if my mother couldn't stop him in time, he'd get on the phone to his old sketching buddy Jack Shadbolt, who had since become one of Canada's most famous painters, and lambaste Jack's new work. "You're a charlatan, Jack! All sound and fury signifying nothing!"

My mother never discussed these rampages of his, let alone the reason for them – the bottles hidden in the studio and the emergency supply in the garage. When the shouting started, Joyce would create a distraction, turning our living room into a stage for a one-woman show complete with skits, dance routines and commercials. Our parents applauded with desperate pride in the Adorable One, who was cuter and perkier than I would ever be.

Meanwhile I quietly wondered why my mother had cast her lot with a madman. He didn't even look like a normal father. Other dads wore Red Sox caps; my father owned a bathing cap, which he wore to my undying embarrassment at the town pool. Other dads owned barbecue tools and grilled hot dogs in the backyard; my father had a collection of walking sticks and never took a "constitutional" without one. For the rest of Durham, "constitutional" had to do with the freedom of proud Americans; for my father it appeared to be just the opposite, an emblem of proud, unbending foreignness. One day a neighbour looked up from washing his station wagon and said to my father, "Tell me, Maynard. Why do you always carry that damn stick?"

My mother had no patience with my melancholy musings about the difference between Daddy and other kids' fathers. She'd look up from her project of the moment (a wardrobe for Joyce's miniature bear, a tutu for my ballet recital) and put me in my place. "He's a brilliant, original man. Of course he can be moody, but that's the price of exceptional gifts. You're lucky to be his daughter."

Lucky? Cindy Crandall's father took her camping in the White Mountains; my father wouldn't go anywhere unless he could get back by teatime. Instead he took us sketching, a procession of Maynards armed with pads and walking sticks. I lagged behind, the only one to refuse a stick, pretending I didn't know these oddballs. Out in the country where no one could see us, I dropped my guard. My father found beauty in the most unlikely places, pointing with his stick and marvelling at full voice. Look! A fallen log. Look! A shadow crossing our path at an interesting angle. Once he homed in on – of all things – a telephone pole. He bent down and pulled me close, eye to eye, until I saw what he did: a slash dividing the sky into planes. I crouched on a rock to capture the bones of the moment as my father had revealed them to me, and something leaped in my chest when he admired my drawing. In fact, he admired it so much that he tore it from my sketchbook and took it away to the studio. The next time I saw my composition, it wasn't mine anymore. My mother pronounced it "too stark" for her taste, but it still ended up in the place of honour over the fireplace. She didn't dare question Daddy's creative breakthroughs.

The attic studio was the soul of Maynard Hall. When my father's work went well and the house rang with his exultation ("Thrilling"; "Extraordinary"; "My finest work yet") he'd invite us all to the inner sanctum. These visits unfolded with a sense of ceremony. First the ascent to the harsh climate of the attic (with no air conditioning or heating, the studio was either insufferably hot or cold enough for two sweaters). Then the circle of contemplation under the skylight, where the easel stood. At last, the high point, the critiques. "Try looking without your glasses," he would say. "The extraneous details disappear and your eye is drawn to the essence of the piece." (It never occurred to him to dilute his vocabulary for children.) He liked searching comments about form, line and symmetry. My sister and I spoke that language; the best way we knew to make him smile was to help him rethink a murky corner. My mother hung back like an anxious guest who has worn the wrong clothes to the party of the season. She'd exclaim at how "lyrical" a painting was, but Daddy paid no attention. His magisterial disregard seemed to say, "You're a very clever woman, my dear, but you simply cannot think like an artist."

She continued to tell me she was happy, although one corner of the house sent the opposite message. At the foot of the basement stairs sat her laundry room, lit by a single naked bulb.

Sometimes I had to go down there to hang a load of washing on the wobbly indoor clothesline. It was like descending into a pit. At a time when detergent commercials featured giddy house-wives competing for "the whiter white," my mother's whites were a flagrant shade of grey, like the machine itself, with its per-manent crust of spilled laundry products. We all laughed at those laundry-obsessed TV moms who appeared to have soap suds for brains, but none of us questioned the underlying message: if a wife truly loves her family, she'll devote her whole being to their care. Down in the basement with my hands in a tub of cold laundry my mother had flung into the machine with gritted teeth, I felt the sodden weight of our collective expectations without understanding why this simple chore made me so queasy. I practically sprinted back upstairs to the real world of big airy windows hung with plants so lush and green that we didn't need curtains. I thought I was escaping the darkness and the musty odours, never seeing in that place what is obvious to me now – my mother's silent fury, pushed deep into the bowels of her dream house. The room practically shouted what she never did: "You artists think you're so special! Why is everybody in this house special except me?"

In some ways our house was the Land of Plenty. Every drawer, shelf and closet brimmed with stuff that my mother couldn't bear to discard (it might, who knows, be essential some day). Miles of rickrack and yellowed lace; an explosion of old plastic bags dotted with crumbs from long-gone loaves of bread; teeter-ing stacks of magazines: *Life*, *The New Yorker*, the women's titles my mother wrote for. In the basement she kept dusty canned goods bought ages ago at scratch-and-dent sales and forgotten ever since (if the Russians dropped the bomb, the Maynards would feast for weeks on artichokes, pimiento-stuffed olives and seasoned breadcrumbs). Two trunks in the attic – one for me, one for Joyce – held our complete creative works, except for the offerings sent to Grandma in Winnipeg.

And words, words, words – an endless, drenching cascade of them. Both my parents had a passion for poetry, but my mother, with her legendary memory, was the one who poured it over my head, unable to contain her joy in language. Before I knew the names of the poets, I absorbed the flow and force of their words. I met the bishop on the road, I met a traveller from an antique land, I saw the tiger burning bright. I discovered a landscape of tantalizing mysteries. Two roads diverged in a yellow wood, which opened onto cliffs of fall (frightful, sheer, no-man-fathomed), which overlooked Alph the sacred river running through caverns measureless to man, which wound its way to the tulgy wood, home of the whiffling Jabberwock. I heard the mermaids singing each to each and came to believe that they would sing to me because, as a citizen of Maynardland, it was my birthright.

Then there were the words my mother wrote. Until she established herself as a professional writer, they consisted mostly of the letters that formed a running commentary on our supposedly charmed lives. She always had a letter to Grandma on the typewriter or a fresh carbon copy in the middle of her desk, as if she knew I would read them. I couldn't resist, not just because they brimmed with wit and colour, but because they told me all was well in our house. We were unique, we were brilliant, we adventured together in a kingdom of the imagination. My mother had said so again and again, and my mother was the fountain of knowledge.

But for all its abundance, Maynardland was the land of Not Enough. My mother was the keeper of comforts and the rest of us competed for fragments of her overburdened mind and heart. Daddy came first for the unspoken, obvious reason: if she couldn't stop him from drinking, then at least she could slow him down. Joyce and I found strategies for catching attention: she would eat only nuts, grapes and chicken wings (never a breast or a leg); I developed an ailment I called "the bare feeling," the only description I could find for the emptiness that gnawed at me. To have my mother all to myself, I would have given any number of crooning mermaids.

Bursting through our front door after school, I'd throw my books on the teak table and make a dash for the kitchen. If I timed it right, I could have a one-on-one with my mother. I'd perch on the cracked vinyl stepstool that faced the stove (the only item in the house that had survived her ban on ugly things) and warm myself with her conversation. We would talk about why we both loved *The Secret Garden* and whether Marilyn Monroe, that explosion of gorgeousness, could possibly stay married to her latest man, the dour intellectual Arthur Miller. We mused on the hidden lives of women my mother knew: Gail's hopeless love affair, Carolyn's self-destructive streak, Barbara's wayward son. By age ten, I had the goods on them all and was exploring their motives. What some would call gossip, my mother called "the study of human nature." She was not a malicious woman; she was driven by boundless curiosity. Everyone she met was a story to her, a collection of pungent and beguiling secrets concealed behind Peter Pan collars and ballerina skirts. Lips would quiver; boasts would betray insecurities. Confessions would slip out between bites of date-nut bread. My mother attuned my ear to the underground spring that courses through all speech and silence, heard by women of intuition and ignored by men. (The only trait Daddy shared with other fathers I knew was disdain for the vast and poignant intrigues of the everyday.) When my mother shared the truths she had teased out, I felt like her best friend in the world.

One day as she stirred the soup I asked, "Why was I born?"

She didn't even pause. "Because we wanted to have you."

"But Daddy didn't want any children. You said so."

My mother pursed her lips. "He was just a little nervous, that's all. Once you came along, he was crazy about you."

Crazy. She had that right, anyway. I considered this business about wanting to have me. Sure, she wanted a little girl. But that wasn't the same as wanting *me*. There must have been at least a gajillion little girls she could have had instead, all lined up among the Never Born like shiny new dolls still in their boxes. Pretty ones, cheerful ones, obedient ones who didn't argue about their chores, fight with their little sisters or, worst of all, criticize their fathers. Surely among those girls there was one with all my good points and none of my annoying deficiencies.

⁓◦⊙◦⁓

My mother got a call from my teacher, Mrs. Sawyer: *We need to talk about Rona.* Lonely, shy, not working to potential . . . that was the gist. On an IQ test I had tested dull-normal because I spent more time looking out the window than filling out the little squares. A gifted child like me! Something had to be done.

My mother broke the news over a plate of fresh chocolate chip cookies (when she had something difficult to tell me, she tried to make it seem like a treat). "You don't seem very happy," she explained. "I've noticed and Mrs. Sawyer has noticed, too. So we think it's time to do something about that."

Of course I wasn't very happy. But why was this such a big deal all of a sudden? Ever since I could remember, my parents had described my sister as the sunny one and me as the resident cloud. You could give me a hand-sewn wardrobe for my favourite doll, as my mother did one memorable Christmas, and I would say, "I don't really mind that the evening coat has a crooked hem." My games had a bitter edge, like one called "French Revolution," in which my friend Linda and I sent our dolls to the guillotine. I didn't have many friends, just misfits like Linda, who towered over everyone else in our class. The other kids laughed at Linda's dresses, which were always too short, just as they laughed at me for going to the opera with my mother.

To me a certain bleakness of mind was like winter in New Hampshire: just a fact of life. Now it seemed my mother had arrived at a different interpretation. I didn't fit the upbeat narrative she was spinning in her letters to Grandma. I was broken and I needed fixing. That's what this "help" was all about. "You're going to see a very nice woman named Mrs. Warren," my mother said. "Wait till you see all the toys she has for you to play with."

Mrs. Warren had plenty of toys, all right. She could have stocked a rummage sale with beat-up stuffed animals that looked as if little kids had drooled on them. She had a miniature oven, a red plastic ironing board, a few Tonka trucks that had barely survived a road accident and a baby carriage containing a naked Tiny Tears doll – the most boring doll ever invented – with a bald patch on her scalp. Who played with this stuff? It made me miss Linda and the French Revolution game. I wouldn't have minded sending Tiny Tears to the guillotine (there was a wagon to use as a tumbril), but I sensed that Mrs. Warren would take a dim view of that.

While I did my best to play with the dollhouse, she peered at me through glasses that she wore on a chain around her neck. She kept interrupting me with questions about what I was doing. Couldn't she see for herself? It offended me that grown-ups thought they knew what I needed, when they clearly had no idea. Because I didn't have enough friends at school, I was supposed to make friends with an elderly woman in a sweater set and lace-up shoes. And they called it "help." Meanwhile, my mother sat in a small beige room with a man named Dr. Burkheim. A psychiatrist, she said. Exactly what went on there, I never understood. "He's helping me to help you," she would say. I had a good notion what would help me. My father could act like a real father. But he never set foot in the Child Guidance Clinic.

There was one good thing about those sessions, but neither Mrs. Warren nor Dr. Burkheim had anything to do with it. The clinic was in another town, and my mother had to drive me there. On the way we talked, just the two of us cocooned in the car. No interruptions from Daddy, looking for his tweed jacket; no phone calls from Grandma; no impromptu perform-ances from Joyce. My mother remembered exactly how it felt to be a child, and as she drove she talked about the little girl she had been, devising wickedly ingenious games with her friend Hazel. "We used to kill flies and line them up for ants to find. They made such a satisfying spurt. You wouldn't think so much white gunk could come out of such a small creature. The ants made short work of it, I must say. Some of them cleaned up all the gunk while the rest staggered off with the carcass. It was truly thrilling, like watching Africans lug a dead lion away, right there in Birch Hills, Saskatchewan."

"You didn't know what Africans looked like. You didn't have a TV."

"I didn't need a TV. I had a grainy photo in *The Book of Knowledge*. To me those volumes contained the whole world."

If only I had a friend like that – a girl who could discover the world in a book. Most kids wondered why I preferred reading to hopscotch, but Freidele Bruser would understand. "When you were a little girl, were you ever lonely?"

"I had a sense of difference; that's how I'd put it. There were never any other Jewish children. We did have a Chinese man in Birch Hills and Hazel used to make fun of him: 'Chinky chinky Chinaman, catch his pigtail.' She had no idea what's it like to be an outsider. I did, of course. I couldn't bear the way she taunted that man but I couldn't bring myself to say so. I wanted so much to belong." She took her eyes off the road just long enough to look at me. "Rona, I know how hard it is for you. There aren't many children like you in Durham, but before you know it you'll leave this town and find a place where you belong. You'll have extraordinary friends. When I went to Radcliffe I thought the gods must have assembled the friends I was making, it was that exciting. 'O brave new world, that has such people in it!' Did I ever tell you I knew Vladimir Nabokov . . . ?"

That day we stopped for ice cream, double scoops. In the sweetness of the moment I forgot that my mother had lost her brave new world.

After a few months of visits to Mrs. Warren (they were never called "therapy"), my mother told me that I wouldn't be going anymore. "You seem a lot happier now," she said as she slid a batch of dream squares into the oven. She smiled as if she needed to believe this, and I didn't have the heart to tell her that nothing had changed. Not for the better, anyway. I was losing our private time in the car. But my mother had enough problems. She had bills she couldn't pay without a loan from the bank. She had Daddy and his moods. Grandma had just come home from the dentist with a mouthful of blood after losing all her teeth. On top of all this, she should worry about my little-girl sorrows?

The bare feeling gaped in the pit of my stomach, yawning wider and wider until it seemed to erase my flesh and bones. I was sitting on the vinyl stool and yet I felt no more present in the world than all those happy, well-behaved children my mother could have had instead of me. In a house of words, I had no words for what I was thinking. The sacred river dried up. The mermaids sank to the bottom of the ocean with seaweed stopping their mouths. My mother said, "So what do you think, Rona? Isn't it nice to wake up in the morning and look forward to another day?"

RIVALS

The letter to Grandma that lay on my mother's desk looked just like all the rest. As usual I scanned it, looking for my name. Not a word about my plan to win the school spelling bee, first rung on the ladder that would take me all the way to a podium in Washington. I could practically hear the applause. All the kids seemed to think I was unbeatable, even though they didn't even like me. Just wait till I won the national trophy. They would cheer for me and want to be my friend. How could my own mother be so blind to the biggest project in my life? Halfway down the first page, something came at me like the fang of a serpent: "Rona will be a pretty girl, but Joyce bids fair to be a stunner."

Tell me you don't mean it. Tell me you're not sending this letter. Tell me I'm as beautiful as my sister.

My mother rolled her eyes at me. "Honestly, Rona, I'm surprised you don't have more important things on your mind. Some of us are beauties, most of us aren't. That's life."

What kind of consolation was this? Beauties had the edge; *that* was life for a woman. To get my photo on the cover of *Life* magazine, I'd have to be beautiful like Gina Lollobrigida or dead like Anne Frank. The women in the Maidenform ads all owed their thrilling adventures to beauty: "I dreamed I walked a tightrope in my Maidenform bra." "I dreamed I swayed the jury in my Maidenform bra." Jutting breasts, tiny waists, couturier clothes (but only from the waist down, the better to show off their bras) . . . those women weren't relying on brains alone. My mother had told me herself that she ought to be a few sizes slimmer; she never passed a mirror without sucking in her stomach. Her sister Celia was slim, and anyone could tell that this bothered her. Yet here she was, pretending that beauty didn't matter.

At least I could still beat my sister at writing and drawing. On Saturday morning I set up my coloured pencils at the teak table. I was going to make a fashion magazine full of slinky dresses that I wished my mother would wear instead of stiff tent-like numbers from the discount store. All the shoes in my magazine would have pointed toes; all the models would wear glossy beehives to show off their dangly earrings. If I couldn't possess beauty, I would invent it.

Across the table Joyce claimed a station for her own artwork. Instead of fashion models, the Adorable One drew herself: big eyes under a jaunty fringe of bangs, lips upturned in that ever-present smile. Underneath she wrote, "COME AND CUDEL WITH ME." Then she bounded to the dining room window, where she held up her drawing like a sign. The window looked out on a lilac tree that our mother happened to be pruning. She wore an old shirt of Daddy's and no lipstick; a kerchief hid her shiny curls. One glimpse of Joyce's sign and she let the shears fall to her side. She had sweat stains under her arms, but I could tell it wasn't just hoisting the shears that had brought a glow to her cheeks. With her free hand she waved to my sister. They stood there looking at each other, and I saw a yearning flicker across my mother's face. I had never seen that expression before, and my mother didn't see me taking note of it; her eyes were fixed on Joyce. I thought it must be jealousy that made me so uneasy, but I didn't really want such a look from my mother. Let Joyce have it if she craved attention that badly.

Rona and Joyce. The thorn and the rose. The rock and the sand. We were born that way, one to resist and the other to yield. I shrank from embraces, the baby who spurned her own mother. Joyce held out her arms to the world, the kind of baby total strangers reach out to touch. Our mother craved touch, and in Joyce she had someone who delighted in her touch as no one had since she was a child, sheltered in her own mother's lap, the little Russian doll nested in the large one.

I don't remember when the ritual known as cuddle time began; I only recall the churning shame of what I saw. Every morning Joyce jumped into the double bed where my mother was sipping her coffee. There they would snuggle, exchanging kisses with silly names: cuties, nibbles, suctions. No one thought to close the door where I stood willing this show to be over. My mother reclined against the pillows like Venus painted by Rubens, with my sister's hair fanned against her breasts. Joyce flashed what looked like a smile of victory: *I'm the favourite, you're not*. I told myself that if my mother enjoyed this, I shouldn't object. She was right about everything. I hated my jealousy, but not as much as I hated the thought of lying in that bed instead of Joyce.

"Cuddle time is stupid," I told my mother.

She laughed. "Well, of course you'd think so, my cold little fish. Sometimes I wonder what you're going to do when you get married!"

"Nobody else's mother has cuddle time. It's creepy."

"Rona, it's just a game we made up. We don't play like other people in this family any more than we talk like other people or fix up our house like other people. Difference is a gift, not a curse. I thought you'd know that by now."

What I knew was exactly the opposite, the anguish of difference. In a family of outsiders, I was the one on the margins. My mother had decreed that touch was the language of love, its most perfect expression a secret to be shared with her daughter. I could have been that daughter, but I refused to learn the language and now I was dumb to her. She pitied me for it. That was the worst part.

⁓⊙⊙⁓

Only one person could interfere with cuddle time. Grandma. When she visited from Winnipeg, she slept beside my mother in the blue bedroom and hung her identical button-front, shawl-collared dresses in my mother's closet. A glass for her dentures appeared on my mother's desk. Sometimes I saw them floating there, whiter than real teeth.

When she had her own teeth, Grandma could crack Brazil nuts with them. Her legend preceded her, told and retold by my mother. She raised houseplants from the dead. She'd once lifted the hind end of a car that was mired in mud, all by herself. And then, wouldn't you know, she pushed it. Her powers bordered on the supernatural. One night in my mother's Radcliffe days, before she found the will to marry my father, she was nearly raped by a good-looking soldier she had met in a bar. At least no one knew what a fool she had been to let him walk her home across a deserted park. But someone had an intimation. Grandma sent her a letter that said, "Tell me you're okay. I had a terrible dream about you. A big snake was chasing you." The night of Grandma's dream was the night of the attack, the soldier tearing at my mother's clothes until she broke free, screaming, and ran home in tears.

Every spring my mother wrote a Mother's Day letter to Grandma, who showed them off to all her friends. I could never quite believe she had written them. Unlike her other letters, they brimmed with Hallmark metaphors ("My mother is a smile warmer than a handshake and a laugh like silver bells"). They expressed fealty more than love, and I was part of the tribute handed over to the queen of her world:

> I am never prouder of [Rona and Joyce] than when they seem, in one way or another, to remind me of you; and never happier than when I feel I have achieved with them something of the ideal mother-daughter relationship that I have always shared with you. So, here is my Mother's Day bouquet: I offer you my children.

I shuddered at the very idea. Grandma wasn't my idea of a role model. Her operatic scorn encompassed multitudes: *goyish* cooks who were afraid of onions, widowers with the brass to remarry, Jews hiding their origins with gussied-up names like Lewis, when Rona Bruser well remembered their patriarch, Hymie Leibowitz (he proposed and she turned him down). A *nebbish* buys himself a fancy pinstripe suit, overnight he's the Duke of Windsor? Grandma didn't envy people with money; she suspected them of buying the position to which natural graces did not entitle them. She feared nothing but was ever on the lookout for threats: inferior merchandise tricked out as first quality, anti-Semites waiting to shaft the Jews. She trusted the shrewdness of her eye, the steel of her own determination, the allure of her incongruously girlish laugh. When she joked about the sex appeal of Harry Belafonte – a *schvartz*, but a fine figure of a man, how he could move – she seemed to entertain the thought that he might welcome her hand down that unbuttoned skin-tight shirt.

Before Joyce became the family stunner, there was Grandma. "It used to make me sad that I didn't inherit her beauty," my mother said. "She positively blazed with it."

Grandma blazed, all right. She radiated confidence in her own uniqueness and the light that it reflected on all that was hers. She just knew her baking was more delicious than other women's, her outfits more polished, her family more gifted. Denied real beauty by nature, she created the illusion of it. Photos from her prime show a pleasant-looking, *zaftig* young woman with a mischievous half-smile and a fashion model's instinct for the flattering gesture.

By the time I knew her, she took up space in every sense of the word. A woman of girth, she viewed her fatness as proof of her triumph over want. "You wouldn't want a thin Grandma!" she used to say. "So many wrinkles!" There were folds and folds of her, although her brocade corset made her as tight and sleek as a galleon. With the Cuban-heeled oxfords she called *chubatoras* and a handbag that could have held a telephone book, she looked even bigger than she was. Only her hat was tiny, a pillbox perched coquettishly on her icy hair. She took unconcealed pride in her full-length mink, a retirement gift from Grandpa and her one luxury. For what it must have cost (even on sale, as she would have insisted), they could have filled a closet with shawl-collared dresses and bought a year's supply of roasting chickens. The mink was more talked-about than worn (she had nowhere to go but the grocery store and the nursing home where Grandpa lived). She liked to speculate on who would inherit her prize – a topic most often raised when my mother let her down with a compliment withheld or a shopping expedition postponed. She always spoke of her death with a kind of relish, as if she planned to be watching from on high while we divided her possessions, exclaiming at the taste of the one to whom we owed this bounty.

⚘

My mother was on the phone with Grandma. It couldn't have been anyone else, the way she twisted the cord around her fingers while feigning absorption in bundt pans and orthopedic shoes. She spoke in a teacher's-pet chirp until her real voice burst out, seething with frustration: "Mums, I *have* a home! My home is in Durham with Max and the girls." This meant Grandma wanted her "home" in the one-bedroom walk-up in Winnipeg's North End. My mother had never lived there, never really thought of Winnipeg as home after all those little towns where her family had alighted for a while with their cargo of tarnished hope. For Grandma's sake, Joyce and I went to Winnipeg with my mother for our summer vacations, sharing a Hide-a-Bed in the airless living room. But the Winnipeg visits never settled the matter of Grandma's loneliness, her longing for Fredelle.

A day after the phone call, my mother made an announcement. "Guess what, girls? We're going to have a real family Christmas this year. Grandma's coming!"

Joyce began to hop like a wind-up toy. "I'm going to have a Christmas show for her, I'm going to make her a present!"

How could this be happening? Grandma couldn't even taste pork without carrying on as if she'd been poisoned; her own children never had a Christmas tree, and she had no use for "Hanukkah bushes." Now she was going to hang tinsel to "O come, all ye faithful"? I said, "But she's Jewish. She won't have a good time."

"Oh, come on! She'll have a wonderful time. She'll get right into the spirit. You know what a sense of fun she has."

Compared with Daddy's Bible-thumping, missionary mother, Grandma was Lucy Ricardo. But her idea of humour was mocking *goyish* ways. *Goyim* served grey meat with no tasty caramelized bits; they cared too much about hockey games and not enough about writing contests.

Every year Christmas at our house meant no-holds-barred submission to seasonal cheer, *goyish* style. Our tree brushed the ceiling, so heavy with ornaments that it had been known to topple under its own weight. After that my father tied it to nails in the wall. We scorned artificial trees, yet our fragrant fir was a spire too perfect to be real, thanks to Daddy's rearrangement of the branches with shears and wire. We always pronounced our latest tree the most beautiful of all, and every year I wondered how we'd keep this up. But we always did, thanks to Daddy, our Christmas impresario.

The previous year he had outdone himself. He had painted a choir of angels on the window at the head of the stairs. He didn't tell us what he had in mind; he let us watch the miracle unfold. Kneeling in his jeans with a dancing brush in his hand, he worked upward until an angel's face appeared in every pane. Their curls fluttered in a celestial breeze; even their halos seemed alive. At night they shone against the sky like our own private stained-glass window. They sang of peace on earth until spring, when my mother finally wiped them away. I'd been waiting ever since for their return; now they weren't coming back after all. Grandma wouldn't like them. Only baby Jesus was more *goyish* than my father's blonde angels.

—◦◦◦◦◦—

My grandmother didn't believe in God, let alone Jesus. She had her reasons. Where was God when the Cossacks rampaged through her *shtetl*?

She remembered them ripping her family's home apart. She would have been a toddler then, hiding under her mother's skirt. Amid the crashing of dishes, the shouts and threats, my great-grandmother stood her ground as she had done since her youth, an orphan girl making her way with a little money sewn inside her cloak. I don't know how she got the money, where she was going, or what she endured on the journey that knotted her thin lips like barbed wire. Her name was Freidel (Grandma named my mother Freidele, a diminutive, in her honour). It was to Freidel, not God, that my grandmother owed her survival. If anyone laid a hand on a child of Freidel Slobinsky's, it was going to be Freidel herself.

Freidel and her husband, Abraham, had five children, two sons and three daughters. In their time and place, every daughter was a burden, a dowry to be raised from scraps of nothing. But this alone does not explain Freidel's treatment of her daughters. As Grandma told it, Freidel sent the boys out to play while the girls cleaned like scullery maids. The boys ate fresh jam from the pot on the fire; the girls got the scum from the surface. To Abraham, Rona was something of a pet; he would take her on his errands and show her off to friends. To Freidel she was the lowest of the low, known as "Ugliness."

Grandma, of course, was not the most reliable of narrators. Even in the story she told most often, until it acquired the force

58

of an anthem, the details kept changing with her mood. The man was a Cossack, he was a passing workman. She was digging beets with her bare hands, she was playing among the roses in a rare moment of idleness. He raped her in a field, where thorns and pebbles dug into her back; he raped her in the shack where he kept his gear. One detail never changed: she was nine years old. Nor did the denouement, a beating and a scolding from Freidel: "Ugliness, I warned you, never give a man the opportunity."

"I didn't give him the opportunity! He picked me up and carried me away."

"Who's going to want you now? I'll be stuck with you forever!"

—◦⦿◦—

Rona must have been about twelve when the family sailed to Canada in search of opportunity. Farmland awaited them in the corner of Bird's Hill, Manitoba, that was known as "Jew Town." On the pier in Liverpool, Freidel made an announcement. Her smallest child, Lucy, was too frail and sick to make the journey. They would have to leave her behind. Rona wouldn't hear of it. She carried the baby on her back and looked after her all the way to Manitoba. From then on she and Lucy were inseparable, a family within a family. Grandma's other siblings didn't count; she had an arbitrary notion of kin.

In Bird's Hill she dug potatoes for a dollar a day, working barefoot to save her only pair of shoes. She dreamed of being somebody, and so did her father. No farmer at heart, he moved the family to Winnipeg, where he set up a thriving warehouse and in time became a founding father of Jewish charities. Young men lined up to dance with Abraham Slobinsky's lively daughter; young women burned with envy. Of all the suitors she could have married, she chose an artist, another Russian immigrant with nothing in his wallet and the wide world in his head. Her father took a dim view of this nobody, Ben Bruser, but Ben loved Rona as she wanted to be loved, with a bright, reckless abundance. Still, she took her sweet time to say yes. She declined his first proposal, driving Ben into the arms of the first woman who agreed to marry him. On his way home from the engagement party, emboldened by a few drinks, he went to see his Ronachka and threw himself on her mercy. She drove a hard bargain. They would marry, but the spurned fiancée would have to marry first. Refinement, *edelkeit*, required no less.

While he waited, he sent letters on paper with the texture of fine linen, each one embellished by a watercolour. Grandma never had many jewels to show me, so she displayed her letters instead. My favourite showed a curly-headed moppet hugging a bunny, with the caption "Oh, I wish I was a rabbit!" Not all of his exploits were deemed fit for children. He was such an artist with his roving hands that Rona yielded well before the wedding. He didn't lose his desire for her until he lost everything he was.

For the rest of her life she was the caretaker, the stout-hearted manager of challenges that would have overwhelmed a lesser woman. Ben Bruser was a *mensch*, with a heart as wide as the prairie sky, but what he knew about practical matters could have fit on the tip of his paintbrush. Together my grandparents launched and lost a succession of general stores in little prairie towns with no other Jewish families. These ventures were collectively known in the family as "Grandpa's store," although the truth is that Grandma should have run them. As they say of successful executives, she would not have shrunk from tough decisions. I can picture her saying, her voice clear and firm: "I'm sorry but I'll have to let you go. Nothing personal, in times like these we can't afford you. Leave your keys and your ID card with my assistant." Today she might have a corner office at Wal-Mart. In those days she did her best to fix her husband's blunders while scrubbing every surface in the store until it gleamed.

Grandpa's great talent as a retailer was creating the most beautiful window displays ever seen in the likes of Birch Hills and Plum Coulee. He would give you the shirt off his back; Grandma would do the prudent thing and sell it to you. She happened to be wearing a new dress, for once, when a customer came in and admired it. "Just a minute," said Grandma, ducking out. She emerged minutes later in her old, faded dress with the new one in her hands. "Only worn today so I'll give you a special price."

Queen of grit, sacrifice and survival, that was Rona the First. In addition to her other near-magical powers, she could create a sense of grace from nothing. Norman Rockwell could have painted the scene, if he'd had a Jewish immigrant period. Talk about *edelkeit*: hand-sewn dresses with embroidered hems for Freidele and her older sister Celia. Jelly in a crystal bowl, a metronome on the piano. To buy her girls an encyclopedia, Grandma sold her quilted coverlet. What wouldn't she do to give her children all that she had never had? One daughter in particular: Freidele, the favourite. A good daughter, always ready with a new accomplishment to raise the family banner of success.

With such a daughter, who needs a son?

There had been a son, her first baby, stillborn. Uncle Ephraim, mentioned once in the middle of her kitchen banter with an offhand laugh, as if he'd been a cake that hadn't worked out because of a mistake in the recipe. Grandpa cradled Ephraim in his arms; Grandma refused. Ephraim never existed, she claimed, so it was *mishigas*, craziness, to mourn him. With her usual certainty, she told me why he died: "He was too fat. All that cream I drank while I was expecting. Grandpa thought it would make the baby strong." I believed her story, believed she had gorged Uncle Ephraim to death.

Looking back, I doubt if Grandma really wanted a son. She could not have seen in a boy what she apparently saw in my mother – a miniature version of herself, only smarter, better and more lovable. Her first daughter, Celia, was beautiful and no slouch in the brains department, but stubborn and not much of a cuddler. Then along came Freidele, eager and pliable, the kind of baby a mother could encircle.

Freidele and her mother Rona. A sugar cube in a china bowl, a diamond in a wedding band. They completed each other in a physical way that outlasted my mother's infancy: Grandma would follow her to the toilet rather than interrupt their conversation.

Another little girl briefly joined my grandparents' family – the orphaned daughter of Grandma's older sister, who died in the flu epidemic of 1918. Grandpa had tender feelings toward all children, even the kids who came to his store to buy a few pennies' worth of candy. Grandma parcelled out attention to those who deserved it – her own. The niece didn't qualify, so she was packed off to the Jewish orphanage in Winnipeg. Love, to Grandma, was not unlike borscht in the old country. The more hungry faces around the table, the smaller the servings.

My mother used to tell this story deadpan, ignoring its darker side. Grandma, so bounteous in her love, was swift and unbending in her judgments. She had something of her own mother's ruthless pragmatism. You wouldn't want to cross her, as my mother knew she'd have to do if she chose Max Maynard. In the mind of an educated woman weighing her options there must have lurked, somewhere, the fears of an awestruck child.

Her mother had the power, if not the inclination, to punish her with banishment. And to lose her mother would have been to uproot the tree of life.

In fact, the bond between my mother and Grandma held the promise of betrayal from the start. To succeed in the thoroughly gentile academic world and fulfill her mother's hopes, Fredelle had to lose all visible traces of her immigrant origins, starting with her immigrant first name, Freidele. Grandma's old-fashioned ways became faintly embarrassing to her. How could she nudge her *shtetl*-born mother into modernity? When Grandma came to visit her at Radcliffe, she saw the perfect opportunity: dinner in a French restaurant.

Grandma beamed as my mother ordered *rôti de porc poêlé* for them both. So clever! You'd think she'd been studying in Paris. And her Fredelle knew just what to order. Sopping up the last of the gravy with her bread, Grandma sighed with contentment. "I could eat another serving but you need the money for your books. You know me, I could make it myself. So what was it?"

"You'll never believe it, Mums. That was pork. See what you've been missing all these years?" Grandma knew next to nothing about Judaism yet she clung to the ancient dictary laws, the primal horror of *trayf*. Her hands flew to her heart. "I don't feel so good. Take me home!"

Perhaps it was *beshert*, fate, that my mother should marry Max. The anti-Rona, he countered the spell of Grandma's engulfing, demanding love with his own brand of magic: that silk raincoat in the Manitoba chill, as if he could make his own weather; a penchant for British expressions like "chum" and "oh, lud." It was always a pastiche, that Englishness: his favourite expletive was the Irish "Jaysus." But as far as my mother could tell, he spoke like a man from a titled family with a country estate and a trout pond, although his forebears came from the working class. Yet with him Fredelle remained a stranger caught between two worlds, the one she had left and the Promised Land that never accepted her. At Maynard Hall she never found the confidence that Grandma somehow managed to exude in cramped prairie houses. She looked the part of a wife, but she had no marriage bed – another respect in which her mother eclipsed her. As a child she could tell when her parents had been making love by the way they jostled and squeezed each other in the kitchen, murmuring in Yiddish about private pleasures. Such jostlings and murmurings never happened at our house.

My grandparents were still in their sixties, barely retired and treating themselves to the first vacation of their lives, when it all fell apart. A drunk driver struck Grandpa in Miami, breaking both his legs and fracturing his skull. The medical bills demolished their savings. Then Grandpa fell ill with Alzheimer's. His vocabulary shrank to one word, "dear," which he could call the whole family without being wrong. Grandma laboured to care for him herself, but was forced to put him in a nursing home. I never knew the *mensch* of the family stories. I knew a hulking shadow who sat all day in an armchair. His smooth, pink face would have been handsome but for its blankness. He made a soft sound that was either chuckling or weeping. I never knew for sure until the tears coursed down his cheeks for sorrows he could no longer name.

⤜⟨◎⟩⤛

Christmas was coming. At the airport Grandma swallowed me with her distinctive hug, as soft as the mink and as hard as the corset. It had a scent, lemon drops and lavender sachets. As I squirmed, she reproved me: "Don't be such a stranger! Guess I'd better have a nice long visit this time so you and your Grandma can get reacquainted. Won't that be fun?" *You really crack me up, Grandma. How old do you think I am, anyway? I'm eleven, too old for this stuff. Try it on my pipsqueak sister.*

In the first week of Grandma's visit, our house became a command post for her domestic projects. The vacuum cleaner roared like a wild beast that she had collared; houseplants in brand new pots were hustled from window to window like patients in an old-fashioned sanatorium. Every room smelled of bleach and floor wax; the oven disgorged a stupefying abundance of cookies. Things vanished as Grandma tidied them up – my word lists for the spelling bee, my father's new book on the Bloomsbury Group. He attempted a smile that became a wince: "My good woman, you are a force of nature." (He didn't have a name for her – not the stuffy "Mrs. Bruser," the too-familiar "Rona" or the inconceivable "Mother.")

Grandma seemed to swell like an enormous bird; compliments, intended or otherwise, always had that effect on her. "You know me, Max, I love to help my daughter. A head like hers, she has better things to do than clean." My mother frowned as if she were hearing something different: *My daughter has let things slide around here.*

By the second week, the house was so clean that even Grandma had trouble finding hidden disaster zones. Now we were really in for it. With time on her hands, she dogged my mother's steps, filling every minute with her stream-of-consciousness patter about strangers back in Winnipeg: "Goldbaums' girl married a *goy*, of course they're heartsick, *zoll zeyn*, so be it, I hear Luba's having a colostomy, eighty years old and they don't let her go in peace, of course, the doctors want to make a little *gelt*; Rose came by for tea, when she gets going about her grandson there's no stopping that woman and what has he accomplished, bounces a basketball, nothing to Rona and Joyce, for this she fills my head with her *kvelling*?" Her three favourite themes, braided like *challah*. No matter where you started out with Grandma, you ended up musing on defection to the *goyim*, grisly operations and the innate superiority of her family to everyone else's. If my mother tried to change the subject, she was put in her place: "Before you know it, I'll be pushing daisies. Nothing left of me but Grandpa's letters and my mink. A beautiful fur, somebody can wear it for years."

"Oh, please, Mums, you've got more stamina than all of us combined."

In Grandma's presence my mother seemed to wilt. She stopped quoting poetry; Grandma didn't care about dead *goyim*. She lost her zest for outrageous anecdotes; Grandma's conversation had worn her out. She would snap and then sigh, ashamed at her own ingratitude. In my mind I called to her: *Come back to me. Be your strong, funny, magnificent self for me.* A stranger had taken her place, and this new person was about as magnificent as the frazzled woman in a painkiller commercial that I liked to mimic. The TV woman spits to her mother, who is trying to give her a hand in the kitchen, "Mother, *please*! I can do it *myself*!" Now I couldn't laugh anymore at the pitiful *mother-please* woman, who was going to be the shame of her family if she didn't deal with that headache. She was one of my own.

In Grandma's third week with us, Christmas rushed by. Grandma was determined to make special deep-fried pastries for the occasion. Rosettes, they were called. Apparently, nobody knew how to make them anymore. Nor did anyone seem to sell rosette irons. Tracking one down required an odyssey through every housewares department in the area. My mother sat with

Grandma in pre-Christmas traffic; she elbowed her way through hordes of shoppers seeking deals on bubble lights. On Christmas morning I understood why nobody bothered to make rosettes. Who wanted to eat deep-fried pastry with nothing inside? The platter of rosettes sat barely touched beside the tree.

Sometime after Christmas, my mother ran outside in her nightgown to warm up the car for my father. Next thing we knew, she had cold sweats and a fever, as high as any Grandma had seen in years of nursing her family. A doctor came, the only one willing to drive through a blizzard. It didn't look good: "Pneumonia, too weak to move in this weather. Good thing she has her mother to look after her. Touch and go."

That night our house rocked with fear. I sat down with my spelling bee words, but this time they made my eyes ache. My father retreated to his study, emerging only to stumble down the hall to the bathroom with exaggerated care. Joyce had gone to bed early, her face buried in a pile of stuffed animals. I peered at her through the half-open door and then left her to the comfort of the animals. In our house, you had to be crazy to disturb a sleeping person. From the kitchen I heard the clump-clump of Grandma's *chubatoras*. She would know, she would tell me.

"Is my mother going to die?"

Grandma was attacking the bottom of a pot with a Brillo pad, hard enough to shake the flesh on her arms. Lank tendrils of hair had worked their way loose from a squadron of bobby pins. Her face sagged as if it were melting but her lips were tight with resolve. She looked at me as if from the far end of a cave. "One thing I know, it's sickness. All kinds, all places. People gone in their prime, just like that. Women today, they don't know the things I had to learn. But it was for the best. I know what to do."

She had turned my bedroom into a sickroom for my mother. While she cleaned up, I slipped into the blue bedroom and opened the closet door. I found my mother's work shirt, the one she had worn the day she pruned the lilacs, and held it to my face. It smelled of her and everything she touched around our house – raked leaves, dusty books, stale perfume from the bottle of Tigris that had sat on her dresser ever since I could remember. I breathed in the garlic from her hands, the ink from a fresh typewriter ribbon, the faint green crust of Comet she left around the bathtub, ashes from the fireplace and onions browning on the stove. *You can't die. You can't leave us alone with Daddy.*

I slept on the living room couch while my mother's illness dragged on. At night I had the Christmas tree all to myself, the branches holding out their bounty of glitter like false promises. Ghost branches now, their needles scattered where the presents had been. I listened to my father banging down the hall upstairs to the bathroom. He was going to stain the floor carelessly again, and this time it would be Grandma shaking her head. With her around, he had curbed his loudest nocturnal excesses, the crashing chords and the sermons, but I found myself missing the bizarre soundtrack of ordinary life at Maynard Hall.

Grandma snapped the thermometer like a baton. She sent Daddy out for rubbing alcohol and through the open doorway I saw her knead my mother's naked body with the big, powerful arms that had lifted the car from the mud long ago. My mother's skin was the colour of a mushroom; she mumbled in delirium. It embarrassed me to see her without clothes, without words. She didn't sit up that day or the next. But during a winter thaw she finally rose from her bed. With her first breath she thanked Grandma for saving her life. With her second she looked

at herself sideways in the mirror and announced that she must
have dropped a couple of sizes.

Grandma put on her mink and flew home to Winnipeg. In
her suitcase she carried the rosette iron and two new shawl-
collared dresses that my mother had bought her. I can imagine
what she must have carried in her head – the truth about our
lives at Maynard Hall. She had cleaned up the bathroom floor
every morning, as my mother surely knew. That spring her
annual Mother's Day letter had an unaccustomed gravity:

> My dearest, my darling Mother –
>
> I am thinking, of course, of how you carried us
> all through those dreadful first weeks of
> January. . . . I would not, heaven knows, wish for
> pneumonia, nor did I have to take sick to
> realize how very dear you are to me. But
> being sick was truly a kind of fresh revelation
> of your strength, your understanding and your
> utter loveableness. . . .

She never spoke again of Grandma's "understanding," and
Grandma never said "I told you so." What had once been my
mother's private shame was now a secret they guarded together,
compounding both her loneliness and her sense of obligation to
Grandma. My mother didn't have to tell me this. I could read
her like a book.

I didn't have the same knack for spelling, despite my dreams
of triumph in Washington. I placed third in the class bee
without even advancing to the school competition. That day
I came home in tears because, after mastering the likes of

"onomatopoeia," I had misspelled the lowly "possessed." My mother seemed amused. "So, let me get this straight. You're in tears because you didn't win a memorization contest? Well, Rona, may this be the worst calamity that ever happens to you! Sweetheart, I'll be crossing my fingers!"

HANDSOME DEVIL

When my father was a young artist in Victoria, with more ambition than money, he took a job teaching at Lampson Street School. He cut a dashing figure, bounding out at the end of the day with a sketchbook under his arm. Sometimes he found a sedan waiting at the curb, with a stout, middle-aged woman at the wheel. The sight of her mesmerized the children. Imagine, a lady who could drive! They had no idea she was famous. Her name was Emily Carr, and she had come to take Mr. Maynard sketching.

Soon enough, Emily soured on her protegé. She thought he was playing fast and loose with her ideas, and she wasn't entirely wrong. A painting that hung in our living room – a white church surrounded by brooding Douglas firs – looked exactly like one of hers, down to the last trunk and bough. I knew because I'd seen it in a book. On top of being crazy, my father was a poseur, a thief of visions. When a visitor admired our painting ("so powerful, such reverence for nature"), I felt compelled to set the record straight. "It's just a copy. Daddy took the idea from some woman named Emily Carr."

My mother's lips cracked in an icy smile (just like me to raise such petty details when nobody in Durham had heard of Emily Carr). She said, "Rona hasn't yet discovered the concept of homage but she has an exaggerated passion for ethics. Sometimes I think we're living in a courthouse, the way this child keeps us in line."

Afterwards she let fly. "How ironic, Rona! You presume to judge your father, but you've acquired his talent for causing offence. You seem to think you're the keeper of a higher truth, but let me tell you, the world does not look kindly on those who make free with the feelings of others."

My father's past was an ocean of mystery. He appeared to sail across it in an open boat, barely holding his own against the wind. He had somehow arrived at the safe harbour of Maynard Hall, yet the set of his mouth suggested hazards on the journey that were mostly of his making. From the school-teaching years he had only one story, the one we came to know as "The Little Japanese Girl."

Toshie Takata was the prettiest child in the class, a Canadian like everyone else. Her parents owned a teahouse. In their community, no other families were of Japanese origin, yet at school Toshie was everyone's pet, with a delicacy and grace that attracted the bigger, rougher children. One day my father took the class to swim at the Crystal Garden, a pleasure dome that was Victoria's pride. As the children jumped into the pool, an attendant pulled Toshie aside. No Japanese allowed. Sorry, no exceptions. Toshie had to sit in the stands, holding back tears.

She was in grade five, just like me when I first heard the story. And my father had abandoned her. "Daddy, why didn't you do something?"

My father cleared his throat. "It was 1934; such practices were commonplace then. There wasn't a great deal anyone could do."

"But, Daddy, it was segregation. You could have stood up for her. You could have said, 'Either everyone swims, or everyone goes home.'"

Was that so much to ask? Down south, black people were staging sit-ins to integrate swimming pools and lunch counters. They weren't afraid of billy clubs, and I loved their obstinate dignity.

"Ah, Rona, you sound so sure of yourself. I did write a letter of apology to the Takatas, and they seemed quite appreciative."

In 1934 my mother had been twelve years old – like Toshie, the child of outsiders. She too could have been barred from any number of swimming pools, where signs said "No Jews allowed." And Daddy would have let it pass. He didn't have the courage to do the right thing. I knew what Grandma would say about that letter he wrote: "Letter, schmetter. A letter you can tear in little pieces and take to the outhouse for your business!"

⁕

For a cultivated man of his time, my father didn't send many letters. He'd begin them late at night, in his cups, then have second thoughts in the morning. My mother, meanwhile, seldom let a day pass without mailing at least one single-spaced letter and filing a carbon for future reference. She used to mention two letters, both to Grandma, that she chose to exclude from the family archive. One announced her marriage, the other its demise.

I have a snapshot of my parents on their wedding day in 1948 (they had no leather-bound album). My mother squints into the sunlight, her gown a bargain-basement formal with too-tight sleeves. My father, rigid in his three-piece suit, could fit right in at a funeral. They've just taken their vows on the fly. Daddy's new boss at the state university has opened his home for the occasion and given the bride away (she hasn't yet told her parents she is finally becoming Mrs. Max Maynard). A March wind ruffles my mother's hair; distraction tugs at her face, as if she's wondering how to break the news to Grandma.

Six years of courtship, and this was the best they could do.

The honeymoon was a quick trip to Boston. About to board their train, the newlyweds were accosted by a station agent waving a telegram. My mother reached out to see who was sending good wishes, but Daddy shoved the telegram into his pocket. On her wedding night, she searched his pockets and fished it out. A collection agency, threatening legal action.

Her mother must never know. For her mother she would spin a tale of joy. If she had told the real story, her letter might have gone like this:

Dearest Mums,

Life is full of surprises. When Max and I were courting, he used to fill my ears with his talk of Truth and Beauty. Oh, the rapture of it all! Somehow he convinced me that truth and beauty were one and the same. I could quote you the poem, Mums, by a young dreamer who died more than a hundred years ago, but right now I can't bear to think about the words of dead poets because I am alive and alone in New Hampshire, a married woman. Mrs. Max Singleton Maynard.

Yes, I have done it. Can you forgive me? I made the plan and kept the secret for fear of disappointing you. I deceived you and Daddy, the people who love me more than anyone, who deserve so much better than this two-faced love you've had from me.

But there must be justice in the world because it turns out I too have been deceived and so, in a way, I'm closer to you now than ever, curled inside your heart, pinned to you with my own grief. Max has a secret room above our apartment that the landlady lets him use and, Mums, you wouldn't believe what I found there (well, probably you would believe it; you always did see the things I missed – the stone I might trip on, the playmate who wasn't as loyal as I thought). The most extraordinary collection of empty liquor bottles! Fat ones, thin ones, short ones, tall ones. I should take up painting them and set up a booth at a rummage sale: handmade vases, twenty-five cents. The way our so-called finances are looking, we could use a painter with a practical bent, don't you think? I could earn us a second-hand crib for your first granddaughter and a nice brisket or two.

So here I am with a clever old drunk (a magician with words but a drunk just the same) and a head full of guilt because you tried to warn me and I was too proud to listen. Now you're half a continent away and I won't be resting my head on your shoulder anytime soon. (Have I ever told you, Mums, that when I was a little girl, the soft roundness of your lap

*held all the warmth and security in the world?) And
here's the worst of this new life I've made, the part I
can hardly bring myself to say because I thought my
cultivated, fastidious husband was above such things.
He cannot forget my Jewishness; he seems to disdain
it. I am onion-scented gravies too rich for his
stomach; I am the red sash that he considers too
flagrant; I am the too-loud laugh, the too-eager lips;
I am Other, a long way from home . . .*

One morning my mother got up to find a half-finished letter on
the breakfast table, written in my father's hand that slanted like
a hard summer rain. It looked just like the letters he had sent
while they were courting: "Dear my love . . ." Perhaps he wanted
her to read it, with half of his conflicted heart, although this time
he was addressing someone else: his ex-wife in Victoria, a
woman he'd described as a youthful mistake. Now he was
begging her to take him back and describing Fredelle as the
mistake: "Here I am with this clever little Jewish girl . . ."

My mother liked to joke about Daddy's past conquests, as if to
prove how lucky she must be to have won him, this large-living
rake who didn't think of settling down until he set his blue eyes
on Fredelle Bruser. But there had always been a woman too
dangerous to mention. Evelyn Wheeler, his first wife, her very
existence kept secret for fear of bringing shame on our household. I was twenty, on the point of getting married myself, when
my mother finally told me about her. My parents were still
married then, but barely.

"You thought an ex-wife was such a big deal? God, Mother, half the country has an ex these days! What possessed you to keep her a secret?"

"Your father never loved her. There were no children. It wasn't important."

Evelyn was as close to a blueblood as you could find in Victoria, the daughter of a retired railway president. Her impeccable tweeds came from Straith's, the kind of shop that could dress a young woman for tea with visiting royalty. She took an interest in the life of the mind, but Mr. Wheeler had refused to send her to college; he thought book-learning was wasted on women. She married beneath her when she chose Max Maynard. Because my father was barely getting by on a teacher's salary, Mr. Wheeler sent her an allowance. Officially, the marriage lasted from 1933 until the brink of my parents' wedding. My mother kept urging Daddy to get a divorce, and he kept finding reasons to put the whole thing off, raising Evelyn's hopes while planning his escape from her. Max Maynard was the second great loss in Evelyn's life. As a child she'd lost her mother to a mental institution for some mysterious breakdown. Perhaps Mrs. Wheeler was not mad or ill, just unhappy pouring tea for her husband. In her day that kind of unhappiness could get a woman locked up for life.

I have a photo of Evelyn reclining on a beach, a languid beauty with legs that go on and on (how my mother would have envied that body). Her oval face, under one of those snoods that the Duchess of Windsor used to wear, looks both regal and resigned, as if she has been borne on a yacht to attend a party in her honour, only to find that the shrimp taste slightly off and all the guests have had too much to drink. She never remarried.

Growing up, I sensed her presence the way Jane Eyre sensed the mad wife in the attic. Evelyn was the dusty, never-marked exams in my father's desk, the softening radishes in the vegetable drawer, the small signs of neglect that dotted our house like clues to a mystery.

She had something to do with the bare floor and curtainless windows of my mother's blue bedroom. On the wall hung one of Daddy's charcoal drawings, an unlikely love token from their courtship. The scene appeared to have flowed from his hand in waves of despair: a farmhouse alone on a prairie, its windows like two black eyes. A storm has roiled the sky and knocked the bushes flat. Aside from the drawing, the room contained no trace of my father. No suits or ties in that closet, no condoms tucked under the hankies in a dresser drawer. I remember, just once, hearing laughter and creaking bedsprings behind the closed door of my mother's bedroom. It was not unlike the memory of Hurricane Hazel, which toppled huge trees in our town and then retreated into local legend.

My father slept across the hall on the single bed in his study, the darkest room in the house and the only one furnished as he liked. It could have been a monk's cell, if monks had possessions to strew in unlikely piles – corn plasters and Pepto-Bismol on top of *The Divine Comedy*. My father displayed no artwork in the study, just a framed photo of his parents, surrounded by their seven children (my mother wouldn't have it anywhere else). They perched on straight-back chairs in the prim clothing of Edwardian times. My grandfather had the sunken cheeks of a starving man but it was Grandmother Maynard, with her chin like the business end of a shovel and her small fierce eyes, who made me squirm. She seemed to be sizing me up. I could tell where Daddy got his assertive jaw line, which gave drama to his face and only grim determination to hers. She had what looked to me like a monumental plainness, although it may have been a cultivated scorn for any trace of vanity. Her children looked numb except for my father, who seemed about to bolt from the frame. In short pants and a Norfolk jacket, he seemed a picture-book child until you studied his expression. It was at once defiant and fearful, as if he'd been caught in a lie.

I tried to avoid the study, with its distinctive acrid smell, but sometimes I needed a pen or a copy of *Oliver Twist* from the complete leather-bound works of Dickens. On one of the shelves sat a Hellmann's mayonnaise jar containing an inch or so of yellow liquid. I must have looked right through that jar at least a hundred times without realizing what the liquid was – my father's urine. I didn't want to know that when my father drank in the night, he found it a challenge to stagger to the bathroom. He might fall or, worse, leave stains on the bathroom floor. The next morning my mother would make fun of him in front of me and Joyce: "Someone's been missing his aim again! Ah, well! Creating art for the ages must be vastly more important than keeping an eye on the toilet bowl like ordinary mortals." I looked at my father: head downcast, lips tight with embarrassment, a child's hangdog expression on the face of a white-haired man. How could he?

Your father is a brilliant, original man. Except when he can't pee straight.

—◦◦◦—

What my father would not say about his past he revealed unawares. Once he came home with a record, some folk singer he thought my mother would like. He'd been looking for more of the usual symphonies or string quartets, until he strode into the record store and heard the clear, knowing voice of a young woman with a guitar. "Charming stuff," he told us. "I gather the students can't get enough of this Joan Baez."

The jacket photo alone piqued my interest. At twelve, I wanted Joan's face – those high cheekbones, that expression of proud, abstracted sorrow. Then the first ballad filled our living room, and I shivered with recognition. Called "Silver Dagger," the song told a story of betrayal handed down from mother to daughter. The mother sleeps beside her daughter, a dagger in her hand, to protect her from the dangerous attentions of a suitor. Afraid to trust the man who loves her, the daughter heeds her mother's warning and vows to sleep alone for the rest of her life. She has learned too well what men are like:

> My daddy is a handsome devil
> He's got a chain five miles long
> And on every link a heart does dangle
> Of another maid he's loved and wronged.

"Very pretty, dear," said my mother (from my mother's lips, "dear" could have the ring of a threat). "But let me offer a gentle reminder. We need a new roof. Bills are piling up. And some of us are buying records just because we happen to be charmed."

What was she talking about? The song was not pretty. It was fierce and true. Only a woman could create such a song. I wondered who she was, the first woman to sing it, somewhere in the Appalachian Mountains more than a hundred years ago. A woman with a few teeth and a passel of children, not counting the dead ones. She probably couldn't write the words that came to her, not that she needed to. She could look up from her washboard and belt out her testament. The poems my mother quoted had nothing to do with me, but "Silver Dagger" was my story. I kept playing the song until my father shouted down from his study, "Jaysus, have we not had enough of this keening?"

—⟨⟨⟩⟩—

Before any of the women who hung their broken hearts on Daddy's chain, there was one who could have said, "I told you so." His mother, Eliza Teague, known as Lily, a God-fearing woman and proud of it. Lily died long before he met Fredelle, who would have loathed her. She was "a bit stern," according to my father (he might as well have called Everest "a bit of a climb"). When she caught him smoking, she fixed him with a baleful stare and said, as if she saw the pitiable state of his soul, "So you smoke, Max. What *else* do you do?"

He didn't like to talk about his childhood. If I pressed him too hard, he would quote the Gospel of John: "When I was a child, I spake as a child, I understood as a child, I thought as a child: but when I became a man, I put away childish things."

I have pieced his story together from other sources, and one theme stands out: the harrowing force of Lily's religious conviction. If she were in her prime today, she might be preaching to millions on TV, decrying the evils of abortion and same-sex marriage. The sweetness of her name, all leaves and petals, belied her hellfire-breathing passion. She strove mightily to make her children worthy of salvation, but Max never did get the message. A scamp and a rebel, he hid when she called him; he was caught painting on a Sunday when he should have been reading the Bible. (As punishment, his parents locked up the paints for a year.) She should have known the worst was yet to come. At nineteen, Max left his parents' faith. On Judgment Day, when the sun would turn black and the saved would be swept up to sit at God's right hand, the Maynards' apostate son would plummet to hell for eternity. Both his parents knew this the same way they knew that God created the earth in seven days. But it was Lily whose rhetorical flights made damnation so vivid, you could practically smell burning flesh.

For a tin miner's daughter born in 1865, she enjoyed a remarkable preaching career – until she was trapped by the barriers of her day. Religion fired her imagination early. She came from the Cornish town of Redruth, where John Wesley, the founder of Methodism, had once preached to more than thirty thousand people. Lily's parents were staunch Methodists; they must have pointed out to her the vast outdoor amphitheatre where the great man rallied the faithful. As a child, she already showed a flair for oratory. She specialized in temperance doggerel, denouncing the evils of the bottle with such zest that she was offered a world tour. (So Lily claimed; modesty was not among the virtues she aspired to.) At seventeen, she became the Salvation Army's youngest officer, much admired for her pluck. When a drunken heckler got in her way, she knocked the wastrel down.

She aspired to be more than just another hallelujah lassie, however, and her dreams found a focus in the vaulting ambitions that were shaking up the Salvation Army. The Army's founder, General William Booth, held progressive views on the advancement of women. His daughter, Emma Booth-Tucker, ran the international missions and was grooming Lily Teague for leadership.

In 1887, the Salvation Army launched a madcap scheme to honour Queen Victoria's Golden Jubilee. Fifty officers would sail to India, where they would live exactly like the poorest of natives – same food, same clothes, same sanitation – while planting the flag of Jesus. They saw themselves as the advance guard in an officer corps one million strong, an improbably lofty goal, given that India's total European population was then well under twenty thousand. It was a brutal assignment, requiring equal portions of delusion and resolve. Lily volunteered. On the boat she caught the eye of another young officer – my grandfather, Harry – who came to her rescue when the mission went disastrously wrong.

The natives did not flock to convert; instead, they laughed at these foolish European softies who could not withstand the diseases to which they had no natural immunity. As Christian soldiers died at their posts or retreated to the comforts of home, Lily fell dangerously ill. True to form, she vowed to stay the course. My grandfather, fearing for her life, insisted that they leave the Army together, a married couple starting over in their service to God. He fought as hard for Lily as Ben Bruser did for his Ronachka, or Max for Fredelle.

Lily's departure triggered consternation. (Harry was apparently considered no great loss, a mere foot soldier.) Emma Booth-Tucker shook her fist in my grandfather's face and called him a "villain" for "stealing Lily Teague from us." Lily's fine Christian friends in the Army turned their backs on her, and she mourned their loss until she died.

She lost more than friends when she left the Army. The harder loss was a public forum for her preaching. After a few years as Methodist missionaries, she and Harry joined the fanatically rigorous Plymouth Brethren, who devoted their whole existence to preparing for Judgment Day. Compared with the Brethren, the Salvationists were vaudevillians. The Brethren thought music was the devil's work; they scorned the least hint of pomp and circumstance as dangerous vestiges of "popery." (There were those among the early Brethren who shuddered at the very mention of Christmas: what could be more "popish" than "Christ's mass"?) Harry thrived in this band of the elect, but Lily found herself sidelined: the Brethren consigned married women to supporting roles. God over man. Man over woman. Spirit over body. Hers was not to reason why.

On the surface, Lily could not have been more different from Rona the First. Yet my two grandmothers shared some common ground. As strong women born too soon, both found themselves standing behind gentle, idealistic men. Both had no focus for their talents except motherhood. Both were exiles who bore and lost their first children in alien places.

Lily's first-born, a son, died at five months in India, where the Maynards returned as missionaries. They lived between two worlds: one belonging to the "heathen," the other to the status-conscious British Raj, whose members suspected missionaries of "stirring up the natives." The Maynards went on to have seven other children – most of whom, including Max, were born in southern India, in a village not far from the Nilgiri Hills – but the family seldom lived under one roof. While my father was a small child tended by a Tamil *ayah*, his two oldest siblings were at school in England. He used to watch Harry treat the oozing sores of the sick at the mission clinic. But my grandfather, so compassionate toward the natives, was capable of leaving Lily and the children for months at a stretch while he travelled on the Lord's business. In his absence, Lily had to run a large household on her own. Every day she preached the Gospel to the only flock she had – the children – with no one to moderate her influence.

In 1912, when my father was nine, Harry moved the Maynards to Victoria. Soon two foster children joined the family. One of them, Fred Brand, became the longest living survivor of Lily's prayer sessions, which he described to me when I visited him in a cottage outside London that smelled of sweat and sour milk. It was years ago and I foolishly didn't take notes, assuming every detail of Fred's life among the Maynards would be with me always. I even thought we might meet again one day, although Fred was frail and elderly, with thin white hair and wandering eyes. All I remember now is an image of a child's terror seizing an old man's body. The very thought of Lily praying pulled Fred out of his chair onto unsteady feet, as if he felt an urge to escape. He trembled and wept. I felt ashamed to be witnessing such abject vulnerability, and yet for him I was no longer present. He stared past me, hollow-eyed, as he must once have stared at my grandmother. Nearly sixty years had passed since her death in 1929, but he saw her still. At last he spoke, like a lamentation: "She was a black Lily! A black Lily!"

If Fred could not leave her behind, why would Max Maynard be any different? When he fled her home and her sermons, he never really left her, never outran the demons she set upon him. He must have looked for his mother in other strong women, testing and goading them in the inarticulate hope of finally winning the forgiveness that Lily had withheld. In my mother he met the perfect foil. Raised to believe he could do nothing right, he found a woman raised to think that she could do no wrong.

REBELLION

Around five o'clock on a Sunday afternoon, as I lounged on my bed with *The Catcher in the Rye*, someone's car blasted out of our driveway like a hot rod. I rushed to the window just in time to see our blue Studebaker tear down the street, my mother at the wheel. Bound for points unknown, an hour before dinner.

In the kitchen she'd left a ghost meal. A mound of peeled apples, turning brown. A pastry blender clogged with shortening. The *Better Homes and Gardens Cookbook* spread-eagled in a puddle of tomato pulp. That night, for the first and only time, dinner consisted of sandwiches. My father cleared his throat. My sister spilled her milk. No one spoke.

The queen of England might as well have run off to an island with a pirate; that's how baffled I was.

Next morning I found my mother in the kitchen, the pressure cooker already seething. Chicken soup, Daddy's favourite lunch. "So where were you last night?"

The answer exploded as if she'd been waiting to let fly. "Out, that's where! Has it ever occurred to you, Rona, that I might deserve at least a small reward for the work I do around here? That maybe after stocking the cookie jar and entertaining

Daddy's students and cranking out another three thousand words for *Good Housekeeping*, I might want a few minutes to call my own? You of all people should understand that, Miss Can't You See I'm Reading, Miss Don't Come In Without Knocking! For a bright girl you can be surprisingly obtuse. You seem to have forgotten that I spent the best part of the weekend helping you finish that dress you had to wear today, never mind that I've got a deadline to meet. And what did you say to me afterwards? Waving your dainty hand as if I were your maid? 'We're out of Diet Pepsi.' Would it kill you to drink something else?"

So her anger was all my fault. Oh, please! She was the one who scorned store-bought cookies, who prodded me to make my own dresses, who faithfully sent all her magazine tearsheets to Grandma. By this time she made more money writing for women's magazines than my father did teaching literature. (She must have been the only writer in *Good Housekeeping*'s stable who crafted her prose with Milton's cadences ringing in her brain.) If my mother thought she had too much to do, let her try doing less. Holden Caulfield had a word for people like her: phony! (She would have called him the hero of a book, *The Catcher in the Rye*; I thought of Holden as the boy I loved.) That day I got my Diet Pepsi, a whole case of it. But if she wanted me to thank her, she'd be waiting until her precious teak table was ready for a yard sale.

It was 1964, a year of anthems and polemics. Marchers denouncing the Vietnam war, three civil rights workers killed in Mississippi. I linked arms with a cluster of demonstrators in a town with no black people, singing "We Shall Overcome" and wondering when some dashing, blue-jeaned saviour of the downtrodden would be smitten with my inner beauty. I was almost fifteen; my mother was forty-two. She had just acquired a paperback copy of *The Feminine Mystique*, which she carried around like a talisman, filling the margins with notes in her emphatic hand. She kept leaving that book on the kitchen table or the back of the toilet, as if she were daring me to read it. But I had read the article in *Life* magazine, and it told me more than enough about the plague of boredom dogging housewives all over the land. Like a witch with a frowzy bubble cut, author Betty Friedan had foretold my mother's flight from her kitchen: "Sometimes . . . the feeling gets so strong [a woman] runs out of the house. . . ." If this was revolution, I didn't want it. Besides, I'd never be one of those women, those pitiful, tranquillized chumps fuming over their vacuum cleaners. I'd write poetry under the eaves in a Greenwich Village flat, by the light of a candle in a Chianti bottle. No wage-slave husband for me. I'd have a lover who spoke like Richard Burton, looked like Jean-Louis Trintignant and rattled the walls of Middle America like Bob Dylan.

A sign on my bedroom door shouted, "PROTEST AGAINST THE RISING TIDE OF CONFORMITY." The sign had a target: my mother, with her dutiful cocktail parties for Daddy's loudmouth colleagues, who would never recommend him for promotion, no matter how elaborate her canapés. My mother, who prided herself on driving miles out of her way to save a few cents on canned cream-of-mushroom soup, burning up the savings on gas. My mother, who invented and overcame a new crisis every month – drug addiction, widowhood, agoraphobia – for a magazine feature called "My Problem and How I Solved It" (with no byline, she could take on a multitude of sad-sack personas). *Why don't you solve a real problem, Mother? How about "My Husband Is a Drunk"?*

Of course I never said that. What I said, rolling my eyes in case she didn't get the point, was, "I can't wait to get out of this place!"

"Your problem isn't this house, Rona. It's you. When you're old enough to read *Paradise Lost*, you're going to look back on these years and understand that Satan is your soulmate:

> Which way I fly is hell; myself am hell;
> And in the lowest deep a lower deep
> Still threatening to devour me opens wide,
> To which the hell I suffer seems a heaven."

Why couldn't she just tell me to go to hell, the way other parents did when their kids drove them wild? She had to prove she was above such lowbrow tactics, that's why. My mother was an expert on *Paradise Lost*, along with everything else John Milton wrote. Other people had forgotten that, so I was supposed to remember. But I knew the score. "You have no idea what's going on in my head!" I shouted. "You don't know me at all. But I'll give you credit for one thing. You made me strong enough to fight you!"

⁓◦⊙◦⁓

In the life of a woman I had reached the first age of longing. It sharpened and polished me until I danced like a sword in a duel for my honour. I wanted to know how it felt to be naked with a man's naked body on top of me. I wanted Joan Baez hair, long shining panels that never went frizzy in the rain. I wanted to taste magic mushrooms, unlock the doors of perception and gather up truths never seen or spoken in a shimmering garland of words. All of these dreams pressed their absence upon me with the same humiliating force, but the sheer devotion of my longing had a tattered grandeur that gave me hope. It was the banner I carried through the cinder-block halls of Oyster River High School, where the in girls sneaked cigarettes in the washroom and the boys never asked me for a date. None of them, I felt sure, knew a wanting as fierce as my wanting. Maybe no one ever had, except the Holden Caulfields of this world.

It never entered my mind that there could be a second age of longing, when a woman looks back as well as forward, with the urgency of knowing that she doesn't have forever to become the person she dreamed of becoming, before the walls of grown-up life closed in. This was my mother, still looking for a way back to the classroom. She applied for a fellowship and sought a letter of reference from a previous recipient, a young colleague of my father's. "Really, Fredelle!" he said. "All I know about your qualifications is that you host superb parties and are raising two enchanting daughters."

But all was not lost, not entirely.

Out of nowhere the English department phoned her in a panic. They'd just lost the instructor for the extension class at the air force base down the road. The lowest pay, the worst hours. The tenured staff wouldn't touch that gig. My mother grabbed it. For one night a week, she could have a classroom of her own. "Why don't you come along?" she asked me. "Wait till you see the first story I've chosen. You won't read anything like it in that hidebound school of yours. It'll lift off the top of your head."

She intended to dazzle me. And vice versa. We hardly went anywhere together in those days, but I couldn't refuse her challenge.

The airmen had come to class directly from their drills, in sweat-stained fatigues with chest hair bursting from their undershirts. They sat with their legs apart like cowboys on imaginary horses. They had big, nervous laughs and darting eyes. The only other female student, somebody's young wife in a sweater set and pearls, leaned forward on her elbows, marvelling at the first assignment: "Well, Dr. Maynard, you sure picked a corker. That last sentence: '. . . and then they were upon her.' What was *that* all about?"

At the lectern my mother smiled, the keeper of shivery surprises. "You mean you weren't expecting ritual murder in this class? A happy housewife stoned to death by her neighbours?"

No one expected it, me included. She *had* lifted off the top of my head.

We had just read "The Lottery," a short story that to me will always be hers. And she did, in fact, have something in common with the writer; both were misfit faculty wives. "The story came to Shirley Jackson in a waking dream as she pushed her baby's stroller down the picturesque streets of Bennington, Vermont," my mother said. "Her husband was a famous literary critic at Bennington College; Shirley was the town eccentric. She liked to say she dabbled in the black arts, which may or may not have been true. What matters is that the outsider's perspective allowed Shirley Jackson to tear the Norman Rockwell façade off small-town life and reveal what lay beneath: an evil older than the graveyard and as close as the back fence. But it doesn't announce itself with screams or spurting blood, this evil. For that you can catch a double bill at the drive-in. Look at Shirley Jackson's opening images. Warm sunny day, green grass, all those flowers. You half expect some lovable geezer to start singing, 'Oh, What a Beautiful Morning.' The writer lines up her details like a teacup collection, the better to shock you in the end. When *The New Yorker* published 'The Lottery' in 1948, hundreds of readers cancelled their subscriptions. They thought poor Tessie Hutchinson was about to win a Bendix washer, and what was her rich reward? A blood sacrifice in the town square! Her own son coming in for the kill!"

My mother strode among the metal chairs as if through a kingdom of words. Something hidden within her had burst forth, something shiny and lush and brave. The men followed every toss of her hair, every swivel of her hips under the new tweed sheath. She had conquered them and she knew it. To me she was the lesson as well as the teacher – the most enthralling teacher I had seen. She had always told the truth about her gifts in the class-room, and I had not believed her. I thought she'd stretched the facts in her usual way, when if anything she'd downplayed her powers. She said, "So let's talk about the victim. Why a woman? And why this particular woman, Tessie Hutchinson?"

"There has to be a reason?" This from a pimple-flecked airman who looked like a kid. "Maybe Shirley just needed to wrap things up. She could have picked anyone. Kapow!"

"Oho! Feeling cocky today, I see! Now, I wonder what would happen if you flew your plane hither and yon without a reason. You might get shot down over Russia! Kapow, indeed!" Everyone chuckled.

The woman in the pearls offered a few insights that sounded more like questions. "You know something's up because she's late for the lottery? She says she didn't want to leave her dirty dishes for her husband to find? And it's so sad because she tried to do the right thing and she'll never wash another dish again?" Blank looks from the men. Who'd be sad about dishes?

I put up my hand, alight with an idea. "The men in this town run the lottery the way they run everything else. The women don't have any power. They get to run the house and they get to die if they draw the wrong slip. Tessie's a bit of a rebel. She didn't try to do the right thing; I bet she just hated washing dishes. She's the perfect victim because she broke the rules." Nodding heads all around; I could outdo these grown-ups in their own class. "But I wouldn't call it sad, what happens to Tessie. She's not exactly sweetness and light. She practically begs to see someone else stoned in her place, her own step-daughter." I took a deep breath. "The right thing would be stopping the lottery. And that's not going to happen."

My mother looked at me with grave pride. Then she laughed, "I swear I didn't coach her!"

Heading home in the car, I exclaimed, "You were magnificent!"

"You were pretty magnificent yourself. Sometimes you take my breath away with the quality of your perceptions."

She had just fulfilled a wish I didn't even know I had. Underneath all the dreams that pulled me away from my mother, I held fast to the dream of returning.

She slowed down, prolonging the drive. "You know, Rona, we should think about your strategy for getting into Radcliffe. God knows they'd be lucky to have you. But you'll be facing some brutal competition from the prep school kids. Those places really know how to groom a gifted student."

Nobody knew gifted students like my mother. The high school in the next town brought her in once a week to teach enrich-ment classes in writing. With no degree in education, she couldn't get a full-time position. But at least she could lavish her attention on the best. At night I'd find her curled up on the couch with a red pen and a stack of papers, explaining every grade with an essay of her own. Even her marginal jottings were as considered as if they were intended for publication. When she caught a student putting two l's in "Philistine," she wrote, "The acute and aware use only one l."

Among the acute and aware she found me a boyfriend of sorts, David Thurston. David talked about Frodo and Bilbo Baggins as if they were buddies of his. He liked to sing along with Judy Garland. Word had it that David was gay, the ex-lover of an aging actor he had met while working in a summer stock company. "Vicious gossip!" said my mother. "You know how cruel kids can be to anyone who's different."

David was different, all right. He used expressions like "oh, my stars and garters!" But he fit right in at our dinner table, the first guest I ever had with an acceptable answer to my father's favourite conversational gambit: "What is beauty?"

"Well, sir, I've always thought it's the exquisite tension between the real and the possible." *You always thought. What a brown-nose. While other guys were going parking with their dates, you were jerking off to Judy Garland, pondering the real and the possible. 'Exquisite tension'! Oh, sure.*

David couldn't take me parking because, at sixteen, he still didn't have a driver's licence. But my parents had a couch in the basement where he liked to press himself against me with his eyes shut tight and his hard-on digging into my thigh. Maybe he did like girls after all, I told myself. And I wanted to be wanted, even if David's brand of wanting was all I could get. While he bucked in my arms I would pretend he was somebody else and yield to a flush of shameful pleasure.

On our last date he took me to see *A Man and a Woman*. The film starred Jean-Louis Trintignant as a debonair racing-car driver who romances the heroine to the strains of a wordless theme song – all cooing *la la la*s, like something you'd sing to a baby. David bounced out *la-la-la*-ing at full voice. He slipped his arm through mine, showing the world he had a girlfriend: "Wasn't that deliciously romantic?"

I broke free. "Gooey-sweet isn't my idea of delicious."

On the way back to Maynard Hall, we passed the woods where couples went on warm nights like that one. I took David's hand and led him into the trees. I was thinking of Jean-Louis Trintignant when I pulled him down onto a bed of fallen leaves. We rolled together in a counterfeit passion that taunted and stung. I seized his hand and pushed it under my skirt. David jumped to his feet as if he had touched something foul. He looked down at me lying there with my skirt bunched around my waist. "I'd better get going," he said. "There's a Latin test tomorrow."

A test! You've already failed it, you little faggot. And I had failed, too. I was untouchable. No wonder I needed my mother to find me a stand-in for a date.

⁓

"Your day will come," she used to tell me. "I wasn't exactly the belle of the ball when I was in high school. I know how it feels to stand on the sidelines with an empty dance card while everyone else is whirling and twirling."

Before I could whirl and twirl with the best of them, I'd have to get to Radcliffe. That would mean beating out well-groomed students from the prep schools. My parents didn't have the money for prep school fees, but they did have a formidable zeal for grooming. Every year from grade seven on, they oversaw my entries in the Scholastic Magazines annual writing contest. Every year I won a prize, more often several, while Joyce waited for her chance to outdo me. Soon we were both turning phrases on deadline for the contest, reading our drafts aloud while our parents critiqued our work line by line. On yellow legal pads they recorded our dangling modifiers and lazy metaphors. The most elusive and troublesome failing was what they called "a false note." If they sensed one of those in my entry, I'd have to read the offending paragraph over and over until they could both agree on where I had gone wrong and how I should restore my broken prose to wholeness. It seemed the real contest was between my parents over who had the most demanding ear. But as the resident typist, my mother always prevailed, editing until the last minute. (Daddy had never learned to type.) By the time she whisked my entries to the post office, I no longer thought of them as mine.

Still, if her version got me into Radcliffe, was that so bad? She was the Radcliffe-trained teacher; I was a mere supplicant at the gates of learning. Once Radcliffe accepted me, I'd have other extraordinary teachers. Then I wouldn't have to worry about that damn contest.

The year I turned sixteen was my golden year in my mother's eyes. She took one of my prize-winning stories to one of her editors at *Ladies' Home Journal,* who published it with a burbling sidebar: "'Prodigy' describes the 15-year-old author of PAPER FLOWERS to perfection. Rona Maynard talked at nine months, sang in seven languages at a year and a half . . ." Only one person could have disclosed such things, and they made me cringe. (I could just imagine what my brattier classmates would say: "Hey, Prodigy! How 'bout serenadin' us in seven languages?") As it happened, my mother's campaign was just getting started. When my story was cited in *Best Short Stories of*

1965, she proclaimed the news far and wide: "Rona's in the same company with Malamud and Roth!"

"Mother, you're exaggerating. Malamud and Roth had their stories published in the book. Mine was just cited on a list."

"Don't be so modest. The admissions officers will take note, I assure you."

Joyce had taken note, that much was clear. She had what our mother called, with visible amusement, "a bad case of nose-out-of-joint." Sister of the writer, indeed!

But I hadn't exactly written "Paper Flowers"; that was the trouble. Upstairs I put "A Hard Rain's Gonna Fall" on my record player and reread my story. The first sentence pleased me: "We were 15 when we rebelled against society." Every word was mine. Then the false notes appeared, every one introduced by my parents. I arrived at the pivotal scene, in which my heroine, a girl much like me, decides to drop the madcap friend who has shared her fantasies of adventure: "Suddenly I noticed her dungarees. Rips everywhere and they were spattered with mud. And her hair! It was dirty – just plain dirty. She needed a good shampoo." What was wrong with torn dungarees, for God's sake? I would never talk like that, but my parents did. They reminded me of the ten thousand talkers Bob Dylan was singing about, whose tongues were all broken. And I had spoken their words, a phony at the core. On the record player, Dylan vowed to speak his truth from the tops of mountains and the depths of the darkest forest. I thought he was speaking for me because I could not speak for myself. Maybe I wouldn't. Ever.

⁕

When the latest *Good Housekeeping* fell through the mail slot, it looked just like all the rest. Cleaning tips, meat loaf recipes, moronic ads: "Dear Betty Crocker, I've been married a year. Jim hasn't said one word about my cooking since the first week. I'm worried . . ." Now, there was a dilemma my mother could solve. I flipped to the "My Problem" section to see what she'd invented this month. There it was: "Every Child Needs Two Parents." Milquetoast dad finally taps inner strength by cracking down on mouthy teenage daughter who needed the steadying hand of male authority. Long live family harmony! All hail the omnipotent father!

For once her story wasn't pure invention but something far worse, the funhouse-mirror version of a real fight between Daddy and me. The memory still burned, whether she knew it or not. Behind my back, she'd made him look like a hero instead of the drunken tyrant he had really been. I found my mother at her desk, furiously typing, and waved the magazine in her face. "How could you sell me out like this?"

"Sell you out? It's an anonymous story, for God's sake. Composite characters enacting an archetypal drama. But to be perfectly blunt, we do need the money to keep you in the style to which you've become accustomed."

I ran outside and walked until my feet hurt, a teenage version of those poor, frantic housewives in *The Feminine Mystique*.

The real story, like the one Mother wrote, began at the dinner table. We had just returned from a family outing to see *What's New, Pussycat?* and on the way out I'd walked right past the Carlsons without so much as saying hello. Bob Carlson was a colleague of Daddy's, and my perceived slight drove my father wild. "You should be ashamed of your insolence!" he said. His lip curled the way it always did after an extra drink or two, and his fork clattered to the plate. My sister stopped playing with her food; my mother's eyes telegraphed a warning.

"I wasn't being insolent. I didn't see the Carlsons. I was lost in thought."

"You apparently believe that your thoughts are more important than the norms of civilized society. With your rudeness you defiled those norms in front of everyone in the theatre."

"Oh, really? Aren't we supposed to be a family of thinkers? Truth and beauty and all that? I don't see what manners have to do with truth and beauty. They're just an empty ritual."

"Your delusion would be ludicrous if it weren't such a threat to the very survival of our species!" (What had I done, dropped the atom bomb?) "The 'empty ritual' that you have the audacity to criticize is all that separates man from beast! You owe this family an apology!"

And then he was upon me, jumping from his chair to seize me by the wrists. This had happened so often that I knew what to do: go rigid in his grip and draw strength from my silent fury. *I won't apologize, you pompous old hypocrite. You've said yourself Bob Carlson is a second-rater. I wouldn't be surprised if you've said it to his face at one of your stuffed-shirt cocktail parties. Talk about flouting social norms! Go on, do your worst.*

My sister looked relieved: *Thank goodness it's not me.* My mother didn't even stand up. The old story. I thought it would end there, as it always had.

Not this time.

My father smacked me and dragged me up the stairs to my room, lurching and bumping past the window where he'd once painted Christmas angels. So many nights in my bed, craving a man's touch, and this was what I got – a thrashing in front of the family. I screamed in a voice I didn't know; I kicked like the incorrigible savage he believed me to be, yet the savagery was in him. I turned against the beast of his despair with a hard, cold anger that obliterated everything else he was, and everything my mother hadn't done to help me.

For days I didn't speak to my father. At last my mother pleaded for mercy. "He's the only father you have," she said. She had that right, anyway. I longed for a father who could guide and protect me. Since I was clearly out of luck, I wished for what I could hope to achieve. I wished for revenge.

-⊛-

The only place I still liked to visit with my mother was Harvard Square, my future home, where the flying-haired Radcliffe students raced from class to coffee date toting book bags full of Proust and Dylan Thomas. I coveted everything about them, even their clothes: hoop earrings, Marimekko dresses, hand-made leather sandals that laced at the ankles, Grecian style. I loved the raffish young men who waved to them from the seats of motorcycles.

My mother took me to the shops where, in our fantasies, we'd buy jewel-coloured cushions and carved wooden boxes for my dorm room. We sat together on the broad steps of Widener Library, where Thomas Wolfe had once set out to read the entire collection. My mother quoted *Look Homeward, Angel*: "O lost, and by the wind grieved, ghost, come back again." She couldn't show me Felton Hall, her home in what she called "the magic years," where my father had come bearing tulips in the middle of winter. The place had been demolished years ago.

Back home we role-played the interview, honed my application letter. My mother's big worry was the teacher recommendations. "Your teachers don't have the finesse to write the kind of letter you need. They'll probably dash something off on their lunch break."

I came home from school one day to find that she had taken charge of things. On the teak table lay a fresh carbon copy of her letter – already in the mail – to Mrs. Edward S. Stimpson, Dean of Admissions at Radcliffe. Oh, God, she was pleading my case. "My aim is not to 'get Rona into Radcliffe,'" she had written, pointedly identifying herself as an alumna and an experienced university teacher. So why was she writing – to find a pen pal? "We think of Rona not just as a girl of unusual intellectual capacity, but as a person of *gift*. Whatever she does . . . she does with true artistry." Spoken like the queen of Maynard Hall. Whose application was this, anyway, mine or hers?

I was about to confront her when these lines stopped me: "Rona does not give her heart easily – to people, ideas or institutions – but when she does, her loyalty is absolute. She is singularly free from any kind of meanness. . . . She has a great deal of independence and moral courage." I liked to think that was true. Maybe my mother really did know my real self better than anyone. She clearly thought of her letter as a gift to me. And although it was no more welcome than the mangled birds that our cat would deposit at the door, she had written it with love, even admiration.

I wanted to be worthy of her tribute. I said nothing.

My mother chose my outfit for the Radcliffe interview – a mini-dress with a Peter Pan collar, a kittycat bow and a fake vest outlined with rickrack. It looked like something a kindergarten kid would wear, but why waste my breath? The admissions officer had a gentle voice and an appraising smile. She lost no time getting to the crux of the matter: my reasons for choosing Radcliffe. My mother and I had rehearsed this very question many times but somehow the answer escaped me. I thought of my mother in the waiting room, flipping through a magazine that she'd be too agitated to read. Did she guess that I was looking out the window instead of making my case? Was she beaming the argument to me with her will and her concentration? When the answer finally came to me, I knew she wouldn't like it. I also knew it was the one true answer I could give: "Actually, I'm still thinking about that. I don't know if Radcliffe is the place for me."

⤙⤛⤜⤚

"How did it go?" my mother asked.

"Fine." That would hold her for a while. Good thing we had a bus to catch and a rush-hour subway ride to the terminal. Not even she would quiz me under those conditions.

Purses and elbows pinned me to my spot in the jerking train. When I felt the first squeeze between my legs, I tried to step aside. No room. Then another squeeze and a probing finger in the gusset of my pantyhose. This couldn't be happening – a stranger's hand where David Thurston's hand would not go and where my own hand never went, either. From across the car my mother smiled at the girl I had so diligently impersonated, the one who would soon be off to Radcliffe. But now I was being punished for my charade. I looked down and saw a man's arm disappearing under my mini-dress. I saw every hair on that arm as it crawled up and down. And then I saw the immovable face of my torturer. Sunken cheeks, eyes hard as rivets. His expression said, "Be a good girl and I'll be done with you in a few minutes. You're not going to scream, are you? You're not going to say a word about our secret." I didn't. If I spoke up, a subway car full of strangers would know what a dirty mind I had. He had picked the right girl, one who knew how to keep a stoic silence. I had done it when I put on the mini-dress, when I found the letter to Mrs. Stimpson, when I let the false notes into my story. The train swayed. My mother mouthed something I couldn't make out. My whole body felt hollow inside, as if nothing remained of me except that dumb interview dress with the kittycat bow.

On the bus home to New Hampshire, the truth came out. Not the part about the man with the rivet eyes; the part she had been hungry to know. When I told my mother what I'd said to the admissions officer, her face clouded and she shook her head. "Oh, Rona, you're too honest for your own good!" She didn't say that Radcliffe would never take me now, but I could tell what she believed. And as luck would have it, she was right.

⁓◦◉◦⁓

The week I left home, there was nobody there. My parents had taken Joyce to Mexico; they'd miss my high school graduation. My mother didn't see any reason to watch me collect a diploma from a school I had detested, even though I was making a speech. My topic was freedom, and now I would finally be free. Wasn't that the only thing that mattered? My mother said, "You'll like having the run of the house. An independent girl like you."

She had planned a graduation gift for me. Her friend Gail would drop it off at Maynard Hall on graduation day. The doors of the wide world were blowing open, and I would cross the threshold unseen. In September I'd be off to my fifth-choice college, the only one that would take me. The country was full of accomplished, gifted kids, including many who'd surpassed me on the College Board exams.

Gail arrived while I was ironing my dress for graduation, class of 1967. She looked pained as I unwrapped my mother's gift. "My goodness! You'll get plenty of use out of that!" she said bravely.

A plastic hand mirror with a sunflower on the back. That's what my mother had left to mark this day. What had she spent, $1.98? Gail brushed my cheek with her bright red lips. She smelled of hairspray. "Break a leg tonight, kiddo! And *bon voyage!*"

I put on *Sgt. Pepper's Lonely Hearts Club Band,* turning it up loud because no one was around to complain. (My father couldn't tolerate noise, except when he was making it.) Then I took off my glasses the way I always did to study my reflection. The girl I saw in the plastic mirror wasn't anyone I recognized. She had a new pixie haircut – either terribly chic or a terrible mistake – and a puzzled expression, as if she'd arrived a week early for a party. Her face had a fragile side and an angular one that could have come from two different girls. She was nothing close to the fairest in the land, but might be pretty by candle-light. The Beatles sang, as they'd been singing all day, about needing somebody to love and still needing that person when you're sixty-four. On *Sgt. Pepper* a girl slipped out of her house in the dark and left her clueless parents to wonder where they went wrong, but life was getting better all the time and Lucy showered the sky with her diamonds.

FALLEN

He said, "I've got to meet your father." He lay naked on the grey, rumpled sheets where for hours he had rolled and tumbled with me like a Labrador retriever with a Frisbee. I had stalled him to the point where any other guy would have called me a shameless little cockteaser, but this one had decided that I just needed time to comprehend his place in my life. He looked up at me with rapt, unhinged devotion. With a man-to-man talk, he intended to settle my future. His name was Ian; I had known him for about eight hours. Of all the goofy things he had said since the clothes came off, this stuff about my father took the prize. He hadn't even asked about my mother, poor sap.

I said, "You wouldn't like my father. He has this question he insists on asking all my friends: *What is beauty?* He doesn't think much of the answers."

"Well, he hasn't heard *my* answer. 'Beauty, Mr. Maynard, is your daughter. She's gorgeous and sexy and sweet and I'm just nuts about her.'"

Nuts. Yes, that was Ian. Where did he get these ideas about me? I looked at him, blond and furry, with the soft beginnings of a beer gut. He sprawled on his unkempt bed like a god painted by a master of the Italian Renaissance. The god would recline on red velvet, with admiring cherubs overhead instead of a sixty-watt bulb. Yet Ian had the god's defining feature, an attitude of entitlement, and all because of that scrap of flesh between his legs. He gloried in his pleasantly average body. Meanwhile I sucked in my stomach, just as my mother always did. How she would savage him – not that he would notice.

I could picture the scene:

> *"So, Ian, aside from our Rona, what makes your heart beat faster?"*
>
> *"Well, Mrs. Maynard, guess I'm your typical Canuck. This time of the year, I'd have to say hockey. Don't know if you follow the Maple Leafs, but I've been a fan since before I could skate. I'm betting on them to take the Stanley Cup again this year. But now that they've traded Mahovlich to the Red Wings . . ."*
>
> *"Ian, you amaze me. Here I am, Canadian to the core, and not once have I thought of myself as a Canuck. Or followed the Maple Leafs, I must confess. Does Rona even know who this Mahovlich fellow is, I wonder? Of course, if you should choose to talk about Ingmar Bergman, she'll give you quite a run – a skate, dare I say – for your money."*

I found myself wanting to protect him, this bounding puppy of a man who had attached himself to me on Bloor Street, outside one of those shops that sold hookahs and faux-brass bangles from India. He offered to take me home for dinner: T-bone steak, iceberg lettuce and cello-packaged tomatoes. No one else in Toronto had ever asked me to dinner except my mother's sister, Aunt Celia, who was kind, lively and a wonder-ful cook, but not the sort of company I craved at age nineteen. Besides, she'd just had me over for *coq au vin*. If I didn't go home with Ian, I'd be eating greasy shepherd's pie again at the dining hall. He looked like the kind of guy who'd listen to Dylan and keep a plastic bag of revelation-grade dope on whatever he was using as a bedside table (real tables were *so* suburban). Oh, why not?

Ian preferred Gordon Lightfoot to Dylan, but I was right about the dope. Some friend of his had brought it back from Jamaica. In the middle of the night, as the Bathurst streetcar clattered by outside, he rolled us a joint. "This will relax you," he said. It didn't. Malignant fantasies bloomed in my head, spread-ing tendrils of panic and disgust. I saw my body as a giant plastic game, with a fluorescent key for every place Ian had touched. The keys buzzed and flashed with gaudy abandon, but he was never going to win. No, he would pay for reducing me to this. I saw him running through a forest like the doomed, breathless hunter in a Greek myth my mother used to read me. The hunter had caught sight of a goddess bathing naked, a sight forbidden to mortals. She set his own dogs upon him; they gave chase with their tongues hanging out, baying for his blood. I saw the imag-ined Ian torn to pieces while the real Ian looked at me as if I were the disintegrating one. "It's just a bad trip," he kept saying until I fell into a heavy-limbed semblance of sleep.

I woke to find him in the kitchen, eating peanut butter out of the jar. At the sight of me he shook his head. "When I met you, I thought you were the best thing I'd ever seen. Couldn't believe my luck. Now I just think you're strange."

—◦◉◦—

It was 1968, disillusionment and violence resounding in the headlines: hundreds of Vietnamese civilians massacred by U.S. troops at My Lai, Martin Luther King and Bobby Kennedy shot dead, American cities on fire. I had recently fled my fifth-choice college, a bucolic haven for trust-fund preppies, to attend the University of Toronto – another school of last resort (more prestigious American places had all turned me down). I was continuing a family tradition, leaving my native country, but with none of the drama that surrounded my female forebears when they set forth on their adventures. For me there was no ocean crossing with a sister on my back, no infant buried in a foreign place, no consuming love affair pursued across a border.

Nor was there much adventure to speak of. Toronto was my mother's turf, where she had earned her master's degree, an early protegé of Northrop Frye. U of T was a good school, she said, but I knew she had been miserable there as she tried to forget Max Maynard. She had promised Grandma she would see Jewish men in Toronto, and she found one who was mad about her, a young philosopher named Howard Taubman. He had glasses and a receding hairline, but his letters quivered with desire. Just before I left for Toronto, she read a passage from one of them aloud to me:

> You're like a diamond, immersed in dark velvet, curving and caressing the stone that shines through a thousand blacknesses with a magic potent gleam. Fredelle, this is no electric storm I feel, that crashes and plays and passes quickly away. It's a sharp, strong unyielding steel bar that passes through my heart and joins it to yours, that's burning and searing my flesh away.

My mother struck a pose as she read Howard's letter – hand on heart, lashes aflutter. I knew what she was thinking: *Max would never mix his metaphors like this. I should take a red pen to Howard's prose.* Howard loved the flesh-and-blood woman she was; my father loved the idea of her, and the kingdom of the mind they would rule together. I was her stand-in prodigal, returning to the scene of her choice between a man and a vision.

In my spare time, I walked the streets for hours, not sure if Toronto had a place for me. I breathed in the fist-shaking giddiness of the times. Rochdale, a communal "free university" with no professors or structured classes, had just opened its doors to the stoned architects of a new educational order. We still had professors at U of T, but students had begun to avoid those who still gave exams. In the campus cafeteria I picked up my free guide to female masturbation, complete with anatomical diagram and the reassuring advice that my boyfriend should not feel threatened by my empowered, myth-defying hand, because "a hole needs to be filled," as if sex were road repair and men a bunch of peons with shovels. It felt that way to me. By this time, I'd gone home with a number of young men, not one of whom became my boyfriend.

In the midst of all the swaggering defiance, Toronto retained an air of Scots-Canadian rectitude. I had never met so many men called Ian, or imagined that a major city could be so thoroughly white. A classmate shrugged off my inquiry about race relations: "We don't have those problems here. You can shop and ride the subway all day without seeing one of them" (no black folks, no burning ghettoes). As far as I could tell, it was Americans like me who aroused suspicion. The Guess Who's "American Woman" blasted daily through campus cafeterias; eyebrows arched knowingly when I confessed that I had never heard of Margaret Atwood (I could quote Leonard Cohen, but he was a famous troubadour). My origins kept eliciting the same politely supercilious comment: "Draft dodger, eh?" My fellow students informed me that, despite what I'd been taught in school, the United States had lost the War of 1812. Worse, we Americans had sent Richard Nixon, "Tricky Dick," to the White House. We didn't have the good sense to elect an outspoken intellectual like Pierre Trudeau, who had just moved into 24 Sussex Drive.

I watched for my mother's letters, single-spaced on the same yellow paper she used for her manuscripts. She was working on her first memoir, *Raisins and Almonds*, stealing time between magazine assignments and parties for Daddy's colleagues. But it was everyday life, not art, that filled her dispatches from home. She analyzed the self-defeating behaviour of assorted friends, brought me up to date on scandalous divorces, and poked gleeful fun at Dr. Joyce Brothers, the celebrity psychologist whose magazine column she was ghostwriting. Dr. Brothers had just submitted notes for a column on "Why Women Like Pornography," which my mother dutifully turned into an argument with her usual flair, only to discover that the editors were expecting something else entirely: "Why Women Hate Pornography." As she put it in her letter, "The magazine prints every month a new photograph of their resident psychologist, often looking into her files. Daddy suggests that next time I be featured looking out of the drawer." I read each letter at least twice, so I could savour every anecdote. Mostly, her letters made me laugh.

Then there was the letter entirely devoted to her furious campaign against my sister's grade-nine English teacher, Barbara Topping, who had denied Joyce an A. My parents knew about this blow before Joyce did; they'd already confronted Mrs. Topping on the matter of their daughter's talents:

Joyce has of course argued with Barbara all
term, but her written work has been impeccable
(more than that, at times brilliant) and she
hadn't the slightest doubt about getting an A.
I knew the shock of that B would be terrific,
so I found an excuse to get Joyce out of school
early that afternoon, before reports went out.
You will sigh, "overprotective," I know – but
believe me, 'twas well. . . . Joyce became quite
hysterical, screaming and screaming ("She hates
me, I hate her, I'll never go back!"). . . . I could
throttle Barbara. . . . Barbara is cruel to Joyce. . . .
She let slip a revealing comment in our interview: "When Joyce criticizes other people's
writing, I can just hear you."

Overprotective? That wasn't the half of it. Craziness was
running rampant at Maynard Hall. Who was enrolled in grade
nine, Joyce or my mother? The way I saw it, Barbara Topping
had a point. Of course Joyce sounded like my mother. I should
know; I did, too. Rereading the letter, I found hardly a mention
of me. "You are not (thank goodness) on my crisis list," my
mother had written. No doubt I would be if she knew I had
picked up a man on the street and gotten stoned out of my skull
with him. She'd have blasted me with Shakespeare:

Th' expense of spirit in a waste of shame
Is lust in action; and till action, lust
Is perjured, murderous, bloody, full of blame,
Savage, extreme, rude, cruel, not to trust.

So perhaps it was for the best that my mother had Joyce to torment with her obsessions. But I wouldn't escape this fiasco. Somebody had to start acting like a grown-up. I sat down to consider my reply:

> It depresses me to see all three of you working yourselves into a frenzy over something you can't possibly control. There's no reason why Joyce's English grade should be a crisis for the whole family – or even for her. . . . It seems to me that one reason you're so outraged is that you're projecting the whole episode onto a much larger scale, seeing it as one phase of some epic crusade against the forces of mediocrity. . . . Naturally I too have a tendency to think that the Maynard way is the only way . . . [but] the strength of your own convictions ought to be enough. . . . All this advice-giving has really worn me out.

My mother wanted help on another front, too. Like me, she had a sister who was painfully pretty – tall, fair-skinned and, worst of all, slim. When they were growing up, boys used to make fun of bookish Fredelle, but they competed for Celia's attention, drawn not simply by her looks but by something more profoundly irresistible. Celia had what my mother once called "an assurance, a pleasure in herself as a girl, a quietly gleaming poise." While these graces aroused my mother's envy, Celia's life provoked her unconcealed disdain. My aunt had no job or university degree; she kept a home for her husband, a Jewish businessman, and their two daughters. She took courses on subjects that intrigued her, but my mother dismissed them as the make-work projects of a bored and boring housewife. When Celia welcomed me into her home, I saw for myself how harshly my aunt had been judged. She would sit on her sofa like a particularly elegant girlfriend, long legs curled under her and head cocked to one side, with a bemused smile that said, "This is just a heart-to-heart between the two of us. Isn't it complicated to be young?" In her smile I saw glimpses of my mother's, but with none of the sharp edges.

"Your visits mean a lot to Celia," my mother would say. "I hope you'll go again soon. She's so lonely." Wasn't that also what she'd said about Grandma: *so lonely?* As my mother told it, she herself was the only one of Ben Bruser's women to have dodged the curse of loneliness. For years I thought it was youthful self-absorption that gradually ended my visits to Celia. I couldn't articulate the other reason, the guilt in my mother's voice. Later I came to realize that I didn't want to do on her behalf what she could not do on her own, create a bond with her sister. Before long, it was too late. Celia was diagnosed with Alzheimer's while still in her fifties. My mother visited her in a nursing home until Celia's husband asked her to stop. Her visits, he said, were upsetting Celia.

I slouched at the back of the class, doodling flowers on the cover of my notebook. I would have stayed in bed, but had been awakened by a hangover. So here I was with a ladder in my pantyhose, barely awake for Professor Burnside's final class on *Paradise Lost*. A plea clanged in my head: *Don't let me be pregnant, don't let me be pregnant.*

Professor Burnside was said to launch covert vendettas against female colleagues. But he liked A students and I was among them, with a near-ferocious zest for dismantling the greatest hits of English verse. One penetrating comment from a classmate, and I'd put up my hand, determined not to be out-shone. In my haste to speak, I was known to cut fellow students off in mid-sentence – until we got to *Paradise Lost*. Milton wasn't for me. No sense of humour. So bombastic. Tells you right on page one that he's about to do what's never been done in prose or rhyme. And pulls it off, if justifying the ways of God to man is your idea of a rip-snorting read. Of course, it's Satan who gets all the rip-snorting lines, as everybody knew who had actually slogged through those interminable angels to get to the good parts. Who'd want to worship a God like Milton's, a vengeful blowhard who kicks Adam and Eve out of Eden for eating an apple that He, being God, knew from the get-go they wouldn't be able to resist? Correction: Eve would not be able to resist. The Fall of Man gets blamed on a woman who's not content to be Adam's helpmeet. Her pretty head turned by Satan, she thinks she deserves to be special and smart. One taste of the apple and she also has to be sexy, reaching out for Adam as if she really wants what no woman is supposed to want.

God over man. Man over woman. Spirit over body. This was the world view my mother had chosen to study. I pictured Fredelle Bruser in her homemade dress – like Eve, a proud young woman who wanted more. My father made promises and she believed him.

If I had taken Burnside's advice to our class, I'd have read aloud from *Paradise Lost* every night. How was I supposed to do that, with the girls next door playing Iron Butterfly's "In-A-Gadda-Da-Vida" at top volume and cases of beer being heaved about? But I liked hearing Burnside read. At the lectern he opened his copy of the poem, its spine torn and its pages interleaved with index cards. He must have been carrying that book around for about a hundred years. He looked at us – the yawning ones, the frantic scribblers, the daydreamers like me – as if he doubted we would grasp the point but was hoping for the best. Then he spoke: "We have come at last to the edge of Eden. Here the first man and the first woman, the parents of us all, begin their exile to the place where all of us mortals make our home. This fallen world, with its innumerable failures and losses. When the old masters painted this scene, they followed the Book of Genesis. They gave us the cowering and crying of two humbled sinners laid low by their own weakness. Milton gives us a deeply flawed but thoroughly human couple who can still hold fast to what they've got – each other. Milton's final scene is not the end of anything. It is a brave and poignant beginning of many things – of married life, of human history, of the journeys that subsequent poets have taken, all the way to our own time and beyond. So if you remember nothing else from *Paradise Lost*, I hope you will remember this passage." He cleared his throat and read with a catch in his voice:

> Some natural tears they dropped, but wiped
>   them soon;
> The world was all before them, where to choose
> Their place of rest, and Providence their guide.
> They hand in hand with wand'ring steps and
>   slow,
> Through Eden took their solitary way.

Shuffling of papers, stamping of boots. At the door Professor Burnside stopped me. "I see you've found Milton a bit of a push."

"I guess I'm not into the Fall of Man. *Paradise Lost* is . . . well, it's disturbing to me."

This amused him. "Very good! So I haven't been wasting my breath after all. Great poetry is meant to disturb. If you want to nod off with a nice cup of chamomile tea, you can always try that sentimental huckster Rod McKuen. But I suspect you're a bit too discerning for that. Runs in your family, I hear. Aren't you the daughter of Fredelle Bruser, the Miltonist? She cut quite a swath, I hear. Tell me, where is she teaching these days?"

"She's not, I'm afraid. They didn't want a woman at the local university. She ghostwrites Dr. Joyce Brothers' column in *Good Housekeeping*. But she does it with Milton's cadences in her head." I knew I was selling my mother's writing short, but I hoped to make Burnside squirm.

"A shame," he said.

⁓◦❦◦⁓

What should be a man's first gift to a woman he loves? I had a few ideas: earrings from somewhere exotic, a unique and beautiful book, dinner at a place where the tablecloths were white and not made of paper or plastic. A young man had decided he loved me, and in my hands he placed a cardboard tube. "It's an eclipse watcher. I made it myself, to protect your eyes while you look at the eclipse of the sun."

I shoved the thing back as if it were a used hamburger wrapper. "Actually, I don't plan to watch the eclipse. So you might as well use it yourself."

He could have walked away. He could have decided I was worse than strange, or given me a piece of his mind. He didn't. His name was Paul Jones, and we had met in a campus production of Chekhov's *The Seagull*. I played Masha, the black-garbed depressive, whose first line is "I am in mourning for my life. I am unhappy." Paul was my father, the comic relief. He turned out to be sufficiently amusing offstage that I agreed to a coffee date. When I mentioned my conflicted career as a writing prodigy, he didn't seem all that impressed. He said, "I will be your toughest critic."

This Paul Jones was speaking my language, the biting tongue of Maynard Hall. Whether he knew it or not, he was proving he could take on my mother. He was my age, twenty – born in England, raised in towns all over Ontario, an exile and a wanderer, like my forebears. He told me he was proud that all of his possessions could fit inside two cardboard suitcases. He lived in a rented room with no furniture, just the mattress where I woke up beside him one winter morning, knowing I was home. This was not the same as being happy. But when had I ever been happy at home? He saw me as the person I was, not as the glory I might reflect on him. In Paul I recognized someone who could love me without loving, or even liking, what I wrote. He combined the intuitive understanding I had always wanted with the rigour I had come to expect, growing up in Maynard Hall. And he clearly was not one to stumble in the dark with a drink in his hand and the Furies at his back, like my father. We rented a third-floor walk-up and made our first joint purchase, a twenty-five-dollar TV. In June I decided it was time for him to meet my parents, but he'd better know what he was in for. "They'll haze you. They're brilliant, creative people and they need to prove it. Try to be patient."

After hitchhiking all day, we got as far as a ditch in northern New Hampshire. All night we sat there, shivering. At last I phoned my parents and persuaded them to rescue us. They arrived in their second-hand Oldsmobile, my father clutching the wheel, my mother beside him in a shirtwaist dress buttoned to the neck. Their faces had sagged since I left home, but the familiar Maynard scorn still flared in their eyes as they looked Paul up and down. I knew what they were thinking: *So this is the fellow who has just moved in with our daughter.* Tangled hair, grass stains on his pants. Bad enough that he couldn't spring for bus tickets; worse yet that he couldn't even flag a ride at White River Junction. At dinner Paul could not define beauty to my father's satisfaction. Then my mother weighed in. "So tell me, Paul. What do you plan to do with your life?"

Paul rocked back in his chair, stroking his beard. "I would like . . . to be consulted."

"Really! A young man of lofty ambitions. Oh, in case you haven't noticed, Paul, that chair you're rocking in so blithely is not a rocking chair. You wouldn't want to leave a broken chair as a souvenir of your visit." We hadn't yet spoken of marriage, but my mother beat us to it. "Rona needs to find the right fit for her talents. She has years of exploration ahead. I certainly wouldn't want to see her married at age twenty-one. Although, of course, if she were marrying the president of Harvard . . ."

I retreated to the kitchen to cut Paul another slice of pie. There Joyce offered her two cents' worth, whispering, "Rona, you are positively subservient to this Paul Jones."

So much for our first family dinner at Maynard Hall. The next brought another debacle, a clash between my parents. In all my years under their roof, I had never seen them fight. There had been the odd outburst in the middle of the night, usually involving the car keys and my father's fitness to drive. But those fights didn't count; I knew them only as disembodied voices. Now my parents were fighting at my mother's teak table, while the roast capon grew cold on our plates. And of all the subjects they might have crossed swords about, they had chosen the state of the English department, where Daddy had taught since 1948. He would never teach anywhere else, and would always be the lowest paid professor.

He said with a carefully composed half smile, "We have managed to transform ourselves in recent years. I'm quite impressed with the new men we've managed to attract. Very fine fellows indeed. For instance, young Henderson, the Miltonist —"

"That nincompoop! Really, Max, you astonish me. Henderson wouldn't know an original thought if God and all the angels hurled it down from the heavens to crush his empty head."

"Jaysus, Fredelle! You and your accursed pride. You presume to judge a young man of distinction, but you know nothing, nothing at all."

"Nothing? One of us knows nothing, and I am not that person. If memory serves, you didn't even complete your master's thesis! Let me remind you, Max, that I am a Miltonist. A better one than that second-rate gang has ever seen!" She pushed back her chair so hard that it banged the sideboard. Then she ran upstairs and slammed the bedroom door.

Joyce burst into tears. "Daddy, you started it. You owe her an apology."

My father didn't look at her, or any of us. He crumpled at the head of the table as a snort of shame escaped him. While Joyce continued to plead, I led Paul into the living room. "God, I'm so embarrassed! They've never done this before. I don't know what came over them."

"What's the big deal? They're married, and married people fight."

"Not these people. They've always been different – until tonight. I can't stand to see them like this. I'm sorry you had to see it."

"Okay, so they both overreacted. You carry on about your extraordinary parents as if they're more than human. They're not. If you have to worry, why don't you try worrying about something real."

In August Paul rolled over one morning and asked, "When are we going to get married?" I hadn't thought I wanted to be married. Marriage was for young fogies who aspired to bedroom suites and two-car garages. All our friends thought so. When they heard about our plans, they would say, "Can't we talk you out of this?" They couldn't. We both wanted to tell the world that we had found our place in it. The first date we were offered at City Hall seemed charged with meaning – October 20, 1970. My twenty-first birthday. I remembered my mother's warning about not wanting to see me married at twenty-one. Then I sat down and wrote her a letter that positioned the wedding as I hoped she would one day see it. I began, "Good news . . ."

She phoned to tell me all the reasons why this news was not good. How long had we known each other? Seven months? And just what did we plan to live on? Hadn't it crossed my mind that a young man whose goal was "being consulted" might not be the best of providers? Of course she and Daddy would respect my decision, but I should understand that my family would not come to the wedding. Joyce would be busy at her keenly competitive private school, where she'd been sent to escape the likes of Barbara Topping. As for my parents, they were expecting house-guests on October 20. "Besides, we think of you as married already. It's only a civil ceremony. You won't be floating down the aisle in a long white gown, after all."

I could have told her she had already skipped one passage in my life, high school graduation, and that she wasn't getting off this time. I could have said that her callousness enraged me. But I said none of these things and could not even feel my own anger. I had only one thought, one goal: getting my parents to the wedding. "You can entertain your guests some other weekend," I said. "I'm only getting married once."

MARRIAGE

On our wedding day we awoke to a banging at the door. Those damn Jehovah's Witnesses just wouldn't leave us alone. *We don't want to be saved, got it? Find some suckers down the street to take* The Watchtower *off your hands.* Then I remembered who had promised to arrive for catering duty at nine-thirty sharp. My mother, with my father as sous-chef, and three kinds of cookies, brought all the way from Maynard Hall. They had left my sister at home, even though she'd begged to attend my wedding. School was more important, according to my mother.

What was it she'd told me to buy? Bread: check. Pickles: check. A couple dozen boiled eggs. Better put the water on pronto.

"Rona, Rona. I asked you specifically for white rectangular loaves. This bread won't roll nicely for pinwheel sandwiches."

I had gone to Kensington Market for dense, round loaves of dark rye, flecked with poppy seeds and caramelized onion. "But I love this bread. It's from the best Jewish bakery in Toronto."

"Well, it's your wedding. But this knife! What on earth have you been cutting with it, cardboard cartons?"

We were hosting a reception after all. The original plan,

going straight back to class, seemed too slapdash even for us. What to serve? I'd given my mother a week to figure it out. Now here she was in my kitchen, turning our wobbly chrome table into a command post. "Max, watch your fingers with that knife; we don't have time for a hospital run. Paul, you might clear your math problems off this table – unless they could use a liberal garnish of egg salad. Rona, where are those pastries Grandma sent? . . . What do you mean, you *ate* them?"

I had nothing to do but choose the outfit I would wear to cross the threshold of womanhood. My mother didn't approve of the long quilted skirt and Mexican shawl, which left the plum-coloured velvet mini-dress I had loved since grade ten. Too bad I was out of pantyhose. On my way out the door to restock, I collided with Paul, his arms full of my twenty-first birthday gift: the *Compact Oxford English Dictionary*, inscribed "To my wife, Rona." I couldn't imagine a less appealing gift. My mother had always been my lexicon; without her around to offer instant definitions, I relied on educated guesses. "Oh, Paul. When have you ever seen me open a dictionary?"

"Never, of course. That's why I bought you this. An English major should use a dictionary."

My mother watched us from above with her platter of billowy pinwheel sandwiches. "My dear Paul, I've spent twenty-one years contemplating what your bride should do. And a lot of good it has done me! Tell me, is that the tie you're planning to wear?"

He looked down at the thing. Knitted by one of his sisters, it dangled well below his belt. "That's okay, I'll just cut it off."

Our wedding day unwound like a bright ball of yarn, skittering and bouncing and rolling under things, one surprise after another. I didn't know it was possible to be married in two minutes flat, or that Paul's best friend would burst in from

Montreal just as the doors were closing, or that my husband of about half an hour would carry me upstairs to our apartment amid the cheers of revellers bearing gifts in plastic shopping bags. I could not have predicted that his parents and mine would never meet again, much less that in fourteen months' time he and I would be parents ourselves. But I had known all along that the sandwiches would be perfect, bursting with so much filling that you had to lick your fingers. My mother had pronounced them "comic, better suited to a labourer's lunch pail than a wedding reception." For that alone I would have loved them.

Like my mother before me, I have no wedding album. I'm lucky to have any photos at all: we nearly forgot to buy film. All but one of the shots exude raffish good cheer: the bridal couple grin distractedly, parents make amiable small talk, well-wishers drift in and out of the frame. My father, who to date has viewed this marriage as one of those whims that the old and wise should tolerate in the young and feckless, pulls me to him with a brave, tender smile. Then there's the shot of my mother and me. Rigid in her black leather coat, she stands guard beside me, her massive purse wedged between us. We have both removed our glasses, intending to present our best faces for the camera. Mine is blurred with weary detachment, as if her very presence is dissolving me. My mother looks like a teacher staring down a wayward student.

Back at Maynard Hall, she sat down to spin a tale for Grandma. Her mother would never guess that she had anything but hope for our marriage. She began:

Dearest Mums,

Our little wedding has come and gone, and the Paul Charles Joneses are happily installed at

30 Robert St., surrounded by their gifts (two Acrilan blankets, a set of place mats, assorted chrome lifters and turners and a fondue-maker). Let me tell you, there is nothing to giving a wedding. The books are wrong. . . . ("Six months before, get estimates from caterers. Five months before, decide on colour schemes. . . .") All you have to do, I see, is be on hand the night before – and work very hard if there's to be a reception.

We'd been married for about six months when the health centre called about my test. The doctor could see me the following morning. Sorry, I would have to come in for the results. As if there was some kind of mystery! Maybe they thought I'd fall apart if they didn't frame the news just so. After all, I was only twenty-one. You can't live on love, can you? Not with a baby.

The doctor was a woman, for a change. A mother of two, she said. "I'm so delighted that you're keeping the baby. And you'll stay in school? Good for you! Tiny ones are so adaptable. You won't need a crib, he can sleep in an empty drawer. Your friends can watch him while you go to class. Bet they'll be fighting for the chance. I see your due date is December 6. A Christmas baby! So with a little bit of planning, you can get your term papers out of the way, rest up over the holidays and get back into the swing of things."

The baby, an accident, already had a name: Miranda. How could my first-born be anything but female? Grandma, my mother, Aunt Celia . . . they all had daughters. Poor Uncle Ephraim hadn't taken one breath in the world, which had to be some kind of portent.

I began to long for Miranda. We'd share all the special pleasures my mother had shared with me: paper dolls, fairy tales,
outings to the ballet. She would treasure her pink satin toe shoes,
as I used to do, and keep her secrets in a diary with a brass key
smaller than a thimble. Yet to bring her into the world, I would
have to give up the furled sweetness of her, blooming under my
empire-waisted dress. As long as I carried the promise of her life,
I didn't have to justify my own. I'd been thinking about graduate
work in medieval literature, but only for lack of any other ideas.
I didn't want to be a medievalist; I wanted to be Miranda's
mother. Paul said, "What makes you so sure it's a girl? What
would we call our son?" We couldn't agree on a name for a son,
couldn't even discuss the matter without an argument.

That was the least of our problems. My husband's way was
not the Maynard way. He liked to sleep all morning (how my
father would have fumed at this indolence). He took me to task
for making scornful remarks about people who read *Love Story*
or listened to Mantovani. When I announced my plan for fixing
up our living room (gold carpet, schefflera in the window), he
didn't exclaim at my good taste, because he knew it wasn't really
mine. He said, "I see we're turning this place into a low-rent
Maynard Hall. Too bad we can't afford a teak table."

I had chosen a husband with the strength to resist my
mother. I hadn't bargained on any resistance to me. In every
challenge, I detected a symbolic departure from his rightful place
at my side, an occasion for tears in the dishwater and anguished
scribbling in my journal, when in fact the departure was mine, an
instinctual returning of the heart to my mother's house.

She sent cookies. She sent money (we had none, except a
student loan and scholarships). She sent reminders not to
fritter it away: "Let me, zooming in on your household, take

one small – I hope, neutral – example: your telephone. I do not know how much extra you pay for a cradle phone that sings. I would guess $36 a year. You have then chosen a singing phone in preference to 18 chickens, 72 dozen eggs, two pair of boots, 12 good paperbacks . . ."

The summer before my fourth year at U of T, I went to Maynard Hall for a last pre-baby visit to the place I still called home. An electrical storm buffeted the plane. The daytime sky became a backdrop for the Book of Revelations, blackness lit only by thunderbolts. We pitched and rolled while passengers closed their eyes, murmuring soundlessly. Even the crew looked stricken. On less harrowing flights I had braced myself for doom, but this time I trusted in my amulet, Miranda. To spare her, the gods would spare us all.

Miranda had shaken something loose in the Maynards. Or so I thought, absorbed in the adventure of my motherhood. In fact, the world as we had known it was breaking apart, pulled by forces that we either didn't notice or strove to ignore. My sister would soon be off to Yale, leaving our parents alone for the first time in twenty-two years. To my silent satisfaction, she appeared to envy me (Joyce had always cooed over babies, I had always ignored them). My father was about to retire – a suitable occasion, he and my mother thought, for a show of his artwork in one of the university galleries. The university refused, so the show would be held in our house – produced, like my wedding, by my mother. She'd been baking for days; Joyce and I would pass the cookies around while Daddy's colleagues contemplated their purchases (total sales: $800).

Meanwhile she'd been completing *Raisins and Almonds*. In a few months' time, she would hold it in her hands: a book of her own, shaped for the pure, soaring satisfaction of it, and not to fill her allotment of magazine pages. Yet if she spoke of her pride in this milestone, my mind must have been elsewhere. Because Miranda filled my head, I assumed she had to be my mother's obsession too.

That fall my mother wrote me a letter like nothing I had ever seen from her. It was all about me, infused with a passion so disarming that she turned to poetry – Yeats, this time – to support her point.

Dearest Rona,

It is a kind of shock, when I see you, to realize how much you matter to me. Of course I think of you a great deal – wonder about you, look for your letters . . . but generally with a kind of remoteness. There you are, living your life; here I am, living mine. This fine detachment deserts me when we meet. 'And thereupon my heart is driven wild:/She stands before me as a living child.' Strange that English, so rich a language, should have but the one word for responses to lover, husband, parent, child. They are so different. A child's feeling for a parent is always, I suppose, crossed by contrary currents: duty, habit, desire for protection and resistance to being protected. . . . A parent's love for the child has in it an odd sort of ferocity. (You will understand better what I mean when Miranda lies in her bunting.) Do not harm her, life. Lay a finger on her, Fate, and you reckon with me.

On Christmas morning, 1971, labour pains awakened me at three in the morning. We bounded out of bed to open our presents beside the evergreen branch that we'd scrounged for free at the lot around the corner (lacking decorations, I had trimmed it with bangles and beads). It teetered in an empty bottle like a blissed-out hippie. If not for our shared excitement at the imminent gift of Miranda, we might have bridled at the Christmas books we'd chosen for each other: *Five Weeks to Winning Bridge* (I couldn't imagine learning) and *How to Live on Nothing* (he couldn't imagine eating dandelions picked in vacant lots).

That day in Ottawa, Margaret Trudeau, the flower child of Sussex Drive, gave birth to a Christmas baby. Two days passed before I gave birth, the flower child of Robert Street. A boy, round and pink. What would we call him? I had pictured Miranda as wrinkled and sallow, a baby to be cherished for her pilgrim soul; this baby had the kind of Gerber cuteness that reduces total strangers to clucking admiration. I had seen him emerge from me in the overhead mirror; there was no one else's baby he could be. Still, I didn't recognize him as mine. No one else seemed the least bit troubled. Paul teared up. The doctor had praised me: "Isn't she terrific?" (I had powered my way through so-called "natural" childbirth, equating anaesthesia with Wonder Bread, Muzak and other abominations.) My mother and Joyce, on the phone from Maynard Hall, exulted in the lustiness of my changeling's cry. But when a volunteer brought me the first portrait of my son, I sent her away and burst into tears. *Poor little bugger. No wonder you look dazed. Of all the mothers you could have been sent to, you ended up with me.*

Paul brought me home through wet, heavy snow that clogged the windshield wipers of the aged cab. At this rate the airport might shut down. *Please, not before my mother's plane lands.* She was on her way with a shopping bag of cookies and cinnamon rusks; I was saving the first diaper change for her (I'd already forgotten the nurse's hasty lesson on diaper folding). An hour passed, then two, while the baby wailed and the windows rattled in their frames. Paul asked, "Shouldn't we change him? How hard can it be?"

And then there she was, in her white fox hat, stamping the snow from her boots. She enfolded my son as if he belonged to her. "Oh, Rona, he's beautiful."

So many flawed creations I had offered to my mother for the finishing touch. Dresses with crooked seams, pie crust that fell apart on the rolling pin, stories with mysterious grammatical errors. This one didn't need any touch-ups. Benjamin Jones, age four days, was already perfect. Or would be, with a little attention. "My goodness, Rona, what have you been doing all afternoon? He's soaking, poor child! Now, let's see . . ." She began to fumble with the diaper. Thousands of diapers she must have changed, not that you'd know it.

"Grandma will be thrilled that you've named him after Grandpa."

"But we didn't. Benjamin's the only name neither of us hated."

"Let Grandma have her illusions. She's all alone with her memories. What will it cost you to make her happy?"

My mother took over. Paul turned on the TV.

That night I dreamed our home was made of rotten beams held together with string and masking tape. Every time I tried to tighten the string, another beam gave way. I woke in tears, looking up at my mother. She stroked my forehead the way she used to do when I was sick in bed. "You're just exhausted, that's all. Now you know why they call it 'labour.' There's a name for this, the 'baby blues.' But it passes. You have an enchanting baby and a husband who loves you and a family in Durham who know how gifted and special you are. You're a very lucky young woman." This must be what she thought I wanted to hear. But if my mother didn't believe it herself, then why should I believe it? She thought I never should have married, let alone become a mother. Instead of money in the bank, I had a singing telephone. This was luck?

-⁎⊙⊙⁎-

I did not have the baby blues. I had a numbing, intractable malaise that hung over me for months, distorting everything I saw. In a story I loved as a little girl, Hans Christian Andersen's "The Snow Queen," a demon's mirror shatters into millions of pieces that lodge themselves in people's eyes and hearts, turning beauty to ugliness. I was like those people. In real life the demon's mirror is called depression, and a chronic, low-grade form of it had dogged me since childhood. Depression made me wonder why I was born, made me follow Ian home, made me confide in journals instead of people. It made me the odd person out in a family of oddities; because of it I'd been sent to Mrs. Warren and returned "happier," whatever that meant. The truth is, I didn't believe in happiness. Not for me. Not for anyone interesting. Was Anne Sexton happy? Bob Dylan? Allen Ginsberg?

I believed there was such a thing as craziness, and I thought I knew what it was. It landed you in a locked ward, like Anne Sexton, or it made you a parody of the hell-raising artist, like my father. I knew nothing about depression – how common it is, especially among women, and how likely to recur. I didn't know that the number-one risk factor for depression is a previous episode. Or that a new mother – her hormones in flux, her body transformed and her whole life disarranged – is at risk for post-partum depression, which turns a so-called blessed event into a cruel and shameful ordeal. Seen through the demon's mirror, a beautiful baby can become an emblem of failure at the most complicated, mythologized and transformative task any woman can undertake – motherhood.

It never crossed my mind that there could be any help for my condition. Besides, to seek help would have been to confess my failure.

I spent my nights in the nursing chair, frantic with weariness. With one arm I held the collected poems of Wallace Stevens, the subject of my next term paper, but the words floated like plankton on the current of my despair. With the other arm, I gripped my perfect baby, the rosy interloper who had come to me instead of Miranda. He deserved a smiling, milky goddess who thrived on sacrifice. That wasn't me, nowhere close.

My bathrobe had fallen open, revealing a body I no longer recognized – swollen breasts, a stomach like a prune. Good thing I couldn't see my face, the red eyes and grey shadows. *You did this to me, my cherub. Go on, take another bite of me. Isn't that what mothers are for? I don't need sleep, precious one, sleep is a luxury reserved for you – and that father of yours, who can sleep through anything.* I had no dreams, only waking nightmares. I saw myself on the topmost floor of a skyscraper, dropping Benjamin from a window, Grandma's little *mensch*. What would she and my mother think if they could see inside my broken, addled head? That's Rona for you. Stubborn and selfish. Doesn't know how to love.

In "The Snow Queen," love is the answer. A boy with an eye full of demon glass is rescued by his dearest friend, a girl whose only resources are loyalty and pluck. She makes her way to the kingdom of ice, where the Snow Queen has him in her thrall, and brings him safely home. Who would rescue me? I raged at Paul for escaping to the classroom and the library, where he shelved books to make a little money. I called him cold, he called me hysterical. "If you don't have any respect for me, why don't you leave?" I would cry. Leaving would show some gumption, I thought. Some pride and self-respect. If I knew how to love, my husband would love me. But here he was, eyes fixed on the TV screen. My mother was right: I never should have married him. Maybe I should push him out the window with the baby.

Meanwhile, in the real world, life went on. It wasn't fair. My friends packed their knapsacks for Europe. My father was free to paint full-time, just as he always wanted. My mother was promoting *Raisins and Almonds*, which was becoming a Canadian best-seller. With her memoir of growing up Jewish on the prairies, aware from the beginning that her family was different, she honoured the sustaining power of her parents' love. She spoke to the exile in every reader, the vulnerable child who fears exclusion and yearns for the all-seeing, all-accepting love that parents give only in fantasies. At the centre of her story she placed her long-dead father, the infinitely gentle man whom she adored without question. Her sister and rival rates barely a mention; her mother is reduced to a bustling paragon of cheerful domesticity. Grandma loved the book just the same, seeing a tribute to her and Grandpa's parenting on every page.

My mother didn't tell me much about her own literary success. She was too caught up in the extraordinary rise of the real family star, my little sister. The Adorable One had sold a cover story to the *New York Times Magazine*: "An Eighteen-Year-Old Looks Back on Life." That led to a book deal, among

other things. Joyce's photo on the *Times* cover – impish grin, red
sneakers, Daddy's sweater hanging on her little-girl figure –
caught the eye of J.D. Salinger, the famous literary recluse, who
promptly swept Joyce away to his hilltop retreat in Cornish, New
Hampshire. She had never read *The Catcher in the Rye*; I knew it
so well, I could have told him which character smelled of Vick's
nose drops and whose damn falsies pointed all over the place.
The only man alive who intrigued me like J.D. Salinger was Bob
Dylan. Maybe he'd be the next to fall for my sister. But for the
time being she was in Cornish, writing her book. My mother
looked forward to a more auspicious marriage than mine had
been, never mind Salinger's age (fifty-three) or his bizarre
dietary obsessions (he lived on raw vegetables and nuts). After
all, the man had extraordinary gifts. In a letter she envisioned
her next grandchildren – "the little Salingers, bringing their own
organic lunches."

Not so long ago, in the days of the Scholastic Magazines
contest, Joyce had felt driven to catch up with me. Now she'd left
me in the dust. What was I doing? Pushing a stroller, making my
own baby food. I didn't even go to class anymore; I had no
energy for that. I had dropped out of school.

⸙

I was not the only Maynard to feel outstripped and abandoned.
My father had retired. He had been a campus legend; now he
had no circle of admirers and nothing to occupy his time except
unfinished paintings. They were his official vocation. The real
one was drinking. And that was not the worst of it. Shortly after
Benjamin's first birthday, my mother wrote:

Dearest Rona,

Daddy and I are parting. I suppose this might
have happened in other times, in other ways –
but it has now exploded with catastrophic suddenness. I don't need to tell you how blackly
depressed Daddy has been for almost a year
now, and how helpless I have felt to deal with
his pain. . . . What I didn't know was that he is
in love . . . In spite of the pain, I see clearly that
here now is a chance for change. Daddy can be
with someone who admires him unreservedly,
reveres him – which I cannot do. . . . Well, it is a
sad, sad time . . . I am not worried about your
worrying because I think you will see the separation as the only, the best course . . . This is one
of those moments at which I realize all over
again, What would my life be without my children? We shall all need each other.

My mother seemed to think this would not be dismaying ("I
don't need to tell you"; "I think you will see"). How could she
entertain such a notion? Of course Max Maynard was lashed by
the Furies; I'd known that all my life. But when I tried to tell the
truth, she had always silenced me with her tired old story: he's a
brilliant, original man. If she wanted adoring and dependable,
why hadn't she chosen Howard Taubman?

My father was leaving Maynard Hall to live with Amy
Pratt, a besotted graduate student who had pursued him with
wildflowers and baskets of strawberries. He had not been her

first target at the university, just the first to succumb. Amy had
wild rages and claimed to hear angelic voices. A former colleague of my father's had cautioned him, "Max, your wife is an
extraordinary woman. Amy Pratt is a psychological case." My
father's humiliating desire for Amy enraged my mother, but also
gave her a convenient excuse to send Max Maynard packing.
"You must go to Amy," she said. He begged for another chance;
he wept as he must have done long ago at the feet of his fire-
breathing mother. Lily warned that God would punish him;
she couldn't have predicted that a mortal woman, a daughter of
Eve, could drive him out of Eden. Now he was packing up his
cashmere socks and the double boiler for his oatmeal.

He saw my mother's wrath, I saw her tremulous despair. In
letter after letter, she called out to me. She dismissed her marriage of true minds as a pitiful sham, she contemplated a lonely
future (what else could she expect, a woman of fifty?). My
mother needed me; Paul didn't even seem to like me very much.
Why not split up now, before we ended up like my parents? We
were twenty-three, young enough to start over. "This isn't
working," I told my husband. "I'm going home." Paul didn't
argue, not even at losing Benjamin. Of course our baby would be
going to New Hampshire. A child needs his mother.

I found a lawyer, Mr. Klein. Paul and I went together to his
office halfway between the Victory Burlesque and a liquor store
where vagrants stocked up on cheap sherry. Mr. Klein wore a
glen-check suit that had once been loud. He cleared his throat as
he studied our separation agreement – a list that divided our
worldly goods. Three Acrilan blankets, a set of placemats,
assorted chrome lifters and turners . . . our wedding loot, plus
a few dozen scratched LPs and other oddments barely fit for a
yard sale. About time we packed it in, if this was all we had to

show for two years of marriage. When Paul asked Mr. Klein how much we owed him for fine-tuning this document, he said, "Nothing. You kids have enough problems." My husband whipped out a sheaf of bills just the same. To him this was a matter of pride. To me it was a harebrained display of extravagance, like the fancy phone that so dismayed my mother. The phone had been Paul's idea.

The night before I left, we had dinner at a French restaurant with satin banquettes and crystal stemware on the tables. This too was Paul's idea, along with a bottle of Burgundy, poured by a sommelier who called him "sir." Women old enough to be my mother shot us misty smiles that said, "Bet someone's going to pop the question tonight." I could guess what my mother would say: "Have you any idea how many chickens you could buy for the price of that bottle?" Now I wouldn't have to worry about the price of chicken anymore, or how to tell if the bird was done. No one knew how to roast a chicken like my mother.

I asked if Paul remembered his first gift to me, the cardboard eclipse-watcher that I'd shoved right back at him. "Why didn't you give up on me then and there? You could have saved us both a lot of trouble."

"I thought you'd be worth it. I thought you had possibilities."

Maybe it was the wine, maybe it was the slab of *gâteau reine de Saba*. Maybe my velvet gown was too tight in the bodice. The room closed in on me, the mirrored walls squeezing out my breath. I ran for the door. Minutes later I came to in a pool of crumpled velvet, a linen napkin tucked under my cheek in case I soiled the carpet. Waiters encircled me, diners shook their heads: *These young people, probably on drugs.*

In the morning I did what I had promised to do. The heater in the cab didn't work and I could see my breath as I headed for the airport with my baby. It had been my decision to go, yet I felt as if I were the abandoned one.

⋯⟨◉⟩⋯

Nothing of my father was left at Maynard Hall except paintings (neither he nor my mother could bear to dismantle their museum). My mother had redone the study in turquoise and white; where the photo of the Maynard clan once sat, she'd put a Mexican candelabra in the shape of a mermaid. We ate dinner when the spirit moved us, pretty little platters of this and that: ripe Brie, curried eggs, chickpea salad. We went to bed early, swathed in silence. We spent half the morning in our nightgowns, drinking black coffee and musing on love gone wrong like two girlfriends bonded by the same bitter knowledge. But I was not her friend and the scathing stories she told about my father were not the kind I wanted to hear. The pots he left to burn in a drunken stupor, the lame excuses she had to make. ("He can't teach today, he has a migraine.") To affirm her new vision of things, I shared my own sordid little tale: "Remember when he told you he should have 'married a bitch like Helen Chandler'? Of course, she was a drunk like him –"

My mother cut me off. "He never said that. You're fantasizing. Max was so fastidious about language."

Maynard Hall quivered with betrayal, more than two women could bear. Joyce came home with sunken eyes and wrists like twigs; J. D. Salinger had cast her out. The man of the house was in diapers, a golden princeling, born unaccountably cheerful. To my mother and sister he was pure delight; to me he was something more complicated, joy sparring with remembered failure. I wanted to be able to tuck him away like an irreplaceable toy that must be stored inside the box to protect it from scuffs and scrapes.

138

He spent mornings at a daycare centre, supposedly so that I could write, although I never did much writing. It was something my mother wanted me to do, not something I wanted for myself. Afternoons, I counted the minutes until naptime.

One afternoon he refused to nap: he stood in the crib, shaking the bars and howling. A mother should know what to do, but I didn't know. At that moment I didn't even want to be a mother. I ran outside and stood in the backyard, screaming. My mother's bedroom was open. She was up there at her typewriter, on deadline for *Good Housekeeping*. I screamed until I wore myself out. My mother didn't speak of my outburst. That night at dinner, she wept for my father. "What will become of him? A frail old man with no one to depend on but that mad woman. . . ."

Someone to depend on, that's what I wanted. In Toronto Paul had decided that he was that person. He began to send me letters no one else could have written – by turns funny, perceptive and caustic. I remembered that voice from the coffee-date era. Now it whispered in my ear, teasing and cajoling. My mother was not to be trusted, Paul said. She had sabotaged our marriage. If I wanted to be my own woman, I would have to leave her. My father had once said as much to my mother, but he was not so bold as to court her at Grandma's table. Paul had no such hesitation. He hitchhiked to see me, bearing in his arms a miniature wooden rocker for Benjamin. Even my mother had to give him some credit. It was as if he had swum a fairy-tale moat and scaled a tower to the princess's window. After a few more visits, I decided that home was with Paul. But before I returned to Toronto, I had one final task in New Hampshire.

My father missed the comfort of Maynard Hall. He took to dropping by around lunchtime for chicken soup. In his blue Shetland sweater, he still looked almost handsome, despite his hollow cheeks and arthritic shuffle. Had my mother read the new biography of Virginia Woolf? Remarkable piece of work. Oh, and she must see his new paintings. The finest in years. Hmmm . . . time for a siesta. Up the stairs to the study, the king returned to his castle. No longer drinking, he said. Things would be different when he came back for good.

One morning I was upstairs dressing Benjamin when I heard a ruckus in the garden – my father chasing my mother. I couldn't hear what he was accusing her of, but I saw his hands clawing the air. From the look of things, she couldn't fend him off much longer. Now he had followed her inside, thrashing and shouting. I came to the head of the stairs where he and I had fought in my teens. I remembered his alcohol breath in my face, mingled with the cheap cologne he had worn in an effort to conceal it. I looked down on my parents as if from the top of a mountain. Light flooded in through the window where my father had once painted angels, and it seemed they had flown back at last. But they weren't singing this time; they were wearing breast-plates and brandishing swords. I knew what I needed to do, and that I'd been waiting seven years to do it. I thought I would relish the moment when it came; what I actually felt was an obdurate solemnity. I said to my father, "You don't live here anymore. This is my mother's house, not yours. It's time for you to go."

My father cursed me. He shook his fist. Then he left and never came back.

OFFICE ROMANCE

In the beginning all I wanted was to make a little money and have fun doing it. No point wanting glory; I might end up like my mother. She should be proud of the new practical me, so focused on stretching a dollar for the family. Frozen fish sticks, a used TV, running shoes for Ben from the bargain rack. And one small thing for myself: a bra, the first one I'd worn since high school. I couldn't go job-hunting braless.

I remembered sitting at my mother's teak table, creating pages for imaginary fashion magazines. That had been fun. I could do something like that in the real world. How many applicants for magazine jobs had a brace of awards from the Scholastic Magazines competition and a citation in *Best Short Stories of 1965*?

No one in the business had seen a résumé like mine. Over and over, it opened doors. In I walked with my Mexican silver jewellery and a floor-length dress made of pink and orange drapery fabric (my idea of an editor look, it was much like my mother's hostess outfit, although she had more and bigger silver). Every time I faced the same questions. *Did you work on the campus paper? Maybe you've interned somewhere? Taken a copy-editing course?* No, no and no. *Perhaps you'd like to submit a few article ideas. After all, with your track record as a writer . . .*

"But I don't want to be a writer. I want to be an editor." End of interview.

Writing was what my mother did, what she wanted her daughters to do and what Joyce was already doing on a grand scale. My sister's memoir had cast her in the role of spokesperson for a generation: now she was appearing in *Vogue*, sitting for Richard Avedon, and debating Phyllis Schlafly on CBS *Morning News*. With her own money, she'd bought a quaint old house in rural New Hampshire, fit for a painting by Grandma Moses. How could I compete with that? I wanted to be rid of writing. I wanted to grind it under my shoe, to tear it into pieces and burn it, to stuff writing into a sack full of stones and cast it into the ocean – unless it was someone else's writing. For someone else's writing I would spend hours ruminating, agonizing and polishing, asking nothing in return except a little money and fun.

At last I landed a junior job at *Miss Chatelaine*. Its big sister, *Chatelaine*, had been Canadian women's trusted friend for nearly fifty years, but *Miss Chatelaine* was a promising ingénue, a teen handbook reaching for significance. Book reviews of Margaret Atwood kept company with articles like "Your First Visit to a Gynecologist," all of which I fumblingly checked for punctuation and spelling. I made $9,500 a year, even less than my notion of a little grocery money. My only goal was to make a bit more. When *Miss Chatelaine*'s editor denied me a raise, I complained to a bored-looking man in the personnel department and was told, "Look, you're lucky to have that job. You don't have the qualifications. I advised her not to hire you. But no, she had to do it her way." He threw up his hands, as if the editor and I deserved each other. "She" was Mildred Istona. Not only had she taken a chance on me, she had apparently taken a stand of sorts. But I did not appreciate this. After years of my mother's tutelage I thought that special treatment was my due. I didn't have to feel deprived for long: Mildred moved on to bigger things at *Chatelaine*, leaving the white corner office as still as an empty stage.

It was 1977, the year Elvis died, *Star Wars* opened and Jimmy Carter pardoned the Vietnam draft dodgers. The year Keitha McLean swept in from New York to turn *Miss Chatelaine* into Canada's first fashion magazine. The year I fell in love with my job.

—◦⊙◦—

I had never seen anyone like Keitha – tall as a model, with a loping stride and a mane of gleaming red hair that she tossed to accentuate her points. She made lots of them on her first day at *Miss Chatelaine*. Tossing her fox coat on the nearest chair, she proceeded to tell us that our nice little magazine was about to shake up the whole country, not to mention our lives. "This magazine has *huge* potential and we're going to turn it around," she announced to the gaggle of staffers at the reception desk (we had nothing so grand as a meeting room). "We're going to capture the spirit of the people who are making fashion happen in this country. We'll talk about fashion the way nobody has before, as new ways of living, not just new looks. We're going to do it together as a team. I want to see you all involved in every-thing – covers, captions, you name it. You'll work harder than you've ever worked in your lives. But if you deliver you'll have a great time doing it."

Keitha didn't look like an arbiter of fashion. She had chosen a rakish outfit: ivory silk skirt and blouse with weathered cowboy boots. She'd forgotten her belt; the blouse had billowed free of her waistband. I admired her artlessness and what I took to be her confidence. Although I didn't know it then, she was fresh out of rehab for alcoholism, with no home except a friend's spare room and nothing to her name except a few boxes en route from New York. The previous year she'd been fired from a senior magazine job for showing up drunk at the office. *Miss Chatelaine* was Keitha's second chance to rebuild her life. If she slipped again, she would end up rewriting press releases for a second-rate newspaper. Now here she was, holding fast to her ambition and faking total confidence.

Her stump speech both excited and dismayed me. *Turn the magazine around.* Were we a makeover candidate who had to lose the bad haircut and polyester pantsuit? *If you deliver* . . . It sounded like a warning but, by God, I would be among those who delivered. I wanted my shot at this high-flying project of hers, and she assured us it would be a triumph: "The best talent in this country will be fighting to get into the pages!"

Off she went to rip apart the next issue. Until that morning I had thought it was almost out the door, but Keitha had other ideas. That demure cover had to go! We needed something modern, dynamic. We'd shoot in a swimming pool, with a wet-haired model in a tank suit, goggles looped around her neck as if she'd just finished one hundred lengths, because fitness was the next big thing and we'd been missing it. And please, no more girlish articles like "Your First Wine and Cheese Party"! Street fashion, ska bands, clubs where the trendsetters danced until dawn . . . we'd capture it all in a new section. As *Miss Chatelaine*'s only word person, I was to produce that section right now, on deadline. (Ska bands? What were they?) While I rushed back to my phone, the fashion editor shot me a conspiratorial smile: "Well, Rona, guess we'd better get ready for the new world order. Goggles on the cover! My God, can you believe it? And our new leader's not exactly the latest word in fashion. Did you get a good look at that fox coat of hers? The poor thing's so old, it's shedding!"

The fox coat matched Keitha's hair. Like everything else about my new boss, it had a dishevelled grandeur. Leaving the office that night with a buzzing brain and a plastic shopping bag stuffed with file folders, I noticed it was later than I thought – the butcher shop was about to close. I didn't feel like going home to fry burgers in the dark (our kitchen light bulb had burned out days ago and we were both too tired to change it). Home was where Paul and I scrambled to stay on top of mundane things that claimed all the energy we had; home was dust bunnies and missing socks. Work had just become a full-tilt quest in which the more energy I gave it, the more I seemed to have. At home, I found that I couldn't wait to return to the office for my first one-on-one with Keitha.

She reclined in her chair like a mogul, her Western-booted feet on Mildred's white desk (once pristine but now a jumble of press releases, contact sheets and perfume bottles). "Tell me your hopes and dreams," she said. Hopes and dreams? No one had asked me about those before; until Keitha did, I wasn't fully aware of having so many. Develop stories! Work with writers! And as Keitha might have noticed, we needed better writers. I could rustle up some new talent. Keitha's eyes didn't waver from my face. "New talent? Why don't you start with yourself? I've been reading your file. I don't know why you spend all day checking commas and spelling when you could take a crack at the fun stuff." She had plans for me, she confided. All the best editors could write; they weren't fuss-budgets tinkering with other people's prose. She should know, she'd been a writer herself, with bylines all over the English-speaking world. She needed me to fulfill her vision for the magazine.

This extraordinary woman thought I could be extraordinary, too. I swallowed hard and asked for one thing, a little more money. She threw her arms wide open as if embracing a world of possibility. Her purple silk shirt had sweat stains under the arms. "Hang in, Rona. With me, what you see is what you get. You're in the right place."

How could I not believe her? Once a place of closed doors and lowered voices, *Miss Chatelaine* became a buzzing bazaar: freelancers perched on every available surface, leather-jacketed photographers darting in and out, stylists bearing armloads of fluttering beachwear. They all seemed to have an eccentric signature: a brocade turban, a silver Afro, a glittering profusion of chains and crosses all worn at once. (The skeptical fashion editor, a less-is-more type, quickly vanished; *Miss Chatelaine* was now a more-is-more shop.) The few average-looking people who called on us had secret afflictions: paralyzing migraines or a homing instinct for the wrong men. One writer, soon to be my friend, came in with a raging hangover and a manuscript consisting of pieces of scratch paper stitched together with yarn. Every phone in the place rang off the hook. Meanwhile Keitha sped through the office with a clipboard, hair flying as she issued pronouncements at full voice: "That little twit will never write for us again!" "No red and black – who wants to look like a bullfighter?" God help the staffer who brought her a tired idea. "Show me something new!" she'd yell before slamming her office door so hard the wall shook. As we closed her first issue, she handed me the last piece of copy for polishing: her editorial. When I hesitated, she said, "Everybody in this business gets edited."

Keitha was in her mid-thirties, yet she'd already lived and worked in three countries. She'd been creating drama since her birth in a one-room hospital in Yellowknife, surrounded by miners (the doctor knocked them out with injections to create some privacy for Keitha's mother, who had staggered all alone through the snow to reach the hospital). She had jettisoned a lot in her time: a modelling career, a marriage, any number of lovers. She had left the Catholic Church, but expressed a battered pride in her never-ending struggle to escape what the nuns had taught her. With no children or any formal education beyond high school, she had broken the rules that, according to my mother, should drive a woman's life. Her focus, as far as I could tell, was the career she'd built from unpromising beginnings at a two-bit newspaper in Jamaica. She liked to talk about her successes: the much-imitated lifestyle section she created for the *Montreal Star*, the gifted mavericks she'd inspired at a big New York magazine (no mention of how she came to lose that job).

Exotic as she was, she seemed oddly familiar. I had known another fiercely emphatic woman (my mother) and another alcoholic on the lam from religion (my father). They were both getting on with their separate lives. My mother was in love with a wealthy Jewish man, Sydney Bacon, who happened to come from Toronto and had briefly dated Aunt Celia. He bought her a pretty Victorian house not far from our place, and visited on weekends, bearing gifts (silk lingerie, imported music boxes). Monday to Friday she served tea to friends and worked on various writing projects, not that she had to earn Sydney's love by achieving. With Sydney she could simply be herself, as she never could with my father. He, meanwhile, had given up Amy Pratt and returned to Victoria, the scene of his early promise. There he'd resumed his painting career. Galleries were selling his work as old friends welcomed him home. No longer the rogue they remembered, he had joined Alcoholics Anonymous and was making an effort to stay sober.

For my sister, too, things were looking up. She was sharing the Grandma Moses house with her new husband, an artist who looked like James Dean and had somehow won my mother's approval. They were expecting their first baby. At twenty-seven, I hungered for a project of my own as I had once hungered for romance. *Miss Chatelaine* was not mine, far from it. But Keitha let me believe that it was. With me at her side, she laid plans to relaunch the magazine as *Flare*. Week after week, she devised new ways I could help her.

Rona, I'm sending you to Europe to road-test a tour, three countries in five days.

Rona, you should be writing a career column for us. Rona, have you thought of trying your hand at feature articles?

Rona, I want to start a new section, a guide to the workplace for young women. Figure it out, you're perfect for this.

Keitha understood the power of flattery, but I saw only her belief that I could rise to any challenge she might throw my way. She read my work the way I'd always wished my mother could do, with a focus on clarity and authenticity, not some abstract notion of perfection. "It's a magazine, not the Sistine Chapel," she would say. "You make it as good as you possibly can, and then you let it go because you know that next month there's going to be another one." She believed that *Flare* should walk beside the reader and speak to her like a friend instead of handing down pronouncements from on high. Her watchwords, applied to every story, caption and headline, were "insight, humour and rue."

Every time I handed in my copy, I listened for the proof of my success: laughter from Keitha's office. Her laugh was like a bird call – two trilled notes telling me she was in and, for the time being, happy. On a good day she leaned in my office doorway, exulting in my article on how to buy wine, which began with a zany anecdote about a tip I'd once been given from a grizzled rubby in a liquor store ("Ladies love raspberry wine," he'd said). Talk about insight, humour and rue! Next thing I knew, she'd plunked herself down to reflect on how it is someone of high aspirations can become a shuffling drunk. "Nobody ever wakes up in the morning and says, 'Gee, I think I'll become an alcoholic.' In the beginning, booze solves a problem. It knocks off all the rough edges. And then it becomes the problem." She knew about my father, knew I believed that if he'd really loved me he'd have joined AA long ago. But she never explicitly told me to let my anger go. Instead she meditated out loud on another way to live, her own summary of what she'd learned in church basements with AA's Twelve Steps in her hand. She called it "living like a grown-up." Responsibility, not blame . . . that was the idea, along with an attunement to "whatever gods there be."

"But I don't believe in God."

"God can be whatever gets you out of bed in the morning. Whatever you hold onto when your plans fall apart and you're thrown back to square one. Whatever is true and beautiful in your eyes."

Truth and beauty. A frequent theme in my father's monologues, before a few more drinks pushed him onward to the darker obsession of salvation. He found truth and beauty in art; I was finding them at a fledgling magazine with grainy photos and pages so flimsy you could practically see through them. Creating it lifted me up into a world of possibility and purpose, even when the photo shoot went horribly wrong or the cover story made no sense. I loved the problems along with the magic moments, and I loved the person I became when I threw my arms around those problems, giving them all the wit and mental focus I had. How could I call this "work," when it felt like a rough-and-tumble game that I played with a seemingly golden team of young strivers? They were my community: the beauty editor who changed her hair colour every two weeks, the fashion maven who wore the Annie Hall look before it had a name, the art director who waged a cockeyed but endearing campaign to misspell a headline on the grounds that it looked better that way.

Riding the subway to work, I rubbed shoulders with a throng of twenty-something careerists, all of us wearing navy blazers and carrying new leather briefcases. Sometimes we'd exchange knowing smiles and I'd wonder where my seatmate was headed today. A law firm where she planned to make partner? A bank where she'd one day be appointed VP of some-thing terribly arcane and technical? I'd picture her talking sports with the guys, as all the get-ahead books were urging women to do, and coming home to her "helpful" husband (you couldn't "have it all" without one). Meanwhile I ignored all the women in well-worn flowered shirts and scuffed running shoes, toting sandwiches in plastic bags from K-Mart. They were bound for the places where women had always worked – doughnut shops, typing pools – at jobs no man would ever want. They were just trying to make a living; my kind and I were making history. We were going where our mothers couldn't go, and it crossed my mind that they must envy us. I thought of what my mother had said when she first called on me at the office. "Well, look at this! Your name on the door! And you've got a secretary!"

"Mother, Karen isn't my secretary. She just types a few letters for me."

"Maybe you could convince her to type the odd letter for me.

I'm told my letters are highly entertaining, and I have to type them all myself." She was joking, but she sounded wistful.

—◦◦◦◦—

I was eating lunch at my desk, the usual yogurt and apple, when Karen knocked on my door. "There's a call for you from Ben's school. Some guy who says it's urgent."

Oh, God, what now? I was always getting calls about my rascal eight-year-old. He'd been snapping the blinds, amused by the sound. He'd been caught in some minor misdeed on the playground, while the ringleaders all ran away. He'd been exiled to the cloakroom for making faces and there had expressed his sense of injustice by peeing against the wall. The teacher didn't know about the peeing, but the other kids viewed it as a kind of perverse heroism. In spite of myself, so did I.

I picked up the phone. "Rona Maynard speaking. Excuse me, Mrs. Jones." At the school I used my married name in a futile effort to appear more maternal. The other mothers, mostly older without full-time jobs, were all known as Mrs. So-and-So.

The teacher's voice quivered with rage. "Mrs. Jones, your son threw away his sandwich today."

"He threw it on the floor? I'll have a word with him about littering."

"You don't understand. Your son walked up to the garbage can, just as cool as could be, and *threw his sandwich in the garbage.*"

"So he chose not to eat his lunch. What's the problem?"

"The problem is that I have dozens of kids in the lunch-room. The problem is that your son is something of a leader, and if he throws his lunch away other kids will throw their lunch away, too. And then every second mother in the school will be demanding to know why little Katie didn't eat her lunch. What am I supposed to tell them, Mrs. Jones? That one child, yours, is stirring up trouble for everyone else?"

Who were these mothers, with nothing better to do than pester the school about sandwiches? Good mothers, in the eyes of the teacher. Mothers like mine, who packed a different artful sandwich every day, along with homemade oatmeal cookies. I just slapped some peanut butter on brown and wrapped it up with a banana, as the teacher surely knew. Okay, so Ben didn't like his lunch. I couldn't blame him.

The teacher did, though. Even more, he blamed me.

"That son of yours is bouncing off the wall, Mrs. Jones. You can't expect me to keep him in line because you're too busy to do it yourself. It simply isn't fair. The fact is, your child needs mothering!"

On the rare occasions when a writer attacked my editing, I stood my ground without flinching. But when a teacher cast judgment on my mothering, I always crumpled in the end. I knew how to fix a story; I didn't know how to fix a life, as the school seemed to think I'd better do in a hurry. Someone was broken, Ben or me. More likely both of us. I put my head on the metal desk and wept.

"You look like the world just fell apart." It was Keitha with an armload of papers.

"I'll be fine in a minute." Now I'd been caught crying in the office. The mark of a wimp, according to the get-ahead books.

"Do you want to talk about it?" I didn't. Not with her. Maybe she thought being Catholic had made her an expert on guilt, but she had no idea what it meant to fail a child. In fact, she'd made it clear that my job should come first. When Ben was sick and I had to stay home, she kept phoning with an edge in her voice. Once Ben had grabbed the phone before I did, just in time to hear my boss ask, "So, Ben, when are you going to let your mom come back to work?"

—◦⟨⟨◉⟩⟩◦—

Paul asked about my five-year plan as we polished off the last of dinner: chicken breasts (overcooked in haste), broccoli, a bottle of Austrian wine. We'd had this conversation before, and it always made me bristle. Sensing trouble, Ben headed for the TV.

"I don't need a plan," I said.

Heavy sigh across the table. "If you don't know where you're going, it doesn't matter how you get there."

"I don't want to go anywhere. I love my job. What's your problem?"

Money, for one thing. Didn't I realize how much more I could get somewhere else? Besides, if I didn't get out of women's magazines, I might be stuck forever in a pink-collar ghetto. A journalist friend had made the same point but I expected a softer touch at home. Instead, my husband was goading me: "It's time you got into something more substantial. *Maclean's* could use someone like you."

Maclean's was the flagship of *Flare*'s parent company, Maclean Hunter Publishing. Paul had a management job there on the business side, but the editorial department was said to be a brutal and treacherous place. I'd heard the editor, Peter Newman, described as a "swamp demon." How could Paul think I'd be better off at *Maclean's*?

"But I'm editing articles about body image and women in labour unions. I'm writing three columns for every issue. That's not substantial enough for you? There's not a line in that magazine that doesn't go through my typewriter or under my pencil."

"And they're paying you peanuts. Can't you see what's going on? The more you churn out, the more Keitha saves for the stuff that really counts at *Flare* – photography and models. It's a fashion magazine, for chrissake. You're in a dead-end job and you'll never get paid what you're worth. Keitha's using you."

Keitha, using me. It didn't seem possible. I thought of what she'd told me in our first meeting: "With me, what you see is what you get." What I saw was a surrogate mother who asked what I dreamed of doing instead of filling my head with her own dreams. I loved her, not simply for her bird-call laugh and bruised courage, but for what she had released in me. At *Flare* I did not hold back for fear of falling short. I was writing in a voice that sounded like me, not my mother's. I was under the spell of this new Rona Maynard, the creator and risk-taker, yet it seemed she had been conjured by Keitha's transforming presence. If I worked somewhere else, would she cease to exist?

--◦◦◦--

I went to see my mother in her Green Kingdom. Green and white loveseats, green plants exploding with shiny tendrils, a seaglass-green bedroom, newly renovated at great expense. She seemed more relaxed since Grandma's death, after a long and much-lamented decline culminating in pancreatic cancer. Now she had no more pleading phone calls from Winnipeg, no last-minute flights to discuss treatment options that could only postpone the inevitable. Along with her mother's mink, she had acquired the lustre of freedom, earned with duty, struggle and sorrow. In a white hostess gown that set off the bloom in her face, she poured mint tea into green and white cups. She had lately been indulging a passion for china, and everything she bought had at least a splash of the particular green that appears only in the first leaves of summer.

My mother, the kept woman. Sydney, who adored her but wouldn't hear of marriage, took her all over the world. They crossed the ocean on the *Queen Elizabeth II*, they slept on the finest linen. He came for the weekend with his overnight bag, stopping on the way for flowers and a manicure. When he wasn't around, she might read all day in her nightgown, eating nothing but Brie and crackers. She had an income of her own from writing and speaking, but she took time off whenever she pleased. With her big hats and big jewellery, she resembled a *grande dame*, yet she'd developed a flirtatious streak that seemed positively girlish. No one but my mother would dare to throw a cocktail party for the men who most intrigued her – all of them prominent, nearly all of them strangers. The invitations appalled me: "FOR MEN ONLY. Wine, cheese and conversation with Fredelle Maynard." *Oh, Mother, how could you? No one will come.* I needn't have worried. Seventy men showed up while my mother held court, resplendent in Mexican lace. She was the envy of all my friends, and no wonder. I envied her myself.

"So, Madam Editor," she said. "Your fame precedes you." Just the other night, she'd been talking with a distinguished man of letters who knew my reputation for authoritative work with writers. Maybe some day she'd be known as Rona Maynard's mother. And to think that only yesterday I'd been a shy little creature, terrified of inviting other children to play. "You were so sure they'd say no. You didn't think anyone would want to be your friend. And now look at you, literary Canada beating a path to your door."

"Nobody's beating a path. Who do you think I am, Margaret Atwood?"

"I know exactly who you are. Gifted, original, witty Rona Maynard."

"You're just saying that because you're my mother."

She had something to show me in the basement. There it was, inside what had once been the unused sauna: a nest of soft colourful things, fur throws and velvet pillows. My mother covered her mouth. Her eyes flashed like a teenager's on prom night. *Oh, Mother! A sex room! The only thing you forgot is a leather swing hanging from the ceiling.* "It's amazing," I said, a little tartly. "Only you would think of it."

⁓◦⊙◦⁓

I'd spent close to five years in my first job when my friend Val called from her office upstairs at *Maclean's*. The swamp demon had recruited her as a writer; now he was looking for a sharp young editor. She had told him all about me. "You'll get to run a terrific section. Medicine, law, science, all that meaty stuff you like, plus fashion and lifestyles and pretty well anything else you want. It's practically a magazine in itself. You're going to knock their socks off."

How could she be so sure? Oh, well, better give this a try. My hand shook as I dialled Peter Newman.

He'd been expecting my call.

His office suggested an old world men's club, not that I had ever been inside one. We sat on his leather couch while he did most of the talking, seldom meeting my eyes. He had just repositioned *Maclean's* as a newsweekly, but his team was top-heavy with newshounds who took themselves a little too seriously. He wanted a different point of view, and although he couldn't tell me what it was, he had apparently decided I would bring it (Val must have done quite a sales job). "A magazine is about the heart," he said.

Days later, the job was mine. Again we sat on the leather couch, as he asked one final question: "How much are you making at *Flare*?"

Nowhere near enough; my husband had that right. As *Flare*'s careers columnist, I knew how to sidestep this question. I quoted my own advice: "My salary doesn't reflect my true worth. Let's talk about what I should be making."

"How does thirty thousand dollars sound?" He looked uncertain, as if he feared I might be more expensive. In fact he'd offered fifty percent more than I was making downstairs. I tried not to seem dazzled by this stroke of good fortune. Swamp demon? The man was my champion; he wanted me and valued me and knew I could not fail.

For once I left work promptly at five that night. Paul and I were going out for a celebration dinner. In my head I was already planning stories for *Maclean's* and the outfits I would wear to signal my gravitas. I'd need a new suit, something elegant but unexpected. Bursting out of the elevator, I nearly collided with the vice-president in charge of all the magazines. He had barely noticed me in the past. That day he gave me a twinkly smile: "Now you're going to work for a *real* magazine."

THE DARKLING PLAIN

Maclean's was not a place where ambitious young women had lunch dates. How essential could you be if you sat in a bistro instead of at your desk planning cover stories? But I couldn't say no to my mother, who was treating me on my birthday. At thirty-two, I'd finally achieved what she had always wanted – a job among men, with prestige and a future. Surely this called for a celebration. My mother ordered a carafe of the house white wine, shrugging off my protest that I had to stay sharp for a meeting. "*L'chaim*," she said. To life.

She wore one of her broad-brimmed hats and silver earrings that quivered when she laughed. People turned to look at her, this buxom, white-haired woman with no need for plucked eyebrows or designer clothes. She had something more compelling, an effortless confidence that revelled in its own rough edges. As the coffee arrived, she said, "Open your hands and shut your eyes. I'll give you something to make you wise." I'd been hearing those words from her through a lifetime of birthdays, and I always held out my hands with the sweet, haunting memory of childhood gifts: an antique fur muff that *Little Women's* Meg March could have worn, a rare ballet book from the 1930s. My

mother was the Jacques Cousteau of junk stores; in a sea of irre-
deemable dreck she could always find a treasure. This time she'd
found a gold pin in the shape of a tiny crescent moon. Nestled
inside the crescent was a flower with amethyst petals and a speck
of a diamond for a leaf. "It's lovely," I said. And it was – for a
teenage girl. I'd lost my taste for floral motifs and she had never
noticed. Still, she'd given me a diamond, the only one I had.

"As soon as I saw it, I thought of you," she said. "But you'd
better not wear it just yet. The clasp is broken. You should take
it to a jeweller."

I checked my watch: thirty-five minutes to the story
meeting. My mother placed both elbows on the table and
looked me in the eye, flushed from a second glass of wine. She
took a deep breath, as if she'd been rehearsing this moment in
her head. "There's something else I have for you, Rona. A
project, the most important one you'll ever take on. It's Ben. I'm
worried about him."

Her proprietary tone made me wince. She thought of
herself as the expert on my child, and I'd begun to suspect she
was right. The two of them had forged a special bond during
weekly overnights in her Green Kingdom, when she would pick
him up at school and devote the whole evening to full-on indul-
gence. After a night at her house, Ben always had a princely
swagger in his walk. He called her "Das," a baby name she loved
for its distinctive jauntiness. When he spiked a fever on a
weekday morning, she would drive through a blizzard to look
after him while I worked, bearing homemade chocolate chip
cookies and a clutch of brand-new children's books that she'd
been saving for just such an occasion. I had come to rely on her
devotion to Ben, yet I paid for it in jealousy and guilt. My
mother felt no pressure to mould her grandchild as she had me.

She never judged him, yet she could still judge me without mercy, especially on the matter of my mothering.

Now my mother was saying, "Ben needs more attention than he's getting from you. The last time I picked him up at school, his teacher took me aside and told me how concerned she is. He can't concentrate, he's always clowning. These are signs of neediness, Rona. So of course I said I'd make sure you understood the gravity of the situation."

The old story: my son was difficult, therefore I had failed him. Bad enough that I should hear it on meet-the-teacher night, perched on a miniature chair like a disgraced kid bound for the principal's office (where I was regularly called to account for Ben's mischief). But from my own mother, on my birthday? The litany of blame had never seemed fair – Ben had two parents, after all, plus an agile, restless mind that was always on the lookout for amusement – and yet the charges still activated secret, devastating fears. A good mother is supposed to delight in her child; I took greater pleasure in my job – not because I loved it more, but because it was mine to control as no child could ever be. Especially this child, with his knees perpetually scraped in games I couldn't play and his imagination lit by passions I couldn't share. He designed villages out of Lego; he had memorized the entire plot and cast of *Dr. Who*, a creaky British fantasy serial that he watched every day after school. I'd always thought of Ben as belonging to himself, but my mother seemed to think he belonged to her – and that her mission was saving him from me. So she had taken it upon herself to discuss Ben's emotional health with the teacher. Her zeal enraged me. My voice rising over the clink of the cutlery, I gave her a piece of my mind. "For God's sake, Mother, you could have told the teacher to call me. Paul and I would have been there in a flash. We've never ignored a call from the school. Can't you trust me to solve my own problems?"

"Not this one, I'm afraid. My dear, I must tell you the truth. You are neglecting your child. You're so preoccupied with *Maclean's* that you haven't even noticed what's abundantly clear to his teacher. She beseeched me to help her, and rightly so. For a young woman of your intelligence and character, would it be so terribly difficult to try just a little bit harder?"

My mother's voice shook with sorrow; mine shook with rage and bafflement. *Try just a little bit harder.* The nerve of her. All I did was try. Deadlines and office politics all day, lost school permission slips and dirty dishes all evening. My mother had wanted to exult in my thriving career; now she seemed to want me to be building Lego towers. "So this is your idea of a birthday treat! A broken gift and a lecture on what a rotten mother I am! You have no idea what it takes me to get through the day. Why are you against me?"

"I'm not against you, Rona. I'm *for* Ben. For the elemental human comfort of knowing he's accepted by his mother." She leaned across the table, consuming my field of vision with the brim of her hat and the cold, brilliant blue of her silk shirt-dress. Then she began to recite "Dover Beach":

> Ah, love, let us be true
> To one another! For the world, which seems
> To lie before us like a land of dreams,
> So various, so beautiful, so new,
> Hath really neither joy, nor love, nor light,
> Nor certitude, nor peace, nor help for pain:
> And we are here as on a darkling plain
> Swept with confused alarms of struggle and flight. . . .

I ran to the street and hailed a cab. Just like my mother to duck a challenge by invoking a dead poet. Damn her and her platitudes about the comfort of maternal acceptance. If she wanted to talk about that, I could give her an earful. But not now. I had to save my strength for the meeting. With luck I'd have time to wash the mascara stains off my face before anyone noticed I'd been crying.

--⚬⚬⚬--

After nine months at *Maclean's*, it seemed I had been there forever. The place had a hopped-up, anarchic energy that pinned me to my desk and invaded my dreams. I said I loved my job; the truth is, I'd come to need it the way an actor needs applause or a soldier needs gunfire. It was not so much a job as a do-or-die campaign in which I had to prove my right to stand with Peter Newman's troops as we wrested the latest issue from the weekly onslaught of late copy, missing facts and eleventh-hour cuts to editorial space. *Maclean's* had neither the resources nor the discipline of its American competitors, and these obstacles magnified the sense of ragged heroism that infused the whole enterprise.

On Friday nights when the issue closed late and a tower of boxes filled with jumbo pizzas came in to sustain us, the office seemed to shiver with camaraderie, although just what we were building there was never entirely clear. For some, former campus radicals who'd never lost the fervour of their sit-in days, it was a promised land of truth and justice. For others, it was all about bold new ideas in art and thought. Our separate notions could flourish like competing city states because Peter Newman, despite his formidable eloquence on the page, was in person a man of awkward pauses and cryptic observations that sounded like randomly dictated notes toward the master plan in his head.

I knew the goal involved revealing the country to itself, and that was reason enough to work at *Maclean's*. In fact, the mysteries of the place made it all the more compelling. It could become in my mind what I willed it to be, a glorious, transfixing illusion.

Many young women worked at *Maclean's*, although few had any power. Women scurried through the halls with teetering armloads of file folders; they could sit for hours in the journalist's contortion: phone tucked between shoulder and chin, one hand scribbling notes while the other clutched a Styrofoam cup of stale coffee. They had hair mussed from being raked in frustration and eyes fierce with resolve. I was proud to be one of them, yet I wasn't, not really. Only one other woman had to leave the office at a reasonable hour to look after a child; no one else had a husband on the business side of the magazine, the so-called "dark side," where ads were sold and numbers crunched.

Unlike the men, who wore rolled-up shirtsleeves and sweat-stiffened jeans with an air of entitlement, the women carefully girded themselves for work (silk, tartan, the odd string of pearls). One of them was giving me a first-day tour of the office when I overheard an odd turn of phrase muttered between men like a private code. Could she please explain "the tweed brassiere set"? My new colleague rolled her eyes. "That's what some of the guys call the women who work here. Welcome to *Maclean's*." The old guard expected the worst from me, she added. I had come from a women's magazine, so they'd cast me as an airhead. Their joke had already made the rounds: "Next thing we know, Newman's going to hire the knitting editor of *Teen Generation*."

At *Flare* the hazing of women by men had been a topic for my jobs column, not part of my life. I associated such things with disgruntled hard hats on factory floors, and I could not imagine that Peter Newman's staff would stoop so low. My new boss had a long track record of hiring talented women and his ex-wife, the pre-eminent journalist Christina McCall Newman, had been his respected collaborator. Surely the legendary turmoil at *Maclean's* was an equal opportunity affair. What I hadn't bargained on was the toxic emotional climate – equal parts awe, suspicion and resentment – that Newman inspired in the entire office. He slunk in and out on his way to interviews with titans, a tall, hunched figure whose thick black eyebrows gave him an aura of impenetrable world-weariness. In his absence everyone else would jockey for position and speculate on what he might be thinking about us. His opinions were said to be easily swayed by what he heard from his senior staff, notably a bug-eyed goblin of a man who kept antique abortion tools in his desk drawer and was known to intimidate junior staff by brandishing a whip. The Goblin looked at women the way rubberneckers look at a bad road accident, with attraction curdled by revulsion and shame. One day he complimented me on my perfume; I knew immediately that I would never again wear that scent to the office. Relatively speaking, I got off lightly: he once asked a female colleague to step into the light so he could see through her blouse. He got away with harassing and humiliating women because Newman left us all to our own devices. A famously reluctant personnel manager, our boss did not concern himself with his staff's behaviour.

We all fretted over what the Goblin might be saying – whose work derided, whose team spirit called into question by a false rumour, soon to spread through the office like a lethal virus. Stage One in this disease was a flurry of Newman's curt notes on the tiny sheets of brown paper that we dreaded finding in our in-trays. Stage Two was the firing, whispered among the staff with dismay at the suddenness of it all and ignoble relief that the rest of us were still around.

We pondered Newman's every utterance as if it were the entrails of a sacrificial beast. On Monday mornings we all flocked to the bulletin board, scanning Newman's critique of the latest issue for clues to our ever-changing status. If he had nothing good to say about your section, you braced yourself for a curt brown memo. Then again, his praise could be politically troublesome. In the eyes of certain grizzled old-timers, our boss was a shameless populist who aimed to degrade the magazine with fads and fancies that would sell like potato chips at the newsstand. (I never understood why selling magazines should be held in such contempt – wasn't that our business?) I had barely arrived at *Maclean's* when my one-page story on dinosaurs drew special praise in the Monday critique. Just the sort of thing we should be doing more often, said Newman. *Kid stuff*, said the Goblin's acolytes. *But what else could you expect from Newman's airhead pawn?*

I thought *Maclean's* would take me forward; in fact it was pulling me back to the overheated dreams and incessant competition of my childhood. Like my mother's house, the magazine was a place where women went hungry – for respect, for opportunity, for presence in next week's issue. An extra page for my section meant one less for someone else's, and there were never enough pages to go around. The size of each woman's ration was determined by men – one man above all, Peter Newman, who held the power to raise you up or cast you out. I told myself that my drive and gifts would see me through, but at heart I never really believed this. My mother had told herself the same thing, many medals and honours ago, and look what became of her teaching career. In my mind her story had the force of prophecy.

A few weeks into my new job, I was summoned to the corner office where my grand adventure had begun. Newman sat behind the rosewood desk, nothing on it but a small white card. He cut to the chase: "We have a problem. Not your work; I'm hearing great things. It's money."

How could this be? I'd only just come to *Maclean's* and my section was well under budget. He pointed to the card. My salary card from the personnel department. "We hired you for thirty thousand. Now I see they were paying you twenty thousand downstairs. We've offered you a fifty percent increase. It's too much."

"It's what we agreed to. You put it in writing. I have the letter." I groped from fact to fact like a climber on the face of a mountain, clutching and trembling.

"It's too much. Look, we can deal with this. Why don't we pay you twenty-five? For you that's still a good increase. Then we'll work you up to thirty thousand."

If this conversation went on much longer, I wouldn't be able to speak. I'd choke on my own words. Could he tell? "You offered me what you thought I was worth. Now you've changed your mind. We had an agreement."

I was reaching for the door in a stupor when he said, "Think about it. We'll talk again in a few days. Meanwhile, please keep this to yourself." A few days. A few whole days of feigning self-assurance while my enemies watched me for signs of weakness. Maybe the Goblin was right; maybe I didn't have the steel for this place. I wanted to run to my husband's office on the dark side, but running would reveal my panic. As it happened, Paul couldn't help me. He could only explain, with a look of helpless outrage, what had likely triggered this debacle. The company had salary guidelines, which Newman had inadvertently broken. His corporate masters could squeeze a dollar until it begged for mercy, and they would not look kindly on his deal with me.

Someone on high – perhaps the vice-president who had smiled so benignly on my move to a "real" magazine – must have been applying pressure.

Back at my desk with the door safely closed, I called the one person who could tell me what to do. My mother. She heard my sobbing and she knew: "It's your job." Nothing could surprise her when it came to male duplicity. But this man would not get away with his shenanigans. This time a woman's grit would carry the day. My mother told me to call a friend of hers, a lawyer. With his advice, I held onto the thirty thousand dollars. I had won, Newman had lost. I was right, he was wrong. He had tried – so I thought – to humiliate me, but I had turned the tables, which was only fair.

A few months later a little brown note landed in my in-tray (*Oh, God, what have I done? He thinks I've cheated him, that I'm not worth my salary*). This is what it said:

> Dear Rona:
>
> Just a note to confirm that your probation period is now at an end. It's no exaggeration that we are all wildly pleased with your efforts in the Professions section. Congratulations and keep it up.
>
> Peter

He had apparently moved on. I hadn't. I couldn't forget the salary affair, any more than my mother could forget being cut from the English department. Hugging my burden of resentment as if it defined me, I began to duck around corners lest I pass Newman in the halls. He had told me our craft was about the heart, whatever that meant. To me it was now about do-or-die stands and avoiding unjust blows while I could. But payback time would come. I just knew it.

⁓◦⊙◦⁓

A typical weeknight. Home with Paul around seven (better start frying those burgers fast). Pour myself a beer, throw my coat over the banister. Yell a greeting upstairs, where Ben is watching *Dr. Who*. Slice my finger along with the onion, swear loudly. Drop everything; Paul wants to talk about the damn phone bill. Do I know anything about long-distance calls to Buffalo? A whole string of them to the same number, each one less than a minute? What I know is that Ben has been home alone for three hours, and I'm ashamed. With luck, he won't tell his grandmother.

Paul dials the mystery number in Buffalo. Aha: the public TV station that broadcasts *Dr. Who*. They've just completed a fundraising drive. *Ben, did you make these calls?* He did. A motor-mouth volunteer was threatening to axe his favourite show – and best friend – unless he made a pledge. But what could he pledge, a nine-year-old with no money except an allowance? He breathed into the receiver, mute with anxiety. Then he gave up.

Oh, Ben. Born to two children, raised on the fly and looking it: shoelaces trailing, a smudge on your cheek, shaggy curls brushing the collar of an outgrown flannel shirt. You turn to a TV show for what you're not finding at home. When darkness falls, you switch on all the lights in the house; they blaze like warming fires in a home that is essentially a base camp for the planning of complex adult operations.

My mother was right: I've failed you. Maybe I should try harder. But with what? I've burned through all my energy like a lottery winner on a spree. I don't want to care for anyone, not even you. I want something no grown-up woman should want, and I can't get it off my mind. I want someone to care for me.

A new woman came to *Maclean's*, and she broke all the unwritten rules in the office. She put photos of her daughters on her desk. She wore crayon colours, not understated neutrals. She practically danced down the halls in her patent leather pumps, humming show tunes as she went. I looked up from my work to find her at my desk, hand extended. "You must be Rona! I'm Chris, Peter's new right hand, and whether he's realized it or not, I always know *exactly* what the left hand is doing!"

I didn't think she'd last a month, but I trusted her on sight. Everyone did. As the boss's secretary, she knew the worst yet she chose to see the best. Sometimes she engineered it, although many years passed before she told me her secret. Newman's little brown notes to the staff all passed through her hands, and any memo that did not sit well with her would be quietly consigned to the trash. She was unabashedly maternal. On her daily rounds she would pause to jolly people along with one of her salty jokes. She had a vast store of them, which she told with the unwavering conviction that she could make anyone laugh. I never saw her fail. If the more determined cynics were just being polite, only Chris could elicit such courtesy from them. In that time and place, befriending a secretary was not the way for a woman to expand her influence, yet I couldn't resist her soothing everydayness, her faith in the small social rituals that brightened her corner of the world.

Over lunch in the company cafeteria, Chris would shake her head at my Spartan choices: yogurt and an apple. "Now, Rona, you need more than that to stay in fighting form around here." My mother might have said such a thing, and I'd have told her to mind her own business. But I liked being mothered by Chris. Not much older than I, she projected an artless wisdom that was proudly and thoroughly female. She had firm views about cooking for friends and raising her girls, but not about cutting-edge films or the Supreme Court (unlike the rest of the fractious *Maclean's* sisterhood). With her I could lower my defences. One day I confided my worries about Ben, who'd recently been caught by the police taking coins from a wishing well with a magnet. Chris roared. "Smart little bugger! Sounds like a born innovator, if you ask me."

—◦◦◦—

Different as we seemed on the surface, Ben and I had something in common. I too had been a problem child. At roughly his age, I'd been sent for play therapy to have my troubling quirks buffed away by Mrs. Warren. Now it was Ben's turn, but therapy had changed since my day. As a child, I had been the "identified patient," the family member whose behaviour provides a convenient distraction from larger, more complicated issues no one dares to broach. We couldn't tell the truth about my parents' marriage and my mother's simmering fury, so we focused on one of the symptoms – my unhappiness. This time Ben's antics brought the whole family into therapy, and the focus was not fixing him but changing the way we interacted. In our assessment, the three of us were asked to draw our family. I drew Paul and Ben playing ball on the lawn, and myself looking out at them through the window. The social worker said, "You don't feel part of this family, do you?" That was one of the things we'd have to work on as a group.

My mother had agreed to take part. She swept into our first session as if she were a guest speaker flown in for the occasion. And she made it very clear that she could have addressed the clinic staff. Back when hardly anyone had heard of family therapy, she had interviewed its prime movers for an article. One of them – she dropped a name – had tried to persuade her to co-author a book. "And now here I am, continuing my research from a more intimate angle. The greatest joy of the writing life is the privilege of being a student."

We grown-ups arranged ourselves on folding chairs while Ben retreated with his own social worker. My mother seemed to fill the room with her broad black hat and the matching raincoat that flowed like a mantle. I looked at our wisp of a social worker. *She'll flatten you, poor girl. She was charming your guru while you were still hoping for a smile from some pimply thirteen-year-old. Just see if she lets you forget it.*

We got around soon enough to the birthday lunch. I spoke in a voice I didn't know, halfway between a wail and a war cry. Hard truths overran me, rending their bloody garments and shaking their fists in the air. I disclosed the sense of otherness that had pierced my love for Ben from the start, and my conviction that this had to do with my mother. I admitted to perpetual rivalry – with Ben for her love, with her for a central place in Ben's life. I challenged my mother to help her grandson by standing behind me instead of running me down – I got enough of that at *Maclean's*, just by being a woman. If she didn't hear me, then Paul and the social worker would witness her deafness. It wasn't what I wanted, but it would do.

My mother's lower lip trembled. Her voice dropped to a whisper, the kind of whisper that carries to the uppermost row of the theatre. "Dear child, Ben needed a champion. I thought it was only the Greeks who shot the messenger for bringing bad news."

"Let me ask you something, Fredelle." The quiet voice of the social worker, bless her. "You've told us you did what you had to do on Ben's behalf. Today you've seen the consequences of your decision, the anguish for your daughter and her growing sense of inadequacy as a parent. You've told us you wanted to help. Can you honestly say that what you did has been helpful to your family?"

My mother deflated before my eyes. I had made my point, for once, but now I missed her glorious buoyancy. She didn't say she was sorry, which was oddly consoling, a reaffirmation of her strength. "Apparently not," she said.

PAYBACK TIME

My mother sat at the head of the table, flanked by the remains of her signature family dinner: capon as no one else could roast it, and pie as no one else could bake it – apple this time, fragrant with cinnamon. "A little more pie, Rona?" As if she needed to ask. I always ate a generous wedge followed by at least one sliver. We liked to joke that the calories in slivers didn't count because God only logged the wedges. My mother licked a chunk of apple off her fingers, then she broke off a golden flake of crust. (At Maynard Hall she had confined her nibbling to the kitchen; Daddy was a stickler about manners.) She reclined in her chair and said to her assembled family – Sydney, Paul, Ben and me – "I'll always be grateful to Rona. If not for her, I might still be living with Max Maynard. I nearly took him back out of pity but Rona stopped me just in time. She set me free. And it's abundantly clear that Max is better off on his own. He has what he always wanted, a flourishing career as an artist. O brave new world!"

The pie turned to cardboard in my mouth. I believed her – and believed I had done the right thing when I stood at the top of the stairs at Maynard Hall and told my father, "You don't live here anymore." Someone had to stop the shouting. If we had to replay that scene, I would speak the same lines. But the second time around I would know enough to be afraid. I would fear my own anger at my father – a plummeting sensation within, as if the rightful seat of daughterly love had crashed through me down to the bowels of the earth, burning and tearing as it fell. For years I had waited to make him pay – for his fists pounded on the table, for his nocturnal rants about Hell, for his hot liquor breath in my face as he dragged me upstairs. Yet when the moment came, it brought me no peace. My father had trusted in his home to shield him from a hostile world. And I, sharper than a serpent's tooth, had sent him into exile.

⸺◦◦◦⸺

After my father left Maynard Hall for good, I wrote him off as a hopeless case. For a few years he wandered like Lear on the heath, a wild old man hounded by his own remembered folly. His plans shifted with the winds. He had found peace in rural Sussex; he couldn't possibly stay in such a backwater. He had settled down with Amy Pratt, his young love; he had to flee before she killed him in one of her rages. He belonged in New Hampshire; his arthritis couldn't take New Hampshire winters. With no money to speak of, he travelled light: my mother had convinced him to take alimony from her instead of half their savings. Joyce protested this arrangement, but my mother's ration-ale made perfect sense to me: "Would you want to see him blow it in a few years? Or let Amy get her hands on it? Remember, it's your money, too."

At last he returned to Victoria, where he had once been a firebrand artist and a sketching companion of Emily Carr. What hadn't he abandoned in Victoria? A career, a marriage, a religious faith . . . a whole life, pretty much. But he still had family and friends there who welcomed him back. At seventy-four, my father started over. He took two rooms in the Glenshiel Hotel, a retirement home where the chintz was faded but the rent was low. One room contained a single bed, a few Cézanne reproductions and his slightly threadbare tweeds. The other held his easel and a jumble of paints. From the Glenshiel he could walk to his old sketching haunts on the coast, tap-tapping along Dallas Road with his walking stick and English cap. Again and again he sketched every promontory, searching for the angle that would crack the scene open and make it new. His first year in Victoria, he sent me a package just in time for my birthday. A landscape, spare but exuberant – flourishes of violet and emerald placed just so on black paper. Arthritis had forced him to simplify his style: unable to handle a brush, he was applying paint with a palette knife. Yet I hadn't seen such effortless joy in his art since he painted the choir of angels on the window at Maynard Hall, more than twenty Christmases ago.

For the first time in memory, I found myself admiring my father. I wasn't alone: galleries were planning Max Maynard shows. "I seem to have been discovered," he said on the phone. "There's been quite a flurry of reporters in this humble lair of mine. If I have any more visits from charming young women with notebooks, the attention might prove fatally distracting." *Daddy, Daddy. I know perfectly well what distracts you, and it comes from the liquor store, not the local papers. But I've got to give you credit. You're trying to stay sober.*

Three nights a week he went to Alcoholics Anonymous, recording what he learned there in a notebook that never left his pocket. His fellow members called him "the professor" and reportedly couldn't get enough of his AA speech, a kind of

Dante seminar for drunks. As my father told it, they had all lost their way and were groping through Hell toward the mountain of deliverance. What looked to the outside world like degradation and failure was in fact just the prelude to an epic spiritual journey.

He wanted me to witness his climb for myself. Early in those years of reinvention, he flew me to Victoria for the opening of his latest show, liberally dotted with "sold" stickers. At last he had fulfilled the drunken boast of my childhood: "I am creating my finest work ever." When he took my arm to guide me through the crowd of well-wishers, I initially thought that he was showing me off (he always did like a young woman on his arm). Then I realized the opposite was equally true. These people looked up to him. More than that, they loved him. One woman said, "You ought to see your dad with our daughter. Nine years old and she just dotes on him, those enchanting stories he tells. But I don't need to tell you what a way he has with children. . . ."

My father, a way with children? Not with this child. He never told me even one enchanting story; he was too busy planning how to sneak his next drink. If Daddy really cared about sobriety, why couldn't he sober up for me?

As it happened, he couldn't stay sober for anyone. He flirted with sobriety, promised it his heart and soul, only to betray it along with my hopes. A few good weeks or months would invariably end with a slurred phone call at three in the morning. When his health began to fail and he could no longer manage at the Glenshiel, I told myself, with a stab of guilt, that it must be for the best. Just let him try to drink in the old folks' home. He'd be safe now. And I'd be safe, too, from his phantom voice in the night. "You should come to Victoria, Rona. You should hear me speak about Dante to my fellow pilgrims at AA meetings. A remarkable speech, I'm told. And quite possibly helpful to you. Someday you may find yourself in a dark wood . . ."

⟞⟨◎⟩⟝

I was reviewing my notes for the *Maclean's* story meeting when the phone rang. *Please, God, don't let this be Ben's school.* Someone had indeed been raising a ruckus, but this time it wasn't my son. My father was drinking again, the sly old codger. How had he gotten his hands on a bottle? The man was in a wheelchair – twisted by arthritis, weakened by pneumonia, guarded by a phalanx of nursing aides in the old folks' home. He must have cajoled some woman, flashed that smile and greased her palm. But the Maynard wiles did not impress Dr. Nigel Quimby, whose clipped British voice quivered with frustration. "Miss Maynard, I had hoped to avoid this call but your father has driven me to it. I could itemize the damage his drinking has inflicted on every system in his body – a very fragile one, as you surely know – but I'm a busy man. I have a great many patients who are doing every-thing in their power to stave off life-threatening illnesses. And here is your father, *undoing* all my efforts on his behalf. I'm afraid I've reached my limit, Miss Maynard. Surely there's something you can do!"

I almost choked on my coffee. "Let me get this straight. He's been an alcoholic his entire adult life. People have been trying to 'do something' about it for the past fifty years. And you're hoping I've got the magic bullet. What would that be, Dr. Quimby? A heart-to-heart chat?"

"Your father is very proud of you, Miss Maynard. He respects you. Maybe you can talk some sense into him."

Oh, Dr. Quimby, my dad never mentioned your wacky wit! Hold on just a sec while I make a note in my Day-Timer: "Talk father out of drinking." I'll put it right between "Assign story on the future of the universe" and "Buy kitty litter." And then when I've perfected my instant cure for alcoholism, I'll throw away my editor's clipboard and waltz out of here a zillionaire with a second assistant housemaid to change the litter box. I hung up the phone laughing as if I'd had a few stiff drinks. I yelped and sputtered, convulsed by my private joke, until Chris ran in to check on me. "Are you okay? I thought I heard crying."

Surely Chris would appreciate the comedy of this affair. I waved my mug like a barroom showoff, splattering coffee on my notes for the meeting as I shared my tale, concluding with the flourish: "Fish gotta swim! Birds gotta fly! Alcoholics . . . gotta drink!"

Chris didn't crack a smile. I looked tired, she said. Maybe I should go home early.

That night I made dinner in my old velour bathrobe with a glass of Zinfandel in my hand. I thought about my father, the self-appointed bard of AA. "The professor," indeed! Those poor besotted suckers in Victoria had better pass the hat to endow a chair in deception for him! He had fooled us all, just as he fooled my mother.

I sat on the kitchen floor and wept.

※

"You should go to Victoria before he dies," my mother said. We were curled up at opposite ends of her big white couch, where I had just filled her in on the news from Dr. Quimby.

"I wouldn't count him out just yet. Remember the last time he had pneumonia? They said he'd blow away any minute like a leaf in the wind, and he survived to drink again. When it's really over, I'll feel better."

"I don't think so. I think you'll be sad."

"Why would I be sad? You think I'll miss drunken phone calls in the middle of the night?" Easy for her to sound tender when she wasn't getting the calls.

"He has a gift for rapture, and he's shared it with you. When you look at the trees or read a poem or listen to Mozart, he's there."

"Good. Then I'll be perfectly content with trees and poetry and Mozart. It's the rest of the package I can do without."

I was needling her, and she knew it. She had carried the whole sorry burden for twenty-five years, a silver-tongued chump with an excuse for every class her husband missed and every insult to his so-called friends in the English department. Now that she was rid of Max Maynard, she reserved the right to make expert judgments on his character, as if he were a difficult poem – overrated yet haunting – that she alone had parsed.

She would demolish him as a family man and as a lover (I tried to forget what she'd disclosed about his sexual habits), yet she often shrugged off my own bad memories of him. For instance, what I remembered of the first and only time I ever brought my high school drama group to Maynard Hall for a rehearsal. My parents had gone to a cocktail party, so I thought we'd be safe from unwelcome parental interruptions – until I ducked into the kitchen to get soft drinks for my guests. Through the window, I could see my staggering father flailing away while my mother struggled to restrain him. "You're not fit to go inside, Max! Rona has company! I won't let you humiliate her!"

My father tried to push her away, but lost his balance instead. "Bloody hell! This is my house, not Rona's!"

Years later, on the big white couch, I tried to thank her for keeping him at bay while I cut the rehearsal short. It must have been hard for her, I said. She looked mystified. It never happened. I must be fantasizing.

"Why would I fantasize a mess like that? Is it so hard to believe that you've forgotten?"

"I remember every slip and every slight. What I don't remember couldn't possibly have happened."

⁓◦◦⁓

It must have been some time in my father's last year that my depression returned full-bore. Again I was like the little boy in "The Snow Queen," his vision distorted by fragments of the demon's mirror. My world seemed a broken place: benders in Victoria, bickering at home in Toronto, a gathering chill of disfavour at *Maclean's*, where a minor disagreement with Peter Newman had become a months-long battle that I could not win but refused to concede. My name had disappeared from the Monday critiques and a curt brown note had arrived in my in-tray. On the morning of my annual review, I woke from a fitful sleep and braced myself for the worst.

Newman didn't have a lot to say, and he spoke so softly that I had to lean forward to hear. "There's something missing from your section. I want to see more surprises."

"Then let's talk about how you define a surprise. If I understand what you want, I can produce it."

"If I knew what it was, it wouldn't be a surprise!" For the first and only time in our meeting, he smiled. Instead of a mentor, I was stuck with a sadistic Zen master. And he wasn't done with me. He had some concerns about my salary. I was making more than other people at my level, but I wasn't better. Fighting words, in my lexicon. The Maynards couldn't bear second-raters. "Are you saying that I'm mediocre?"

"You said that, I didn't." How shifty of him to let me charge myself with the crime and then imply that I was guilty. No other interpretation entered my mind. Although Newman hadn't told me that my job was on the line, I drew the conclusion that it was. Payback time had arrived, just as I had predicted.

There was one oasis in my life: my mother's house. The Green Kingdom exuded serenity, from the tropical splendour of the plants that filled the windows to the familiar aromas wafting from the kitchen. It was what Maynard Hall would have been without Daddy, Joyce or Grandma, and every visit rekindled old longings to bask in her total attention, which always proved slightly less comforting than expected.

—◦◦◦◦—

At last I agreed to visit my father in Victoria. He was not the man I remembered. Age and illness had hollowed him out, scooped caverns in his cheeks and eroded his limbs to sticks. His hair was milkweed fluff. Unable to paint or even hold a sketch-book, he drew on paper placemats with a fumbling hand that strove to capture his new diminished landscape, a forest of wheelchairs. I would have found the drawings pitiful, but his eyes stopped me. They smouldered with grave courage, as if he considered it an honour to be drawing at all.

What was he living for? He sat in his wheelchair at a refectory table lined with patients in various stages of dementia. Some cursed, others masturbated furiously. He sighed and dropped his fork into a puddle of unrecognizable mush. "I could wish for a more congenial place to host you, my dear. But this new small world of mine has its unlikely blessings. Remarkable, really, where the mind can go when freed from the shackles of getting and spending."

If I'd had to live in such a place, I'd be cursing louder than anyone. But my father didn't seem angry. Not at the aides who seemed to think a glass of milk was too much to ask. Not at me for sending him away from Maynard Hall. This puzzled me; like my mother, I never forgot a slight. In my father's eyes, there had been no slight. "I was lurching into the worst phase of my alcoholism. I would have remained there if my family had continued, as we say in AA, to 'enable' me. Don't trouble yourself, Rona. The fault was entirely my own – as I have come to understand and acknowledge through the wisdom of the Twelve Steps. One step in particular, where you are concerned: 'Made a list of all persons we had harmed, and became willing to make amends to them all.'"

In the Twelve Steps he had found a new faith, one that gave him what his missionary parents had withheld. They had warned that God would judge him harshly for his sins; AA promised that God would guide him if he made an honest effort to stay sober. Maybe his efforts were good enough for God, but they'd been nowhere near good enough for me. I didn't hate him, although it often seemed that way; I hated the resentment he had always aroused in me, the sour aftertaste of my own accumulating judgments against him.

Bending to hug him, I could feel every one of his ribs. He said, "I'm proud of you, Rona."

"I'm proud of you, too." He smiled as if he'd been hoping I would say this. To my amazement, it was true.

—◦◦◦—

My job had defeated me, reduced me to a sleep-deprived wraith living on coffee, Aspirin and wine. And for what? A permanent headache, a latchkey under the porch for my son, a knot of rage in my stomach at the thought of Peter Newman. Unlike my grudge against my father, Newman-bashing was socially acceptable: at *Maclean's* you couldn't find a more effective bonding ritual. Not content to seethe among themselves, the troops organized a union drive. I signed a union card, thinking of my manager husband on the dark side. Now we had a conflict of interest. One of us would obviously have to leave, and Paul liked his job. I seized the chance for a graceful exit. It was June, 1982. I had lasted just fifteen months.

My resignation was briefly the talk of *Maclean's*. The sisterhood gave me a joke send-off gift, an apron and a fly swatter for my upcoming life of leisure as a home-based freelance writer. Newman gravely told me what a fine career I'd given up, not that it mattered much to him anymore (soon after this conversation, he announced his own departure). The publisher called me into his office to challenge my decision. He said, "What's the big deal about this 'conflict of interest'? Just don't talk about your work at home." Pounding the desk, he added, "Stay and fight!"

What was this, the beach at Normandy on D-Day?

As I left *Maclean's* for good, the last person I saw was Chris, humming "New York, New York" while she bustled by with her files. She ran to hug me goodbye. "Goodbye, darling. Just remember what the song says: If you can make it in this crazy place, you can make it anywhere."

"I haven't exactly made it here."

"That's not what I'm hearing, and I know the score in this office. I'm a quick study. Trust me, quite a few of us are going to be cheering for you."

I stood there for a minute, feeling her arms around me. I didn't know if what she'd said was true, I just knew she believed it.

My father died a month before his seventy-ninth birthday. Amazing that he'd held on so long, after all the insults to his shrinking body. It happened as predicted: an infection blew him over within days. I didn't cry or even put aside the magazine piece I was writing. If I put my mind to it, I could finish before the funeral.

My sister, the organizer, started blocking out the shape of the service from her home in New Hampshire. Daddy would have wanted a flautist and some visual drama for the room; she would bring a hanging he'd designed. Of course she would speak. My mother, the expert on all things Maynard, proposed to send a taped eulogy. She did not even think of attending in person. When the Maynard relatives vetoed the tape recorder, we decided that I would read her remarks. Once again I was her representative, as I once had been with her sister. My most personal contribution to the service was a reading of "Sailing to Byzantium," a favourite poem of my father's.

It was almost Christmas, my father's season, when he'd rearranged the branches on the tree because nature couldn't grow a perfect spire. I told Paul and Ben we'd have to skip the tree this year; I couldn't bear the scent of pine in our house. My mother had told me I'd be sad, but what I felt was more jagged than sorrow, emptiness layered on abandonment. How could I mourn the loss of my father when I never really had him in the first place?

Three of us stood beside the coffin: Joyce, me and Jack Shadbolt, the boyhood sketching buddy who had become what Max Maynard vowed to be, "the most famous painter in Canada." Jealousy had gnawed at my father; in his cups he had often denounced his friend's work. Jack's wife wanted nothing more to do with the man who'd been so vicious to her husband.

Yet Jack had found it in his heart to honour and love this most ornery of friends, and I held onto his loyalty as if it were a staff on a rocky climb. The room where we stood was not what it seemed; it opened onto a crematorium.

They had laid out my father in his glen-check jacket (it was well padded – he no longer filled it). A red rose pierced the lapel, a silk ascot concealed the withered neck. My mother used to wring her hands about his taste for natty clothes they couldn't afford, but through it all she had cherished his style. She never wanted to marry an ordinary man, and his clothes had announced him as extraordinary. I thought of the poem I would read at the service and knew I had made the right choice. My father embodied the poem, and that day I understood it for the first time:

> An aged man is but a paltry thing,
> A tattered coat upon a stick, unless
> Soul clap its hands and sing, and louder sing
> For every tatter in its mortal dress.

The minister was a friend from Alcoholics Anonymous. "Ashes to ashes, dust to dust," he said. We gave Max Maynard to the flames.

HAPPINESS

In a small faded office at the end of a corridor, I met a white-haired woman with skin like well-worn linen. We were meeting just in time; she was about to retire after decades of working with children whose parents drank too much. I brought a reporter's notebook and a list of questions for the magazine story I was writing. Something in her gaze unlocked my tongue. I forgot about the questions and talked about my father. At home that night I found nothing to quote in the notebook, just fragmentary musings that led nowhere. I had blown it, my most important interview for the story. How could I have let this happen?

The woman had also said something that I hadn't even bothered to write down because it wouldn't help me write the story. The last thing she said, it was the only thing I remembered: "Your father's primary illness was not alcoholism. Alcohol was what he used to take the edge off his depression. From what you've told me about his life, it probably started in childhood."

The white-haired woman kept on floating into my mind at the oddest moments. Chopping an onion, mailing an invoice, booking dinner for two, I'd think of her remark about my father.

She wouldn't stop following me, or was it the other way around? Somewhere I'd read that depression tends to run in families. If my father had been plagued by it since childhood, then maybe he had passed it on to me. Looking back, I saw the taint in every stage of my life: the trips to Mrs. Warren's roomful of useless toys, the tailspin of new motherhood, the meltdown at *Maclean's*. Sometimes despair receded but it always returned. And now it had descended on my world with the clang of a metal lid. When I left *Maclean's* and buried my father, I thought that I'd have nothing left to rage against. In fact, I had never been angrier – or felt more bereft. If this was my father's legacy, then I would be stuck with it forever. Thank goodness I was stubborn. My mother, my husband, Peter Newman – they all knew that. I would wrestle this thing, whatever it was. To speak its name, depression, was to bind myself to my father, a weak man who let alcohol wash him under.

⁕

I dreamed I was throttling a kitten with eyes like flames and claws like scimitars. The harder I squeezed, the more it fought for life, biting and kicking, its fur standing up in spikes. I smashed its head against the wall but couldn't even draw blood. The hell-kitten hissed with triumph and I woke up cringing. What kind of nut bar would dream such a thing?

Downstairs the new kitchen gleamed, freshly scoured by the cleaning lady. It had a built-in grill and cupboards that went on forever. Ben and Paul were planning an outing to a Blue Jays game. Our ginger tabby, who always got the worst of the neighbourhood cat fights, rubbed against my legs. On the radio, a chirpy voice predicted fine spring weather. My family had places to go – school, the office and the place beneath the porch where the cat, with luck, might nab a sluggish mouse. I went upstairs to an office under the eaves. From the window I could watch people scurrying to work, briefcase in hand. They had meetings to attend, budgets to prepare and out-trays to heap with flotsam from the great tide of paper that surged from desk to desk. I had a deadline to meet for my story on the children of alcoholics, and nothing would happen unless I made it happen. I worked in my sweats at what I'd always sworn never to do – my mother's work. As a freelance writer, I reduced thorny subjects to tidy, reassuring packages. I buffed away discomfiting truths, pulled consensus out of conflict. Editors told me I was good at this. But not, it seemed, as good as my mother, who made more money and got better assignments. Well, she was sixty and I was thirty-three, as she had pointed out more than once. What right did I have to complain?

The phone trilled: my mother, with news of another job I didn't want. "They're desperate for a managing editor. You could sweep in and whip them into shape."

"Thanks, but we've been through this. I'd rather write my own stories than make other people look good."

"Ah, yes, the lustre of a byline. 'Look on my works, ye mighty . . .' You know, the joy of instant experting can wear a little thin after a while. Besides, I like to picture you directing your minions. My daughter, the executive woman."

"You think I used to be an executive? Come on, it was grunt work."

"Well, you'd be a very good executive. It's something to aspire to. Why not?"

Because this is your vision, not mine, that's why. And it has a flip side, the nurturing domestic me, zipping from a triumph in the board-room, where I dispatch the corporate goblins with a wave of my pointer, to domestic magic at the fireside. Taste my hot chocolate, hear my soothing voice, see me play Monopoly as if I've been longing all day for this moment. My mother had her notion of the way things should be, guarded like the heavy silver choker that she kept in a safety deposit box and brought home to polish for special occasions. She had lent it to me for a black tie dinner, arranging the cold metal coil on my neck with practised hands. All night people admired the necklace, and each time I had said, "It's my mother's."

I always told her I was happy with my freelance career. "Happy" was a word I'd seldom used of myself, and I offered it to her like the spray of red roses that I never presented on Mother's Day. (We had tacitly agreed that Mother's Day was for her and Grandma, not for her and me; the two of us would not stoop to commercialized displays of affection.) Yet she knew I was far from happy; she just didn't know why. All winter she'd been telling me how pale I looked. My answer never varied: "Of course I'm pale! This is Canada, how am I supposed to look? We can't all go to Mexico for a month like you."

I wanted her care, I feared her control. Everything my mother knew, she felt free to judge, and I was not about to let her judge my life. She would never know that I dreamed of killing a kitten, or that my typical day looked like this:

> *Rip page one from typewriter for at least twenty-ninth time. Wastebasket: overflowing. Article: stalled.*
>
> *Wander the house, crying and drinking reheated coffee. One saving grace: nobody sees me.*
>
> *Editor calls to accept last story. Fooled her again. If she had any smarts, she'd be asking for a rewrite.*
>
> *Explode because Ben needs Bristol board and the science project's due tomorrow. Now he tells me! Oh, here I go again, dumping on my poor helpless child.*

Dinner disrupted by latest riff on same old fight. His complaint: I neglect our household because I only think about myself and my problems. My complaint: he doesn't care about my feelings, doesn't even seem to like me. If he has so little respect for me, why won't he get the hell out?

Tears in the dishwater. Only think about myself, do I? Try thinking my thoughts, Mr. Know-it-all, and see how you like it, your head scooped clean of everything you used to love so that nothing is left but what it's going to take to hold on until bedtime. You think I choose to be a bore to myself? Well, here's one choice I still have: I can choose to live. Or not.

I heard bad news about Chris: she had breast cancer. The doctor gave her three years. He didn't want to tell her but she pushed, same way she used to push Newman to do what needed to be done. Pity buzzed through the *Maclean's* network: the lost opportunities, the mastectomy, the children soon to be mother-less. Only thirty-seven! So unfair!

It was unfair, all right. If there were any justice in the world, I'd be the one with cancer because Chris loved her life and I was sick of mine. But in a way I did have cancer – cancer of the soul. And I appeared to be stuck with it. Still, there was something I could do for my friend. I could cheer her up after the mastectomy. For an hour or so I could fake a smile.

She met me that day in a yellow suit and her highest patent leather heels, as if she'd come from an important meeting instead of a sick leave. She didn't simply enter the restaurant; she claimed it for the two of us, calling, "Hello, darling!" from across the room and proceeding to regale me at full voice with over-the-top anecdotes. Her tennis serve: it had improved without that big breast in the way (she'd just clobbered her husband on the court). The nipples used in breast reconstruction: "I saw a whole boxful of them at my surgeon's office, and they're *rubber*! Now, I won't pass up a fake boob but I draw the line at a rubber nipple."

Heads were already turning at adjacent tables but Chris was just getting started. On she went to the tale of her mastectomy. "So I'm lying in the cancer ward thinking, 'Oh, poor me, I've lost my breast.' And then I hear about this poor man down the hall who had just lost his penis. Cancer of the penis! Never even heard of it, have you? Anyway, he doesn't have any visitors. It's all so terribly embarrassing, even the nurses try to stay away. So he's all alone with his wife. Who happens to be blind! Well, someone had to do something so I decided it might as well be me. And off I go down the hall with my IV pole. You know, help another person to help yourself. . . ."

I did know, of course. That's the real reason I had asked her to lunch. I knew she could summon a genuine smile. "Oh, Chris. What on earth did you say to him?"

"Easy. 'Hi, I'm Chris and I figure you could use a good laugh.' Just what he needed, trust me. I told jokes and you should have seen us all crack up – the man without a penis, the wife with her glass eyes and me without my boob. The nurses ran in to see what they were missing, it was that wild."

I laughed. Not a ladylike chuckle but a bursting, soaring guffaw that stunned me because it was mine and weeks had passed, maybe longer, since I heard that sound. My mother and my husband had essentially told me to snap out of my funk; Chris had simply blown it up with her jubilant outrageousness. Her story challenged me. With two irreparably wounded strangers, she had thumbed her nose at fate. She was reaching for happiness moment by moment, building it from the unpromising shards and leavings she found in her path.

I had always thought of happiness as freedom from trouble: no pain, no loss, no disappointment. Absence upon absence, a vast enveloping blankness. I had longed for this, but knew that it wasn't happiness. It was death and I wasn't ready. I had a reason not to die – my family would miss me, sad sack that I was – but that's not the same thing as a reason to live. Since I was going to be around for a while, I would have to change what had passed for my life.

⁓◦◦⁓

No one knew I was phoning the women's mental health clinic. I took a deep breath and then couldn't speak fast enough. *I can't go on like this, how soon can I come in?* Dr. Madeline Lipman, the clinic's director, would see me herself. I remembered meeting her before, safe behind my reporter's notebook. She had the stern demeanour of a professor known all over campus for marking hard. Now she was going to mark my life.

I offered up a theory. "It's my marriage. I wanted something better than my mother had, and I've chosen a different kind of screw-up. It's killing me. I need to leave and start over, but I don't have the courage."

Half the women I knew were leaving their husbands. Their post-divorce fridges held concoctions those men wouldn't eat (spicy eggplant, noodles in exotic sauces); their bedrooms were wall-to-wall Laura Ashley. Divorce had become the new badge of freedom, like the European backpacking trip of my student days. I'd missed the footloose travel while nursing a baby, and now I was sidelined again. All my own fault, of course.

I told Dr. Lipman about leaving Paul when my parents broke up, how I'd made a decision and lost my nerve.

Her eyes narrowed. "Women keep telling me that their marriage is the problem. Abuse aside, they're usually mistaken. More often the problem is their mother. You didn't go home to escape your marriage, Rona. You went home because your mother needed you."

"What are you saying? My father was a drunk, my husband doesn't listen to me, and you're pointing the finger at my mother? All my life she's been the one person I could depend on. Without her my father would have lost his job and crashed the car. And you're telling me she's the problem! My mother's an extraordinary woman. She's had a hell of a lot to overcome but you should see her now. She's funny and gutsy and she loves her life." How could I describe her to this hectoring spoilsport who surely didn't have a hat collection, let alone a sex room in her basement?

Dr. Lipman handed me a Kleenex. "Hmmm. We've been talking about you and your life for a good while now, and it's your *mother's* life that makes you cry. We need to explore this."

"You're letting my father off the hook. Why are you picking on my mother?"

"She chose him. Nobody forced her. If your father hadn't been a depressed alcoholic, he could have diluted her impact on you. We need to reorganize here." She might as well have been judging the state of my lingerie drawer. "I'm afraid we're out of time. I'll see you next week."

What kind of psychiatry was this? And from the doyenne of a women's clinic, of all people? I thought mother-bashing was strictly for old-guard male shrinks who still rambled on about penis envy. "Reorganize," indeed!

I came back next week and the week after that. My antipathy for Dr. Lipman mattered less than the ambition she had kindled. I wanted to ace her course.

⟞⟐⟝

My mother called on the point of tears. "I just got off the phone with Joyce. Oh, life is complicated! She is truly frantic. Things are grim with her and Steve. I think she's eating to comfort herself. I can't bear to think of her, puffy and miserable."

"How do you know what she's eating? Or that she's puffy and miserable? You probably just got her at a bad moment. I talked to her just the other day and she sounded positively chipper."

"If wishes were horses, then beggars could ride. I know her voice better than I know my own. And I know the sound of her anguish."

My sister and her family were living in the New Hampshire countryside, in a picture-book colonial house with woods and a meadow. Of course she and Steve had fights (doesn't every couple?). They also had good times that my mother never talked about. For her and Joyce, every moment seemed to be a bad one, which she later replayed for me in a quivering melody of grief that nobody else could draw from her. The only way to rid my brain of that keening was to phone Joyce myself and then report better news to our mother – a ritual that always left me drained and seething with a grievance that had no name. If she had loved my sister more than me, I could have charged my mother with favouritism. In fact, she loved my sister differently, with a heat fuelled by her sense of loss for the adoring, pliable little girl Joyce had been years ago. Their drama had a way of obliterating or subjugating every- thing else, including my presence. In their orbit I felt like a spectator at a funeral for a living person. Enough of that! I said to my mother, "This is between you and Joyce. I can't carry messages between you anymore. Surely you can tell someone else what's troubling you."

Stunned silence at the end of the line. Then a cry of bewilderment. "But who would I tell? Who?"

—⦿—

Dr. Lipman was pleased with me. She actually smiled, looking almost tender. But she didn't solve the riddle I had put to her. Why would a woman with a multitude of friends – loving, loyal, admiring – be at a loss for a sympathetic ear? "You are not her friend. You're her daughter and you've tried to be a good one. You've followed the rules as she defined them. Now you're changing the rules. To your credit, you've started with the toughest of the lot – the rule that you must never let her down. Of course she'll resist. She'll do everything in her power to make sure you keep on taking care of her."

"Hey, this is my *mother* you're talking about. The one who took care of me."

"We'd better take a look at your notion of care. When your mother skipped your high school graduation to go to Mexico, was that care?"

"She had to get a deal on a flight. She knew I hated that school anyway. It didn't matter."

"To save a few dollars, she missed a rite of passage in your life. It *does* matter, Rona. Then she tried to miss an even more important passage, your wedding. There's a pattern here. The daughter is supposed to leave the mother and make her own life. In your family there's a different rule. In your family the mother leaves the daughter."

"But my mother is not a bad person, she's not!" Was a grown-up saying this, or a little girl? When other kids said cruel things about my mother – *your mother talks funny, your mother is stuck-up* – I had always tried to defend her.

Dr. Lipman didn't understand, any more than the other kids had. She assumed her lecturer's pose – pen uplifted, eyes fixed on some distant point where imaginary slackers were passing notes and giggling. "Your mother is both good and bad, the human condition. The great childhood taboo is admitting that one's parents are capable of hurtful things. It's such a threatening fact of life that the Brothers Grimm had to disguise it when they told the story of Snow White. A coming of age story, handed down from mother to daughter and cleverly packaged to conceal the theme of maternal jealousy. The good queen gets killed off early so she doesn't have to show anything but love toward her precious little girl, Snow White. The wicked stepmother gets to let it all hang out, all that poisonous jealousy toward a daughter who's younger and prettier. It's human for a woman to want to be the fairest of them all. It's just not okay to admit it."

"This doesn't add up. My mother wanted me to have a better life than she did."

"True, but it's not the whole truth. She also didn't want to be surpassed. If you think those desires don't add up, you might want to broaden your outlook. Conflict is what separates human beings from paper dolls."

That night I remembered a story my mother told about the first time she read me "Snow White." It apparently reduced me to tears. When the wicked stepmother is punished by dancing to her death in red-hot shoes, I demanded another ending: "She didn't die, she didn't! She turned good!"

I swivelled in front of the bedroom mirror, sucking in my stomach. Too bad I couldn't do the same for my thighs. Paul watched me from the bed. He said, "No, you're not fat. You're thin and flabby. Why don't you try coming to the Y with me? Bet you'll see a difference in a month or two."

We lived around the corner from the Y, where he was already a stalwart. Nautilus, fitness class, running club . . . the whole sweaty grind. How did people do such things without boring themselves silly? How could they stand to feel their wet flesh jiggling around for all to see? I hadn't gone to a fitness class since I threw away my loathed high school gym suit, with its metal snaps like the ones on baby sleepers. I'd never learned to hit a softball, make a basket, do a somersault or swim the crawl. Willfully inept, I would daydream in the farthest corner of the outfield, running from any ball that came my way as if it were a missile aimed at the glory of my solitude. My father, a powerful swimmer, used to champion the beauty of the moving body (if it was good enough to adorn Grecian urns, it ought to be good enough for me). But I didn't listen to him; I listened to my mother. If she had always been picked last for teams, why should I set my sights any higher? My mother didn't see any beauty in her body. She wore her tubular shifts like armour, concealing her soft, clear skin to the neck. Dressing in front of me, she always hunched her shoulders in embarrassment. I would have called her lush. The word she chose was fat.

She said it didn't matter. (Does anyone care if Shakespeare had a six-pack?) But it clearly did matter that she wore a size twelve after weeks of near-starvation on the *McCall's* Miracle Diet. It mattered even though Grandma – the family beauty, so my mother claimed – wore a size twenty-two and a half.

Grandma naked was an awe-inspiring sight, her flesh cascading in puckery folds until she laced it into a brocade contraption that encased her entire torso. "I have Grandma's thighs," my mother said. "You've got them, too. Legs built for hard work in a hard place." Why had I ever believed her? Paul was right: I was thin and flabby. At thirty-six, I could change that.

I joined the Y with gritted teeth. A month or two later, I did look different. Soon the Y became what my office at *Flare* used to be, a laboratory for the creation of a new self: chiselled arms, flat belly, thighs of steel and velvet. In a wall of mirrors I observed my progress. My reflection lured me to the gym and held me there longer and longer, an image not beautiful but pleasing. I would be vain, by God. I would yield to an ecstasy of vanity. I had found no other corrective to my mother's message.

I bought a new dress with no sleeves and a form-fitting cut. I wore it to a cocktail reception where I immediately spotted my mother from afar. Who else would have come in a Mexican hat, trailing ribbons in carnival colours? In the village where she found it, such hats were worn only by men, and only once a year, during a festival that she witnessed while haggling for pottery. The men tore up and down the one mud street on horseback, full of liquor and machismo, with their ribbons flying. My mother told the astounded potter, a scrawny woman nursing a baby, that she couldn't leave the village without one of those hats. It became her favourite, worn with mischievous pride, as if her possession of this trophy was a covert stand against injustice. But I still flinched at the sight of the beribboned hat, which made her look like an aging schoolgirl. Glass in hand, she parted the crowd to give me a one-armed embrace: "Well, look at you! My most startling accomplishment is that I somehow produced a thin child!"

I was thin, all right – and no longer flabby. Two-hour workouts at the Y had given me the lean, hard thighs of an athlete. Sometimes after one last set on the adductor machine, I would return to the locker room just in time to see the place fill with the Korean women who arrived en masse one night a week. The Koreans didn't come to the Y to sculpt their flesh. They came in pairs to socialize and groom each other. A young woman would kneel in the shower at the feet of an older one, who appeared to be her mother, and vigorously brush every inch of her skin. Then the two would change places. The women had soft Degas bodies, wide-hipped and pink from the steam. They didn't seem to mind my watching them, nor could they have guessed that I wished I too could be crouching under the spray with a wooden-handled brush in my hand, buffing the broad peasant legs of my mother.

⎯⦿⎯

It was parent-teacher night at Ben's school and I would face the interview alone. I dressed to meet the teacher as if I were the one being marked: high-necked blouse, ankle-grazing skirt. All I needed was the right piece of jewellery, something steeped in old-world gentility. My funky silver pieces would never do. Then I thought of the antique diamond pin – the gold crescent with the nestling bud – that had been sitting untouched in its box ever since my mother gave it to me. She had warned me to fix the clasp before wearing the pin. But why wait, when the pin belonged at my throat?

"Your son isn't working to potential," said the teacher. On the subway ride home, I made plans to hire a tutor. I was about to share the news with Paul when my hand brushed my neckline. No diamond pin.

I retraced my steps, running to the subway station through the first snowfall of the season. If the pin had fallen on the sidewalk, I'd never find it now. It didn't turn up on the subway platform, and none of the teachers had seen it. If only I'd brought a flashlight, if only I hadn't been so careless with my mother's treasure. At midnight, weeping, I gave it up for lost.

"We'll buy you another pin," Paul said. "Let's make an outing of it, maybe go to a movie. How about this weekend?" I pictured the two of us choosing something more my style, a bold swirl of silver. It must be for the best that I had lost my mother's pin.

First thing next morning, someone phoned from the school. Good news, she said. The diamond pin had turned up in a janitor's dustpan. It was waiting for me in the principal's office. That day I had the clasp repaired, and then I tucked my mother's gift in its box. I thought I might give it to a little girl some day, but the right girl never came along. She never will during my lifetime. For better and worse, the pin belongs to me.

RHUBARB

The only plant I couldn't kill was rhubarb. It grew wild at the bottom of our backyard. Every spring I would monitor the progress of my crop, from the first shoots piercing the rocky soil to the tender pink stalks just big enough to fill a basket. The basket belonged to my mother, who had trained me to watch for the perfect moment. She had no use for late rhubarb – too fibrous, she said.

It was always around Mother's Day that she came over with her basket. While she picked rhubarb, we'd share insights into mutual friends. With our views we rearranged the world: found mates for the lonely, new careers for the restless, comeback lines for the scorned and mistreated. We decided which books to read next and which brand of virgin olive oil was best. The next day she'd return with my gift – a pie still warm from her oven, the bite of the rhubarb softened by an orange-scented custard. I looked forward to that pie all year, knowing there would be only one.

My mother had learned from Grandma how to bake transcendent pies. Then she passed the secret on to Joyce – who surpassed her, according to a family friend ("but you must never tell Fredelle I said so"). I alone failed the pie-baking test, but perhaps I never wanted to do any better. If I could produce the pie of my dreams, then my mother's pies would lose their specialness. I wanted one corner of my life to be hers, and I chose the rhubarb patch. In summer, when the plants went to seed, it became a tangle of coarse, thick-veined leaves. I was growing weeds, as Paul pointed out more than once. Toxic weeds, at that: if you eat rhubarb leaves, your tongue and throat might swell until eventually you cannot breathe. Surely there was something more docile and pleasing we could grow. But I wouldn't think of ripping up the rhubarb patch. I was not about to part with my annual pie.

My mother and I had entered our best years. I liked my life; she liked hers. Something had shifted in the unseen house where our inner selves used to jostle and vie for space; I had figured out which rooms were common space and which belonged only to me. I had found it was possible to close a door without losing her. In the visible world, we both learned to walk around our hardest grievance, the matter of my mothering. Ben rode his bike between my house and hers, taking a weirdly circuitous route that led past a suburban doughnut shop where she had once enjoyed a cruller. Every time he brought her a cruller; every time she stashed the cruller in the freezer, mindful of the calories. She never threw away a cruller. Years later when I had to empty her freezer along with the rest of the house, the crullers tumbled onto the kitchen floor like hailstones.

It no longer concerned me that we did the same work. Like my mother, I wrote mainly for women's magazines, at first because the work was plentiful and helped pay the bills. I initially thought I was just marking time until stories that men would read came my way. Yet when business magazines began to call me, the work proved oddly disappointing – even cover stories that were honoured at gala dinners. Articles for women hardly ever won public recognition. But in my case they won something else, a community of readers who felt moved to thank me. "Because of your article, I left my abusive marriage." "Your article inspired me to quit my dead-end job and start a business." I never set out to change people's lives or even dared to imagine that I could. The letters told me I had more power than I knew, and they infused my work with a sense of purpose.

I spent my most rewarding days with the phone at my ear, interviewing women across the country. I'd start first thing in the morning to catch the women on the east coast before they went to work, and finish late at night, when the women out west had some quiet time after putting their kids to bed. They'd pour themselves a cup of tea and tell me things they had never told anyone. Sometimes shame had silenced them ("My family doesn't know I've had an abortion"). More often they had thought that their stories didn't matter. Did anyone care what went through Yvonne's mind as she waited for the verdict on her biopsy, or what Angie's mouthy daughter said last night? The pink slip, the twenty-year friendship, the unlikely love affair that outlasted all the dire predictions – I took it all down, the awestruck eloquence of ordinary women seeing, perhaps for the first time, the design they were creating just by living their lives. Before ending the interview, I always asked, "Is there anything you'd like to add?" I heard the clatter of a cup, the eloquent silence of a woman gathering her thoughts. Then it came to her, something she just had to know: "What did the other women say?"

I sometimes felt that all these private, separate conversations were in reality one conversation celebrated every spring when my mother and I picked rhubarb.

—◦◦◦—

My mother came for coffee on a winter afternoon when the house was empty except for the two of us. Outside falling snow blurred her footsteps and the edges of the street. We sat in a living room configured like hers: two facing loveseats and a broad bay window. My colour was dusty mauve instead of her signature green, and my window had moiré curtains instead of plants. Paul and I had decorated the room together, a stressful business involving much eye-rolling and at least one noisy fight in a lighting store. It hadn't worked that way at Maynard Hall, and my mother was recalling those days. "You were sixteen, I think. You said there wasn't a single item of furniture in the house that was Daddy's choice. It had never struck me. You asked why I wouldn't let him have the La-Z-Boy he wanted. You were quite persistent in opening wounds."

I wrote it all down in my notebook, the second one I'd fill that afternoon. *Chatelaine* had assigned me an article called "How I Made Friends with My Mother." I'd proposed this title myself, knowing even then that it wasn't quite accurate. Friends don't have the kind of history we had, but I was telling the story in my mother's tradition, the way it should have happened. That's what the magazine wanted, and what I wanted to believe. My mother said she was proud of my writing career, but her words had the sting of an unwelcome confession: "I remember to my shame that when *Chatelaine* told me they hoped you would write for them, I said, 'Oh, she couldn't. Rona writes very slowly.'"

She told me how it felt to look at the grown-up me and see

all the selves I had been. And of course there were other phantoms – the child she hoped I would be, or feared I was in danger of becoming. She recalled, "You were a toddler the first time I took you to Grandma's. You were going to be proof to my mother of something I had not proved to myself, that my marriage was working and had produced a wonderful child. I had prepped you relentlessly to recite and sing. You had a little book of pieces we'd prepared. I remember with sorrow that you were reciting and couldn't remember what came next. You ran for your book crying, 'Study! Study!' I knew I was using you, and felt bad about it. But to me feeling guilty was a normal part of life."

"Did you feel guilty that time you slapped me?" There was only that one time, her hands windmilling my face while I, four years old, kept insisting, "Didn't hurt." She couldn't land a blow with any force but her knotted brows told me that she meant to break my will. That hurt, and in the end it made me cry. I thought she had won. More than thirty years later, while the light dimmed in my living room, she told me what she lost that day. "You stood up to me, even as a little girl, and I could never stand up to my mother until I finally married Daddy. I always admired you for sticking to your guns. I've been afraid all my life of anger from people close to me, especially from my mother. Her ultimate cut used to be, 'I hope your children never do to you what you're doing to me.'"

With me the challenge was less what I did than who I was, melancholy and intense. My mother said, "I was trying to be happy, with good, happy kids who attested to the health of my household. Joyce learned early the happy family act. You were ostentatiously not like that. You made visible my pain in a way that was painful to me."

My mother shared another thing I had never heard before, and it concerned her lost teaching job. Someone had wanted to take up her cause – a reporter at a local paper. In 1949, he thought it was news that the state university should dismiss a Radcliffe Ph.D. who happened to be pregnant. She told him to back off. "I was terrified that your father would lose his job. So I said I'd resigned voluntarily to stay home with my baby."

It wasn't just other people's anger that she feared. It was her own, concealed behind her housedress and gingham apron. In 1949, a wife's ambition came a distant second to her husband's standing. A man without a paycheque was no man at all, and a family without a male head was no one's idea of a family. I mulled this over while typing my notes from the interview, and then I pushed the thought from my mind. The magazine wanted an upbeat story, a tidy progression from struggle to sweet gratitude, and that's what I delivered. With each revision, another detail fell away until my mother's voice – rueful, pungent, conflicted – was almost entirely absent.

My mother and I were sharing a hotel room in Vancouver. She reclined in the bathtub with a glass of red wine in one hand and the bottle in the other. "Pour yourself a glass. How can I toast us when you're not drinking?"

"They'll serve wine at the reception. I don't want to overdo it."

"Still the cautious one, I see. The shy little girl who hung back while the other kids played. I guess I'll have to make merry all by myself."

We were travelling together for the first time since my teens. A Max Maynard show was opening that night at the Bau-Xi

Gallery, and my mother had volunteered to speak. The invitation billed her as "Mrs. Fredelle Bruser Maynard," as if she were the grieving widow, although she'd seen my father only once between the divorce and his death two years later. At a catastrophic dinner in Toronto he had asked for another chance, and exploded when she refused ("Your mother is depraved," he later told me). Eighteen months after his death, she could put all that behind her. She dressed for the opening in a floor-length outfit she had made herself, with a high collar and sleeves like angel wings – less a gown than a robe that a priestess might wear at some exalted midnight ceremony. Speech in hand, she took the floor.

"Someone said to me the other day, 'How sad that Max did not live to see his work generally recognized and valued.' My comment, then as now, is that Max never doubted his gift. He would have enjoyed applause, but he learned early to manage without it, to rely on his own sense of direction and power. When I met Max in 1943, he announced, 'I am a genius. I am going to become the best painter in Canada.' I thought this nervy and vain. In the years that followed, I came to see that nothing less than such a conviction could have sustained him through half a century of solitary painting in attics and basements. . . ."

I had always done my best to avoid my mother's speeches. Like the set pieces she'd performed as a childhood elocutionist, they involved formal gestures, weighty pauses and compound-complex sentences. In conversation her voice danced, played and teased; at the podium it seemed to freeze as if the least hint of spontaneity could threaten her well-rehearsed command of the entire performance. I could imagine Grandma in the front row, beaming.

"When Max retired I asked the dean of liberal arts to give Max a show in the university gallery and was told that the gallery was reserved for *professional* painters. So Max's first show took place in his own home, with his daughters passing the home-baked cookies. That was when you could buy a Maynard for fifty dollars!" Laughter buzzed through the room, but my mother wasn't laughing.

"So it is with a very special satisfaction – some sadness, a lot of joy and pride – that I view the pictures here today. All of them reflect Max's delight in the natural world, his rare feeling for harmony." She swept the gallery with her hand and I saw the fingers tremble. The tremor jumped to the corners of her mouth. This was the moment when she meant to unveil the real Max Maynard to the admiring throng, but instead he seemed to be revealing himself to her, tearing a hole in her script. He had never really left, and neither I nor anyone else could drive him away – her first love and still, despite everything, the most intoxicating. Sydney had loved her as a woman and his gift to her was the freedom of her own fleshly self, but Max had loved her questing mind and what he gave her was no less than the world as great minds of the ages had imagined it. My mother paused, not for effect. "Most of these paintings are the work of a man old and ill, a man who had suffered crushing blows, yet I see them as astonishingly vigorous, a celebration of life. Let me share with you a fitting epigraph from the seventeenth-century poet George Herbert . . ."

Hundreds of poems I must have heard her quote, raising honoured dead men with her classroom voice, yet she never ran out of fresh poems. She reminded me of the bards who, in pre-literate times, used to carry in their heads the Anglo-Saxon word hoard, the treasure composed of all that was collectively known or dreamed or remembered. She did not need a script for the Herbert poem; she knew every word, or must have thought she did until her voice broke as if the wind were blowing through it.

> Who would have thought my shrivelled heart
> Could have recovered greenness? It was gone
> Quite underground, as flowers depart
> To see their mother-root when they have blown;
> Where they together
> All the hard weather
> Dead to the world, keep house unknown . . .
>
> And now in age I bud again,
> After so many deaths I live and write;
> I once more smell the dew and rain
> And relish versing. O my only light,
> It cannot be
> That I am he
> On whom thy tempests fell all night.

Our eyes met. My mother was weeping.

—◦◦◦—

"I'd like you to read what I've written about you. If you're not comfortable with it, you must let me know." The manuscript sat in my lap, a sheaf of curiosity and dread from my mother's second memoir, *The Tree of Life*. Unlike the nostalgic *Raisins and Almonds*, which had made her name, this book would disclose hard truths that could not be shared while she was Max Maynard's wife and Rona the First's reason for living.

Two years had passed since my mother sat in my living room, speaking one hard truth after another. The transcript of that conversation lay in a drawer because I couldn't forget the truths that had overflowed the boundaries of my magazine story. My mother had more experience as a writer, not to mention more space. Yet the daughter she described in her new manuscript was not the thorny rebel of our interview. She cast me as a dreamy loner, hesitant and fearful to the point of near-paralysis. The kind of girl who would want a gold crescent pin with a bud nestled inside. While I had been such a child on the surface, I didn't recognize myself. The wonder was that my mother could. What could I say? *"Write about the slap. Write about how ashamed you were of pushing me to perform for Grandma."* It's not as if I had the heart to tell such stories. Maybe they belonged in a drawer. I called my mother and told her not to change a thing.

⚬⚬⚬

I dreamed an unseen person held out her hands to me and said, "This is for you." In her palms sat a kitten like no other, its fur a shimmering rainbow of colours. Warmth radiated from the kitten in golden rays like the haloes in medieval paintings. It looked at me as if it had been waiting for my touch.

It was 1989, the year students rioted in Tiananmen Square and the Berlin Wall came down. In October I would turn forty – the age, give or take a year, when the searcher in a woman starts to batter the walls of the life she has made. My mother was pushing forty that day she drove off in a rage without cooking dinner. As a magazine writer, I'd talked with countless women who, at forty, looked around and asked themselves, "What next?" They might have lines around their eyes and a twinge or two in their joints, but they finally understood who they were, and this awakening spurred them to go back to school, launch businesses or, to everyone's amazement, marry for the first time.

So where was my own breakthrough? Nothing had shifted in
the structure of my life; it was other people who were changing.
I met my deadlines in an empty house while my husband
worked ever-longer hours and my son was making plans to leave
home for university. My former magazine colleagues were
winning promotions and looking ahead to the next big move.
Sometimes they would call me to pick my brains about
Chatelaine. "So what's happening over there? Any big changes in
the wind?"

Chatelaine was the matriarch of Canadian magazines – the
country's first, best-read and most definitive magazine for
women, handed down from mother to daughter along with the
recipe box and the family silver. Like a mother with a vast trove
of knowledge and a habit of making pronouncements, it could
inspire, in the same moment, both pride and rebellion. Mildred
Istona had kept a firm hand on the magazine since 1977, and the
consensus among the fractious daughters of the editing community was that she should give way to one of them. As a regular
freelancer for *Chatelaine*, I was presumed to have an eye on the
politics of the place but no credentials for the editor's job. Even
my old mentor Keitha McLean had designs on it. She would tell
me, "You and I could do great things with that magazine."

That I might lead *Chatelaine* myself instead of helping
someone revamp it seemed no likelier to me than it did to my
editor friends. While they were building editorial teams and
presenting strategic plans, I'd been working at my second-hand
desk, talking with women on the phone. Mildred's role in my
life compounded my sense of unreadiness: she had hired me into
the business when no one else thought I was qualified. We had
often disagreed, but never without respect, and I sometimes
found myself defending her when other journalists ran her down.

She was perhaps the least maternal woman I knew, yet I reacted to her the way I did to my mother, with a disorienting mixture of obligation, resentment and protectiveness. So I left the fray to others. Every time a piece of mine appeared in *Chatelaine*, I'd wonder why the most revealing details had been cut.

I was struggling with a magazine piece that seemed dispiritingly similar to one I'd written two years earlier when the phone rang: an acquaintance named Margaret, with an odd request. The Toronto YWCA was seeking nominations for the Woman of Distinction Awards. They had a communications category and she thought I might –

"Sure, Margaret. I know some terrific women to put forward."

"I'm not calling about them. I'm calling about you. I think you deserve this award. If you're willing, I'd like to prepare a nomination."

She didn't know me well, yet she proposed to gather testimonials on my behalf. All I had to do was provide names and phone numbers, along with a bibliography. I thought she was wasting her time, but it seemed churlish to refuse. A few weeks later, she phoned with a progress report. "I'm getting great stuff from your colleagues. They say you've opened doors for them. They're calling you a role model. And here's the best part. Several of them think you should be the editor of a major magazine some day."

I had never made such claims of myself. What held me back was not modesty but a primal fear of repeating my parents' drama. They never downplayed their belief in the superior Maynard talents, but it had proved to be a brittle shield against the world. I had stumbled on a more effective shield, the support of people who believed in me and had nothing to gain from their efforts. Emboldened, I decided to write my own nomination.

I began: "Rona Maynard has devoted most of her journalistic career to the issues that touch women's hearts and engage their curiosity. . . . She was the first magazine writer in Canada to tell a mass audience how feminist psychologists are reinterpreting Freud's oft-repeated question: 'What do women want?' . . . Her pioneering essay on the blaming of mothers for the ills of the world has been cited in at least one scholarly bibliography and reached the public several years ahead of similar efforts by journalists . . ." I was bragging, and women are not supposed to brag. But why not? I had done what I said, and then some.

I sent my package off to Margaret and then forgot all about it. My attention was elsewhere, on my mother. Back from her annual winter vacation, she couldn't find the energy to start her next project, a book on creativity in children. Her famous parties tapered off and she stopped inviting us for roast capon and Negronis. One day she called me and said in a small voice, "Something utterly bewildering has happened. I never thought it could happen to me. I have fallen into a depression."

NETS OF GOLD

I had a plan for my mother. Therapy, then exercise. She was already seeing a psychiatrist who had traced her depression to grief and worry over Joyce. With the exercise program, she would need a gentle push from me. We'd go swimming together at the Y, a little longer each time. "It'll be fun," I promised. "And it'll kick-start your endorphins. Exercise is one of the best things you can do for depression. There's loads of research to prove it."

And what kind of research would that be? Did you find this stuff about endorphins in the Index Medicus *or* Self *magazine?* If my mother had been well, she'd have asked those questions.

That February morning at the Y, she asked a child's questions: "Where do we put our clothes? Is that soap on the wall? Why is it so noisy here?" In the locker room, hair dryers growled and naked yelping toddlers raced down the aisles. A clamour of shouts echoed from the showers. I began to babble: "This is my retreat, a place to unwind with other women." Not that day, certainly not for my mother. I saw what she saw, the maze of identical tiled corridors ablaze with fluorescent light. At least the pool was peaceful in the middle of the morning. My mother would be able to sidestroke up and down in her stately fashion, the water cradling her head.

That day she didn't swim lengths like everyone else. Her swimming had no pattern at all; she zigzagged crazily. I waved and caught her eye. "Mother, this is a length swim. If you follow the lines on the bottom of the pool, you won't bump into other swimmers." My mother's face was blank with bewilderment. The third time she bumped into someone, I led her out of the pool.

I hadn't gone swimming with her since my childhood, when she would sit by herself on the sparse grass at the town pool, tugging the skirt of her swimsuit over her thighs, while I pretended not to know her. She read John Updike; other mothers listened to transistor radios. One August afternoon in 1962, I came out of the pool to find my mother hugging her knees, her eyes shining with tears. "Oh, Rona. You missed a news flash. Marilyn Monroe is dead." Marilyn had just appeared in a *Life* magazine interview, with mussed hair and a look of intractable weariness, reflecting on the dark side of fame. She had talked about secrets she couldn't share, except through her acting; about everybody wanting a piece of her. Perhaps the two women were not as different as they seemed, the luscious blonde whose body every man was said to want and the tart-tongued writer whose body didn't appeal even to her husband. My mother's expression that day was charged with unrelenting aloneness. Nearly twenty-seven years later, at a different pool in a different place, aloneness had transformed her again. But this time I sensed that it was more than the world that was receding from my mother. The harder loss was herself.

⋅⟨⟩⋅

I phoned my mother's GP, whose name had often come up since this malady set in. The doctor was a woman named Ellen who had two young children and treated her patients like friends. "We need to talk about my mother. I'm worried." Out spilled the story of the trip to the Y. "You should have seen her in the pool. She had no idea what she was doing."

"Hold on now, Rona. Didn't you say your mother's never tried to swim lengths before?"

"Yes, but she didn't even grasp the idea of swimming lengths. For a woman as brilliant as my mother to be flummoxed by a swimming pool is just not normal. And she's terribly anxious about her memory. There's a history of Alzheimer's in her family. Her father had it and her sister, too."

"Your mom and I have talked about that. It's natural for her to be anxious. The thing is, memory problems are entirely consistent with depression. And with her family history, she's going to overthink. But let's face it, Rona, past a certain age, we've all got a few memory problems. Can you honestly tell me that you never walk into a room and then can't remember why you're there?"

Consistent with depression. But what if depression was not the problem? I knew depression from the inside, and I knew it didn't look like this. My mother was being erased, that was the problem. How long had it been since she quoted a poem? When other people would say, "Time's a-wasting," my mother might say, if she trusted you to catch her allusion to Louis MacNeice's "The Sunlight in the Garden" (and maybe even if she didn't), "We cannot cage the minute within its nets of gold."

That was then. This was a blurred facsimile of now.

--◦⊙⊚⊙◦--

"We need to talk about your mother." The first person to say it was a friend who'd just taken my mother out to lunch. "Fredelle walked out of the restaurant and didn't seem to know where she was. I had to walk her to the subway station. My father-in-law is a doctor; he thinks this could be serious."

The next friend had just hosted my mother and Sydney for a Passover *seder*. "Your mother took a plate of food that was meant for the whole table and dumped it all onto her own plate. When she read aloud from the Haggadah, she read in gibberish. She had no idea what she was doing. It was painful to see. Some of my guests were so disturbed, they had to leave the table."

It was April 1989. Rhubarb sprouted in my backyard, but I didn't tell my mother. In May I sat down to write her a letter. Unlike all the other letters I'd sent her, this one would not cross a border or an ocean, heavy with news about my doings. I'd written those letters missing her, and this letter was freighted with awareness of the permanent missing to come. It was a Mother's Day letter, the first I'd ever written. On Mother's Day I would be in the Bahamas, working on a travel story. She and I never spent Mother's Day together but this year something compelled me to honour the date.

I took the streetcar across town to deliver the letter. My mother came to the door in her apron, a wooden spoon in her hand and toast crumbs on her sweater. She said, "Something strange has come over me. I was going to make macaroni and cheese, but I can't remember how."

"Let me do it," I said. As if by cooking macaroni I could set the earth back on its axis. The kitchen smelled of burnt flour and the milk had turned. I opened the fridge to find only the motley remnants of food: a cheese rind, turning blue, a couple of shrivelled lemons and a carton of eggs, well past their best-before date. "What are you eating when Sydney's not here? We need to go shopping right now, to get your strength up. No wonder you can't remember things. You're not getting the proper nutrients."

That day I stocked her fridge with food she wouldn't have to cook, cheeses and ready-made salads. On her counter I placed a loaf of whole-grain bread. I filled the fruit bowl with oranges, and then I remembered the letter. At my mother's kitchen table I read it aloud while she looked at me, wonderingly.

Dear Mother,

When I was little, I watched you lace a stew with mushrooms and wine. You taught me that a meal should nourish the spirit as well as the body.

When I still saw my future as a haze of ballet tutus, wedding veils and long-stemmed roses, I watched your world expand as you began to teach and write. You taught me that a woman needs a career suited to her talents.

When I was struggling to build my marriage, I watched you end your own failed marriage and start a new relationship. You taught me that it's never too late for a woman to strive for mutuality and respect in love.

This Mother's Day weekend, you are teaching me still — about dignity in the face of adversity, about faith in the sustaining powers of friendship and family ties, about the courage to fight for what makes life worth living. I am proud to have your example before me.

All my love,

Rona

On Mother's Day I went swimming alone in Eleuthera. It was night, no sound but the surf. I stepped out of my white beach house in the palms and threw myself in the waves. I could have screamed at the moon. I could have been naked. I could have shredded my clothes like mourners in other times and places. No one would have seen or heard.

Instead of swimming, I let the waves carry me and swallow my tears. At last I knew for sure what I had feared all winter. Today's call from Toronto had simply confirmed it. My mother had fallen on the stairs at night. When Sydney rushed her to the hospital, the doctors ran a battery of tests. They found a brain tumour. Inoperable. Nothing to offer her but palliative care. She was sixty-six years old and I'd been betting on her to reach one hundred. My mother was dying.

❧

My mother's kitchen opened onto a narrow garden where geraniums spilled from Mexican planters in all manner of fanciful shapes. She'd haggled for those planters in dusty villages unknown to other tourists, always shipping back too many. If the bird shattered on the journey, she would still have the goat and the mermaid. And the maidens, a whole retinue of them, with broad Mayan faces and flower-encrusted gowns. In the first weeks after her diagnosis, while steroid drugs could still moderate her symptoms and seemingly roll back the months of her unmaking, she liked to sit among her maidens, as brown as the pottery and as still. I had never known my mother to do nothing, not even flip through a magazine, but this new gravity became her. It let me believe she could sit there forever in her silver necklace and straw sunhat, waiting for her next visitor. When I joined her she would say what she had never said in better days: "You always look so beautiful."

Friends came from all over the continent; Joyce had brought her three children. There was always a delivery at the door, a well-wisher on the phone, one of Joyce's poppyseed cakes in the oven. Letters came from students last seen decades ago – among them David Thurston, the gay boyfriend-substitute my mother had found for me in high school. David had been teaching English at Harvard. Although he didn't say so in the letter, he was in the final stages of AIDS. He wrote with a tenderness and grace that dissolved the last remnants of my rage at him for spurning me in the woods. Little faggot, that's what he'd been to me. Now a different word came to mind. Grandma's word: a *mensch.*

The neurologist had warned, "Anyone who wants to have a conversation with Fredelle should do it in the next two weeks." But four weeks passed, then five, and still my mother held court in the garden between her impenetrable naps. I didn't notice the naps growing longer, any more than I noticed tulips giving way to roses that summer when nothing seemed to catch my attention except my mother and her illness. I put my work on hold to spend every afternoon in my mother's garden, stopping on the way to comb the shops for perfect raspberries, her favourite fruit. It was as if, by giving up my own brain, I could somehow restore hers. Meanwhile my mother seemed unshakeably serene, even blithe.

She finally knew what she had and thank God it wasn't Alzheimer's. "I've had a good life," she said to all and sundry. "I would have liked more time but *nisht is nisht.*"

Fredelle, do you have any regrets in life?

"Just one. I would have liked more men!"

Oh, Fredelle, you devil.

She ate whatever she wanted: big wedges of runny Brie, second helpings of cake with whipped cream. Why not, since she'd never wear a swimsuit again? She said whatever came to her mind, whether charmingly addled (to Joyce and me: "You girls are my greatest trousers") or flagrantly mischievous (to everyone: "How many lovers have you had?"). She embarked on her death as a grand project on which she would lavish all the exuberance of the decades that should have been hers. At the end of May she convened a few dozen intimates and admirers for a garden wedding. With her glass of Chardonnay held high, she walked through the geraniums on Ben's arm: Sydney had finally proposed after years of resistance to the very thought of marriage. On her way to the *chuppa* she called out greetings (to her gay friends: "I wish I could marry both of you, but you're already married to each other!"). She wobbled on her feet but I could have sworn it was only from the giddiness of her pleasure in finding, at the far edge of life, what she couldn't have in the thick of it. Sydney smashed a glass with his foot as the rabbi wished long life to the bridal couple. "Would it were so!" said my mother. Sunlight spilled everywhere – on the clinking glasses of the guests, on the froth of red blossoms, on my mother's iridescent silk dress that was either purple or blue, I could never tell which. My mother laughed. I held my breath, and the moment.

⌁⊙⌁

That last summer was a season of rituals, with a ceremony for each of us. My sister pushed the wheelchair and prepared the breakfast tray, always with a flower from the garden. My mother sent a farewell letter to everyone she loved. When her pen began to falter in her hand, I would take dictation in the garden. Her custom-made stationery came in three colours – hot pink, purple, lime green – and had a border of frolicking figures, drawn by Joyce in pen and ink. The effect suggested celebration, and the messages delivered on that promise. The fewer words my mother remembered, the more lavishly she poured her affection on the world: "You and I have been part of each other for long, complicated, amazing, happy years." "Dear Frances, dear Frances, you are deeply dear to my life." Everyone got a letter – friends just met and friends long lost. For Ben my mother dictated, "I send no message, no list of things to do, no prediction of your future, no estimate of your talent. What I send, deep and true, is love."

Just the words I wished my mother could choose for me. Lists, predictions, estimations of talent . . . plenty of those used to come my way in single-spaced pages from her ever-clacking typewriter. As I sealed the envelope, she said, "I'm going to miss Ben. He's sensitive, strong and funny. A really beautiful man."

"Boy, you mean. He's only seventeen."

"No, he's a man now. Soon he'll be falling in love, leaving home. Making some woman happy."

She did not tell me I had been a good enough mother after all. Those were the words I most wanted from her. Even as language slipped away from her, she was crafting her message, avoiding any hint of connection between Ben's character and my mothering. She always did find a way to keep the upper hand. But if I had raised a son who would make a woman happy, then surely I had done something right.

No friend could leave the garden empty-handed. As each guest stood up to go, my mother would call for her jewellery box. It overflowed with bounty from her travels: pendants and chokers, bangles and cuffs, earrings feathered with fake-gold filigree or inlaid with amethyst and turquoise. My mother had a brooch for every mood, a ring for every finger. She decreed to each guest: "You must have something of mine. Your choice." Everyone picked something modest until my mother commanded, "Pick again." After a few weeks of this, the pickings grew thin. A friend from New York took the last silver chain in the box, leaving a tangle of lone earrings that had lost their mates long ago. Suddenly my head was in my hands and a cry rose from a subterranean cavern of myself: "Don't leave me!"

My mother took both my hands. Her touch steadied me the way it used to do when I woke in the night with a fever. "I'm not leaving you. I'll always be with you. Just think of me. It's enough." She drained the last of her wine. "*L'chaim*," she said. To life.

When I was pregnant, women tried to prepare me for motherhood. I had no idea how my life would change, said every woman who had been there. They all hoped I would remember, in the sleepless nights ahead, that they too had once paced the floor with their arms full of helpless, thrashing misery, wondering why they couldn't comfort their babies.

In my mother's last illness, women did what they could to help me let her go. Their words enfolded me like a quilt stitched by many hands. A former colleague's mother squeezed my hand on a subway platform: "My mom passed away forty years ago and not a day goes by that I don't think of her." A friend I'd lost track of called with some advice, based on losing her mother the previous year: "When she's gone you can still talk to her about what's on your mind. You just can't expect much of an answer."

Leaves fell on my mother's pottery maidens. Pumpkins appeared on doorsteps. My mother lay immobile in her sea-glass-green bedroom with the cathedral ceiling, the room where she had chosen to die. How long had it been since she sat in her garden, since she spoke her last word, which was "love"? Doctor Ellen kept saying the end would come soon, in a few days, maybe a week. What I knew was this: my mother had already left, along with nearly everyone else. A few old friends sat with Sydney in the living room, murmuring and shaking their heads while the hired nurse of the moment bustled soundlessly. My sister and her children were back home in New Hampshire, which really wasn't home anymore. Her marriage was ending. It had been in grave trouble for years, as my mother sensed despite my assurances that everything was fine at the picture-book house. I didn't know my sister much better than she had known hers, or perhaps I just wanted to shield myself from the anguish that Joyce alone could inspire in the woman who formed us. I had enough anguish in my life. A few minutes at my mother's bedside was all I could stand before retreating to the kitchen.

I always hoped to find Esther there, making tea. Esther was the Jewish nurse who came to work in Birkenstocks and jeans, her wild grey curls still damp from the shower. She looked like someone my mother could have met at a book signing or a neighbourhood garden tour, so comfortingly everyday that I could almost forget how she entered my life. One dark afternoon she said, "Your mother's a special lady. It's a real pleasure taking care of her."

Special? You should have met her when she could feed herself without dribbling puréed vegetables down her chin. When she could tell stories that would crack you up. When her head resounded with poetry instead of nothing at all. "My mother used to be an extraordinary woman. I'm sorry you never got a chance to know her."

Esther passed me a teacup – Rosenthal china, not one of the earthenware mugs I always picked. "I can tell a lot about a person by how they respond when I lift them. Some people fight me; the special ones help me. They have a way of moving with me so the work goes easier. That's what your mother does. I know it's tough to see the changes in your mother. SBut in my line of work, you just meet people where they are today. And you find there really is somebody there, right up until the end."

⟿⟾

I felt like an actress without a script, but there is no script to guide a woman through the loss of her mother. Like my mother and her mother, like my many times great-great grandmothers going back to the very first, I would have to improvise. *Zoll zeyn*, as Grandma would have said. So be it.

Grandma used to tell a story about the death of her mother, Freidel. "Not a day goes by that I don't think of her," she always said of the woman who had fed her on table scraps and called her Ugliness. Freidel lay dying in Winnipeg while Rona the First, nine months pregnant somewhere on the prairies, could not go to her. A blizzard had shut down the village, half-burying the family store. The only thing Rona could do for her mother was weep and send *sucherlach*, the cinnamon rusks that she baked better than anyone. When she gave birth to her first living child, she feared she would lose this one, too: the baby, Celia, was sickly and slow

225

to nurse. Several days passed before Rona found the strength to get out of bed and make *sucherlach*. My grandfather stopped her at the kitchen door. "Your mother died yesterday," he said.

This happened in 1919. Sixty years later, my mother sat by Grandma's bedside at the Misericordia hospital in Winnipeg, a notebook on her lap and a tape recorder on the nightstand. Grandma was dying of pancreatic cancer – her skin yellow from jaundice, her hair lank and thin. The nurse had taken her teeth away, an indignity she never would have tolerated if she had any strength to complain. My mother murmured reassurance into the microphone: "You still laugh, your eyes still sparkle."

The whites of my grandmother's eyes had turned brown. She lay moaning, except when pain left her breathless. Her speaking voice was wind in dry grass, except when she spoke of her mother. Then she cried out, "Why does she hate me? Why does she think I'm ugly? How can a mother be so mean?"

It was April 1979, a month before the birthday that Grandma never saw. She would have been eighty-seven. My mother was almost fifty-seven. Every day she went to see Grandma at the Misericordia ("the Misery," they called it); every night she slept fitfully, dreaming of her mother. When she could not sleep, she wrote in her notebook, thinking ahead to her next memoir. On the last day, April 29, my grandmother began to heave. My mother's notebook describes the scene this way:

> I put my arms tight around her and sing, first
> "Rozinkes mit Mandlen," a lullaby, and then . . .
> my father's courting song. I am not sure why I am
> doing this, singing off key, except that I want
> swiftly to summon my father's image. At last,
> knowing it will not cost too much now, she will

never cash this promissory note, I say in her ear, "My lovely mother. My clever mother. My generous, loyal mother. My competent mother. My charming mother. My witty mother. My remarkable mother. I love you, Mother." She speaks for the last time, faint but precise: "Thank you, dear."

The decline and death of Rona the First inspired a chapter in my mother's last book, *The Tree of Life*. She struggled to write it, sending her editor a mystifying sheaf of typo-ridden bits and pieces that bore no resemblance to her usual tidy drafts. The finished chapter omits what she said to her mother at the end. Also missing is my grandmother's question, "Why does she hate me?" In the midst of expressing a lifetime and a half's worth of unsaid truths, my mother backed off. She shoved the tape and the unpublished pages into a drawer. After she died, I sent them to her archive at the University of Manitoba, along with all the other remnants of her life that I was too sorrowful and weary to consider. By the time I felt ready for that, I was almost fifty-seven, the same age my mother had been when she buried Rona the First. At a desk in the archives, I played the tape on a September afternoon. I listened to the intertwined voices – one straining for cheer, the other fading away – and could almost hear my own goodbye to my mother, as if we were three women singing in spontaneous harmony. I looked out at the still-green campus where my parents had fallen in love and began to cry.

—◦◦◦—

The last things I said to my mother were like a meditation. They came to me unbidden, with the heft of conviction. Embracing her had never been my style, so it seemed right that I should simply hold her hand and speak. *I have a big birthday coming up. Forty! Can you believe it's been almost forty years since Daddy brought us home from the hospital in the old Buick and the cop pulled him over for speeding? It was a day like today, cold and blustery, winter just around the corner. You knew he was terrified of being a father. And knowing that, you must have been terrified yourself. Today a woman in your situation would not hold on the way you did. Not as long, anyway. She'd have a career, she'd have options. She'd have friends who knew what she was facing and would cheer her on. It wouldn't be easy for her to tell the truth about her life. But at least it would be possible. Sometimes I think of the life you led in the years of silence, and a wave of sadness rolls over me. Other times I've raged at your attempts to save me from a life like yours. But you've given me everything I need to live my life my way and I'll never stop being grateful . . .*

As I spoke the room grew dark and the front door clicked downstairs: Esther, leaving. Where had the afternoon gone? It was time to head home and lean on my husband's shoulder before starting dinner. But I couldn't tear myself away. Silence gathered around me as one word led to another and then to the declaration, "I'd like to be the editor of *Chatelaine* someday."

I expected no more gifts from my mother. She had done enough, and I thought her doing was over. That was before she squeezed my hand.

INHERITANCE

My sister came to help me empty our mother's house. She was taking the Christofle silver to hand down to her daughter; the finest pottery maiden would hold court in her garden. I had neither a daughter nor a garden, but in the hall closet something caught my eye – Grandma's mink, the coat of pride and promises not quite sealed, always mentioned when our mother had a choice to let Grandma down or do her bidding. *I've got a good mink, a beautiful fur, somebody can wear it for years.* Somebody! As if anyone but Fredelle would inherit Grandma's treasure. Now it hung at the far end of the closet, keeping its distance from the lesser coats – the homely muskrat, the raincoat in all-purpose black, the jacket with the missing button. I touched the silky pelt and tried to look noncommittal. If Joyce detected my lust for the mink, she might decide she wanted it, too. She said, "Why don't you try it on?"

I slipped the coat over my shoulders and pulled the collar up to my chin. Pivoting in front of the mirror, I wrapped its dark softness around me like the mantle of a queen. I had never worn mink before, and this one was a storied mink. Our mother used to say that when she wore it to the opera strangers would lavish her with compliments. So what if it was big enough for three of me and an odd length, neither coat nor jacket? "You could have it recut," Joyce said. "They can do anything these days with fur."

I went home with the royal robe. Queen Rona the Second.

Rona the First had strong convictions about mink coats. If you owned one, you had arrived. No other fur would do, and a woman should wait for her moment. For her it didn't come until age sixty-one, a celebration of the retirement that was supposed to bring her a husband's unbroken companionship but instead brought decades of caring for the husk of him. On her deathbed she sized up my mother's new muskrat and said, "You bought a fur coat. I thought you'd wait for my mink."

My mother had her own views on mink. To her it was a bourgeois trophy, like Reader's Digest condensed books and wall-to-wall broadloom. Grandma took such things to be marks of discernment, but then she was a *shtetl*-born immigrant. When the mink finally came to my mother, she left it in her closet to proclaim its distinction behind closed doors. Her mother's mink might as well have been alive, baring its teeth, the way she avoided the thing. Still, she wasn't one to let a good coat go to waste. The first time she wore it, she put her hands in the pockets and drew out a torn envelope on which Grandma had scribbled her widow's shopping list: bread, oranges, milk.

When my turn came to wear the mink, I took it to a furrier and laid out my plan. "I'd like a jacket with cuffed sleeves. Something with a swing to it. A high collar would be nice. How much?"

The furrier sighed. "Figure thirteen hundred dollars, give or take. For that kind of money, you might as well buy a new mink."

"I don't want a new mink. This one's a family heirloom."

The furrier ran his hands over Grandma's mink as if insects were nesting in it. He didn't call it a *schmatte*, not quite. "Look, I gotta tell you, this coat's in rough shape. Whoever left it to you didn't store it right. Feel how dry it is. No offence, but it wasn't much of a coat to begin with. You've got male skins here; female skins are what you want. You're wasting your money to repair this thing."

If there was anything Grandma and my mother couldn't bear, it was throwing good money away. All right, then, I would wear the mink just as it was, for making entrances at parties. In the dark, who would notice the state of the skins? I would conjure the illusion of majesty. It had always been more talisman than garment. At that point in time, a talisman was just what I needed.

I was preparing for the kind of moment that neither Grandma nor my mother had seen – nor Lily Maynard, the hellfire-breathing preacher whose pulpit was the breakfast table. As women in less enlightened times, they all lost out on work that complemented their drive and ambition. They differed vastly in their views of the world, yet they shared a bitter knowledge of their predetermined place in it. They had all stood behind their men and thought, if only wordlessly, "I could do what he's doing, I could do it better." I had a husband who encouraged me to leave my own mark on the world, who had actually taken me to task for setting my sights too low. I had my mother's blessing to pursue what she had been denied. And I had turned forty, the age of potential. It was time to set my course toward the editor's office at *Chatelaine*.

All my life I had resisted competition. It pulled me back to childhood, the pressure to achieve while Joyce nipped at my heels. Let her win if she had to be a winner. I would be valued for who I was, not for what I did. Now there was something I fervently wanted to do, and to do it I would have to compete with other gifted women. Several had gone to work at *Chatelaine* in the not-unreasonable hope of succeeding Mildred Istona when she stepped down. As luck would have it, their timing was off. I was not the only woman capable of editing *Chatelaine*, but I intended to be well positioned when the moment finally arrived.

In January, 1993, I took a second-tier job at *Chatelaine*. The magazine had always been a matriarchal place in which, with few exceptions, the editor rose from the ranks like a daughter moving to the head of the table. On my bulletin board I kept a poem by Emily Dickinson. It wasn't one my mother had quoted. I had found it on my own years before and returned to it often, drawn by the theme of a woman discovering her powers and summoning the resolve to go where they take her. Sometimes I'd look up from a conundrum in a recipe (would that be four chicken breasts, split, or four single breasts?) to ponder the one that Emily Dickinson had posed, alone in her room, ignored by the literati of her time:

> Myself was formed – a Carpenter –
> An unpretending time
> My plane – and I, together wrought
> Before a Builder came –
>
> To measure our attainments –
> Had we the Art of Boards
> Sufficiently developed – He'd hire us
> At halves –

My tools took Human – Faces –
The Bench, where we had toiled –
Against the Man – persuaded –
We – Temples Build – I said –

I became editor of *Chatelaine* at forty-five. It was November, 1994, the year that Jacqueline Kennedy Onassis died and Israel signed a peace treaty with Jordan. Two objects made the corner office my own. One was a glass paperweight in the shape of a bird – a celebration gift from my mother's friend Beatrice, although I thought of it as coming from my mother, with Beatrice as the intermediary. The other was a file folder with a label scrawled in black Magic Marker: *McLean, Keitha*. It contained a few of her articles and the letter she'd sent when my first issue appeared in March 1995. "I see the spunk emerging," my mentor had written. She praised a daring illustration but took a dim view of some blank-eyed, haughty models. "And covers are always a long journey, no?"

Keitha had applied for my job, along with a horde of other women editors. She never stood much of a chance. I was an insider, known to long-time readers and also to the magazine's publisher, Lee Simpson. Keitha was the most suspect kind of outsider, a prodigal. Her editorship at *Flare*, *Chatelaine*'s sister magazine, had ended bitterly ("Keitha is possessed by the devil," her former boss once told me). She bounced around after that, briefly finding a mission at a short-lived magazine for a community close to her heart, people struggling with addictions. Her bid for the top job at *Chatelaine* attracted both pity and dread from people who didn't know her. A *Chatelaine* colleague came to me and said under her breath, "I hope Keitha doesn't get it. I hear she's difficult." My colleague had never seen Keitha in her fox coat and Western boots, emerging from rehab to take *Miss Chatelaine* by storm. "The best talent in this country will be fighting to get into the pages!" she had said. Now it was my turn to seek the best talent in the country. I picked up the phone and asked Keitha to lunch.

There was a lot I didn't know about running a successful magazine, and some of it would take me years to learn. But from looking over Keitha's shoulder, I had learned what is probably the most important lesson. A magazine is a relationship, to be affirmed in every issue. Words and images come and go; values do not. Readers look for integrity on the page, just as they do in their friends.

At first I liked to think of the bond between *Chatelaine* and readers as something I could create and control, but of course I was mistaken. Any magazine joins the efforts of many hands; it is scrutinized by corporate masters. *Chatelaine*, sixty-six years old at the time of my appointment, was a magazine with a lineage. It had had heroes and legends – chiefly Doris Anderson, Mildred's predecessor and an eagle in the dovecote of Cold War–era magazines for women. Doris had championed feminism so early and powerfully that she declined to excerpt *The Feminine Mystique* on the grounds that bored housewives were old news at *Chatelaine*. I did not see myself as an eagle in a dovecote, and times had changed since Doris stepped down in 1977. My task was to stand for an ever-evolving community of readers in my own style. This professional challenge both mirrored and extended the one I had faced personally as a woman descended from strong-minded women. But I wanted the blessing of my mentor.

Loping into the restaurant in jeans and a parka, Keitha looked nothing like the woman who had once worn Armani to black tie dinners. The colour in her face came from the chill outside, not from compacts with designer logos. She studied me as I filled every pause in the conversation with my vision for *Chatelaine*. "This magazine will be the meeting place where busy women can kick off their shoes and tell the untold stories of their lives the way they do among friends, when kids and husbands aren't around. We're going to capture all the grit and humour and candour of women learning from one another over a second cup of coffee. We won't hand down directives from our lofty perches in Toronto; we'll stand right beside our readers on the front lines of change. Woman-tested wisdom is going to be our signature. Because when your teenage daughter is on the street or you've just been laid off and you don't know how you'll pay the mortgage, not all the experts have a framed Ph.D. on the wall. The ultimate expert is the woman who's been there. A woman like you, Keitha. I want your voice in *Chatelaine*. You've been in some pretty tough places, but you've always found your way back. And you know how to tell the tale with insight, humour and rue." Keitha's formula for magazine copy, applied so many times that it felt like my own invention.

Keitha leaned back in her chair, her eyes shifting from me to the snow outside. What had looked like a passing squall was fast becoming a storm. "Insight, humour and rue! Yes, they're still tucked in my survival kit somewhere. Let me mull that over and get back to you. We'll talk in a couple of days." She had two dogs waiting in the van and a long drive ahead to the country home she'd bought with the proceeds of a lawsuit against an ex-lover. She called the place "*Architectural Digest* on the Rideau."

A week must have passed and I didn't hear from her. She answered the phone sounding dazed. "You'll never believe what happened. I don't quite believe it myself. I was driving home, thinking about stories I could write for you, and suddenly the van was flying through the air. I could have been killed but here I am, thanks to whatever gods there be. Must have hit a patch of black ice."

She had not hit black ice. When the headaches started, she went to the hospital for tests and was found to have a brain tumour. "I had a seizure at the wheel," she said. "But it's not as bad as it sounds. The primary cancer isn't in the brain, it's in the kidney. Statistically, that's the best place to have cancer if you're hoping for a spontaneous remission. So I could beat this thing by mobilizing my immune system."

In May, as she grew weaker, I wrote her a letter:

Dear Keitha,

These days my mental pathways keep winding back to you, whether I'm shovelling out my in-tray or walking in the park.

Ever since I've known you (and doubtless long before), you have been a seeker. You've never done anything the easy or obvious way, but you always seem to find what you're looking for – and, along the way, spark surprising, even life-changing discoveries in other people.

I used to dread writing because I knew the shame of a red pen slashing my work. I'd get so anxious about the details that I didn't dare trust my own instincts. From you, I learned that God is not in the details. What counts is saying what you mean, without apology or artifice.

There's a wonderful poem by Emily Dickinson in which she contrasts two courses through life: doing menial work for small-minded task-masters, and chucking it all to build a temple. I've always thought of you as one of those building the temple. You have been my inspiration.

Much love,

Rona

I was writing a memo when Keitha phoned to thank me for the letter. In a faraway voice, she said, "What you said about inspiration . . . it's been on my mind. You didn't use the present tense."

I'd been proud of that letter; now here she was critiquing my grammar for the first time in memory. But she had a brain tumour, after all. No wonder she wasn't herself.

"You said *I've been* your inspiration. I hope I still am."

"Oh, Keitha. You are, of course you are." I thought I'd have the chance to prove it, but time ran out. She died that summer. For the rest of my time at *Chatelaine*, I kept the file folder with her name on it.

In the beginning I loved every aspect of editing *Chatelaine*. I loved the days when everything fell into place as if aligned by forces on high, and the days when nothing went right. A long-awaited article could soar like Baryshnikov or clump on wooden shoes; the latest cover shoot could be a marvel or a botch that sent us back to square one on deadline; the vagaries of ad sales could shower us with more pages than we dared imagine or force us to gut an issue (and many months' planning); we could win an award or find ourselves the target of a boycott by some irate fringe group. And still there was no place I'd rather be than the great throbbing din of the office, where, no matter what happened or didn't, we shaped from the monthly torrent of brainwaves and false starts a magazine that mattered to women. For the first time in my corporate career, I didn't have a child at home waiting for dinner. My husband worked in the same frenetic business, just one floor away – close enough to join me for impromptu lunches, our friends liked to say, little knowing that we both had more productive ways to spend our lunch hours. Nothing stood between me and *Chatelaine*. It swept me up, a bright ocean of possibility. I liked to conclude vacations on a Saturday, so that I could spend Sunday at the office, catching up on everything I'd missed and playing CDs – Muddy Waters, Steve Earle – as loud as the spirit moved me. In the beginning this never felt like work.

The beginning of an editor's job is measured not in months but years. It takes that long to build a cohesive team, attract the essential core group of freelancers and set a consistent tone. For me there were two beginnings: the first four years, when my budget kept shrinking, and a 1999 relaunch in which an enterprising new publisher, Donna Clark, led an unprecedented corporate reinvestment in *Chatelaine*. We aimed to attract a new generation of readers, and over time we made it happen. Even at the height of our building and strategizing, when we fervently believed we were meeting our goal but hadn't yet marshalled all the numbers to prove it, I knew the time would come for me to leave *Chatelaine*, my work there completed. I knew this the same way I'd known, as a child watching the clouds during a seemingly endless summer, that the time would come to go back to school. When that time came, I knew I might resist for lack of courage or imagination. So I told Donna and all my colleagues, "This job is a ten-year commitment. Then I'll find another mission." What that mission might be, I had no idea. My focus was the mission that filled my head, overflowed my in-basket and reverberated in my dreams – building *Chatelaine*'s relationship with readers.

Once a month I cleared a day to write my monthly editorial, "Woman to Woman." It wasn't quite the column I envisioned when I first introduced myself to readers. I had planned to write from the heart about headline-worthy topics like child care and national unity. I was not about to dwell on anything so odd, so irrelevant to others, as my life. I had ceded first-person writing to my mother and sister, and to the essayists whose books crowded my shelves like honoured guests at the party of my dreams. M. F. K. Fisher, Laurie Colwin, Calvin Trillin, Andre Dubus . . . they were Writers; I was an editor. My job was to assemble the talent, not to claim centre-stage. I took pride in the writers *Chatelaine* had assembled, and I had learned from their example. From close observation of *Chatelaine*'s writers, I had seen that memorable writing demands more than insight and wordcraft. The other essential is urgency. If a writer feels no need to speak, why does anyone need to listen? I didn't feel compelled to write about national unity. But there were subjects that did compel me. I decided to explore them. Sometimes I wrote with Keitha's voice in my head.

For one of my first May issues, I wrote about Mother's Day. I wrote for all the women who no longer have a mother to receive a spray of roses or come to lunch – the sisterhood of motherless daughters:

Bereaved daughters talk about the void a friend
of mine calls "mother hunger" – the wish that a
wise older friend would adopt you, the pang of
envy at the sight of a mother and daughter
laughing together over lunch. I have a cousin
who, the first year after her mother's death,
couldn't fall asleep without hugging a pillow, and
a friend who still keeps the silk robe her dying
mother wore in the hospital a decade ago. And
in my own bottom drawer sits my mother's
flannel nightgown, which I still wear on the
coldest nights. More than six years after her
death, it takes me back to her cinnamon-scented
kitchen, where my triumphs and tragedies
achieved a sense of completion as she gave me
her perspective.

If your mother still plants trees and runs
fund-raising drives, you may wonder how much
longer you'll have her and what you'll do when
she is gone. You'll do what we all do: mourn hard
and slowly. You'll come to accept the yearning
that blindsides you when something wonderful
happens – a baby's birth, a promotion – and your
mother isn't there to share it. But don't be surprised if you find yourself breaking new ground.

I know a woman who married for the first
time, in her 50s, after the death of her sickly and
demanding mother. Then there's the longtime
homemaker who didn't seek a job until her
mother died – and is now at the top of her
profession. Such things happen because a

motherless woman need not fear her mother's disapproval or domination. Psychologically speaking, she sits at the head of the table.

When I see women my age chatting with their mothers over lunch, I wish them many more outings together. And when I hear that a woman I know has lost her mother, I do what other women did for me. I write a note, share a memory, offer whatever help I can on her path to her mother's empty house. A gift for supporting each other is part of our inheritance as women. There's no better way to honour our mothers.

I still wish my mother could have seen the response to that column. Women wrote from all over the country – letters that kept coming for years as the column passed from hand to hand. Sometimes they would ask me for a fresh copy to replace one that had disintegrated in a purse or fallen off the fridge door. Hundreds of readers must have thanked me for "Honour Our Mothers," and I thanked them all in return. They deserved no less. Their letters told me that there's nothing unusual about curling up in your late mother's nightgown. Plenty of women have done it, or resorted to some other needful quirk, like saving their mother's bifocals. My experience, which at first seemed particular and isolating, turned out to be almost universal. By telling my story in *Chatelaine*, I was affirming the importance of a largely untold story in the life of nearly every woman.

I decided to leave burning issues to the op-ed pages. What women seemed to want from me was something else – an attentive and illuminating eye on their daily dramas, so easily passed over in the frenzied rush to get the kids to school, the dog to the vet, the report to the boss's in-tray and the frozen pizza onto the table. I knew the conflicting pressures they faced because I'd answered all the letters myself, from off-the-cuff impressions e-mailed on a lunch hour to handwritten note cards with flowers on the front and family photos tucked inside.

For the most part they loved their multifaceted lives. Quite a few of them felt lucky to have so many options; they had seen their mothers chafe against the limits of the past. Yet I detected a ruefulness, a yearning to savour the moments that were rushing by in a blur. This had more than a little to do with the outmoded structure of our readers' lives – the absence of reliable daycare, employer pressure to do more with less, husbands who felt like heroes for "babysitting" their own children. The passionately hands-on fathers so beloved by the media were not exactly a fiction (by this time my own son was among them), but few of the readers who wrote to me had found such a man.

Still, external factors weren't entirely to blame for the wistful note between the lines of so many letters. On the surface these women were nothing like their mothers, yet they hadn't forgotten girlhood lessons in putting others first. How attentively they listened, and to so many people. They listened for the meaning of a baby's cry, for the nocturnal click of the teenager's key in the front-door lock, for the phone call that might be an elderly parent in need of a ride to the doctor. They'd drop everything and listen to the anxious colleague who, at five o'clock, asks for "a minute" that becomes a good half-hour. They tended not to listen to themselves.

Some observers might blame this habit on "low self-esteem." I did not. If women found no satisfaction in nurturing, if they didn't consider it hugely important and worthy of more respect than it generally receives, they would not hold fast to their traditional role while embracing so many new ones. I knew the habit well. I had lived it.

On the face of things, I wasn't much of a nurturer. The thrown-together lunches in Ben's school bag, the Halloween costumes I never made, the lectures from my mother all suggested disdain for old-school womanhood. What I really disdained was my mother's life, but in rejecting her sacrosanct duties I had found other outlets for my caretaking side. All my life I had answered my mother's call, as Dr. Lipman pointed out. At work I wrote thoughtful replies to the most venomous letters and rarely said no to end-of-day requests for "a minute." I immersed myself, from nine to whenever, in an ecstasy of listening.

I thought *Chatelaine* should be the oasis where a reader could hear herself think – the personal equivalent of green space on a buzzing city street. I believed we could do this in the time-honoured way of all humans since the days of the Bard, by telling stories that summoned the dreaming, aspiring self in every reader. Experience had taught me that a woman who knows her own mind is a woman who can make what she wishes of her life, although her path may not be obvious or easy. And so I continued to share defining moments in the making of my own life.

I wrote about the birth of my grandson, the risks and rewards I'd found in a long marriage, the Christmas angels my father had painted. I talked about my stout-hearted grandmothers and my friend Chris, who was then finding the zest to pursue a new love while in treatment for the latest recurrence of the cancer that eventually killed her. Several times I wrote about my own struggle with depression. Readers asked me to keep the stories coming. "I feel as if you're my sister," they would say. Or "I think of you as my friend." I'd never thought of myself as Everywoman. My mother raised me to believe just the opposite. "You're not like everybody else," she used to say. Many people had told me she was wrong. It was *Chatelaine* readers who convinced me.

People started to ask about a book they thought I'd written. They wanted to read it. I always said, "I've never written a book. I don't have time."

⁓◦⊚◦⁓

At work I lived in an endless future. While the rest of the world was barbecuing on the deck, we'd be shooting the story on Christmas dinner. A blizzard might shut down the city as we chose swimwear for the July issue. In the real world there was a past and things vanished into it. My grandson, once entranced by anything with wheels, now longed for electronic toys. I had turned fifty; shadows appeared in my face. I began to make sobering calculations: when my mother was this age, she had seventeen years left (or fifteen years, or twelve). The euro replaced European currencies, the Twin Towers were destroyed. The symbol of my home state, New Hampshire – a natural rock formation called the Old Man of the Mountains – crumbled overnight, just like that.

One Saturday, Paul and I came home from a vacation and a small hard awareness lodged in my brain like a pebble in my shoe. I unpacked the clothes I'd worn hiking in France, shopping in New York, or wherever it was we'd just been, and wished I could still be there. I wasn't curious to see what I'd missed at the office – not on Sunday, maybe even not on Monday morning, either. A passing ennui, I told myself. But it was still around after the next vacation, and the one after that. I no longer loved editing *Chatelaine* and I could never love it again. I had made my contribution. Now it was someone else's turn to remake what I had made there. My ten years were almost up, as ambitious female editors well knew. They were already asking, with unabashed excitement, when I might be moving on.

After the announcement, a friend called to wish me well. "So how does it feel to be giving up the biggest thing you'll ever do?"

"It feels right. What's this nonsense about never doing anything big again?"

"Look, you've got the kind of job people fantasize about. Aren't you going to miss it?"

I told her all the things I wouldn't miss. Interminable meetings, directives from on high, the air-kissing attentions of self-appointed "friends" who wanted me to find a summer job for their daughter or sell multi-thousand-dollar tables for their gala. But although I didn't say so, there was something I would miss – the love I'd invested in it all.

In ten years of black tie dinners, I had not worn Grandma's mink even once. It would have been a pretender at the ball, and in humbler places it was just plain impractical. The weight of it made my shoulders ache and kept pulling the frayed clasp apart so that winter bit my throat. Reaching into the closet for my parka I would stroke the mink from time to time. The furrier was right: those second-rate pelts had dried out long ago. Besides, I was running out of closet space. I had arrived at a time of winnowing; we had moved from our big house to a condo. I gathered up the mink with some shirts that used to be white, the boardroom pumps that pinched my feet and a power suit in an unbecoming colour. Then I took the whole load to the Goodwill drop box and pushed it through with a shiver of relief, as if I'd been waiting many years for this moment.

ACKNOWLEDGEMENTS

During my mother's final illness, my sister and I liked to sit beside her in the garden, reading aloud from the faded carbon copies of her letters to assorted friends and family. A brain tumour had whittled her vocabulary down to monosyllables, yet the letters evoked her lost conversational voice. Unlike her published work, which she always honed relentlessly before the editors saw it, the letters were written in haste while the laundry spun. They express the full range of her character – the anger alongside the loyalty, the self-doubt lurking under the gleeful irreverence.

Since my mother's death, I have reread her letters countless times, mostly just because I miss her. While writing this book, I returned to them again, this time to refresh my memories of our life together. At first I naively intended to tell our story exactly as it happened. My mother never let a few facts compromise a good yarn, but, unlike her, I intended to capture the truth and believed this would be possible. I soon found myself taking a few small liberties – telescoping here, inventing snatches of dialogue there. To my knowledge, no record exists of how my mother actually taught Shirley Jackson's "The Lottery." Her lecture in this book is my own creation, based on her feminist interpretation of a story she admired and liked to teach.

With one small exception, every character in this book corresponds to a real person. I have changed a number of names, but no one is invented. Professor Burnside is a composite based on many people who have reflected with me on art and life. I like to think that my mother would agree with his comments on the closing lines of *Paradise Lost*. But of course she would have outdone him by quoting thematic echoes from at least half a dozen other poems.

Wherever possible, I have used my mother's own words. She left a vast trove of papers, now in her archive at the University of Manitoba. This collection includes her speech at the posthumous exhibition of my father's art, some revealing unpublished fragments and the tape she made of my dying grandmother. My mother's two memoirs, *Raisins and Almonds* (Doubleday, 1972) and *The Tree of Life* (Viking, 1988) sat within arm's reach throughout my writing process.

I felt no need for exhaustive research on my mother – partly because this book is not a biography, but partly too because, as her daughter, I have been learning about her for more than half a century. Many people have contributed informally to my understanding of her, notably Sydney Bacon, Rob Dales, Beatrice Fischer, the late Joan McElroy, Joseph McElroy, Marion Mainwaring and my sister, Joyce Maynard. Joyce's perspective on the woman who formed us both, but in strikingly different ways, is a central theme in her memoir *At Home in the World* (Picador, 1998). Mildred Gutkin, who met both my parents at the University of Manitoba when she and my mother were studying there, generously answered my questions about those years in several illuminating letters. The professor who introduced my parents and inspired my mother to become a Miltonist is the subject of a biography by Sandra Djwa (*Professing English: A Life of Roy Daniells*, University of Toronto Press, 2002), in which both Fredelle and Max Maynard make vivid appearances. A former high school student of my mother's, Anne Drakopoulos, shared her impressions of Fredelle Maynard's charismatic presence in the classroom.

For insight into my grandmother and her family, I am grateful to the Winnipeg relatives who graciously hosted me on a research trip to their city: Ernie Cohen, Fraidla and David Pollick, Debby and Easton Lexier, and Marcia and Jack Raber. The Jewish Heritage Centre of Western Canada provided extensive documentation on my great-grandfather, Abraham Slobinsky (a driving force in Winnipeg's Jewish community), and a tape in which my great-uncle Jack Slobinsky recalls the family's first years in Canada. A *Chatelaine* reader who remembered one of the stores that the Brusers kept on the prairies sent me the anecdote about my grandmother selling her own dress to an admiring customer. I wish I could thank this reader by name, but I have mislaid her letter.

While pondering the formidable women in my family, I read three wise and provocative books on the psychology of women: *The New Don't Blame Mother: Mending the Mother-Daughter Relationship* by Paula J. Caplan (Routledge, 2000); *My Three Mothers and Other Passions* by my mother's friend Sophie Freud (New York University Press, 1988); and *Spinning Straw into Gold: What Fairy Tales Reveal about the Transformations in a Woman's Life* by Joan Gould (Random House, 2005).

Growing up, I knew little about my father that did not come from my mother. Through the years other voices added both light and shadow to her portrayal of him. I am particularly grateful to his niece Faith Reimer, Derek Reimer and Maxine Charlesworth, the late Jack Shadbolt and the late Fred Brand. Doris Johnston, a grade-seven student of my father's at Lampson Street School, reminisced with me over tea about those days. She was kind enough to include a fellow classmate, the late Toyo Takata, who expanded on my father's familiar story of the little girl – Toyo's sister – who was turned away from a whites-only swimming pool.

The late Gwladys Downes, whose friendship with my father spanned most of his adult life, was also close to his first wife, Evelyn. If not for Gwladys, Evelyn would be little more to me than a name and an old photograph. The snapshot I describe in this book is from the British Columbia Archives, where I also found my father's early sketchbooks and a number of other Maynard family photos.

My father's missionary parents, whom he always feared but seldom discussed except in the vaguest of generalities, came into sharper focus while I worked on this memoir. His oldest brother, Theodore, in a spirited autobiography called *The World I Saw* (The Bruce Publishing Company, 1939), traces my paternal grandparents' journey from Victorian England to a mission in southern India, and describes the ultimately tragic impact on my grandmother. Theodore's archive, in the Special Collections Division of Georgetown University Library, sheds additional light on the family. My best memory of a trip to Georgetown is the warm welcome I received from Theodore's many descendants in the Baltimore/Washington area, who had never met me before or even known of my existence. Sam Baldwin took a day off work to meet my plane and drive me around through rush-hour traffic. My first cousin Philip Maynard (who strikingly resembles my father) and his wife,

Aggie, opened their home and their photo albums to me. In honour of our shared history, I left my newfound relatives with multiple copies of Margaret Macmillan's *Women of the Raj* (Penguin Canada, 2005). This richly textured book gave me an appreciation of the hardships my grandparents faced as exiles in India, and of the wild implausibility of their hopes to convert one million natives.

I am lucky to be married to a genealogist, Paul Jones, whose research on British missionary records uncovered some fascinating references to the Maynards. At the Salvation Army International Heritage Centre in Denmark Hill, London, Paul found an article documenting Harry Maynard's arrival in Bombay with the Jubilee Fifty (Harry was the bandmaster). Letters from Harry turned up in the Methodist Missionary Society Archives at the School of Oriental and African Studies, University of London. After my grandparents joined the Plymouth Brethren, Harry filed regular reports to the Brethren's journal, *Echoes of Service*, which Paul found in the Special Collections Reading Room, John Rylands University Library of Manchester. My husband's work builds on previous work by my cousin Frank Woodward, who developed a family tree. Although few of the genealogical discoveries found their way into this book, they strengthened my commitment to the project.

I thank *Chatelaine* for granting permission to include my editorial on honouring our mothers.

The readers of *Chatelaine* convinced me that this book deserved to be written. When words failed me, I would think of the letters they wrote about my columns on my mother, and the stories they told about their own mothers. My agent, Beverley Slopen, championed the manuscript early on. I could not have found a more appropriate editor than Douglas Gibson, who edited *Raisins and Almonds* more than thirty years ago and raised a glass at my mother's wedding to Sydney Bacon.

A number of friends read portions of the manuscript while it was taking shape. For cheering me on in times of uncertainty, I thank Sally Armstrong, Sharlene Azam, Bonnie Buxton, June Callwood, Pauline Couture, Shirley Dawe, Charlotte Empey, Marla Goldstone, Anne Hines, Dianne Rinehart, Val Ross and Catherine Warren. My indispensable husband, a stickler when it comes to the fine points of writing, made helpful editorial suggestions. On top of everything else, he made me laugh.

OTHER TITLES FROM
DOUGLAS GIBSON BOOKS

PUBLISHED BY McCLELLAND & STEWART LTD.

MEMOIRS: 1939–1993 *by* Brian Mulroney
This frank book reveals the life of one of Canada's most remarkable leaders from birth in Baie-Comeau through his time in office, encountering Reagan, Thatcher, Gorbachev, Mandela, and many more.
                    Autobiography, 6 × 9, 1096 pages plus photographs, hardcover

HOT AIR: MEETING CANADA'S CLIMATE CHANGE CHALLENGE *by* Jeffrey Simpson, Mark Jaccard, and Nic Rivers
A leading journalist, a top scientist, and a noted researcher combine forces to produce a sensible "good news" account of how we can fix this problem.
          Non-fiction, 5½ × 8½ , 288 pages, charts and illustrations, hardcover

RAISIN WINE: A BOYHOOD IN A DIFFERENT MUSKOKA *by* James Bartleman
Ontario's former Lieutenant-Governor recalls growing up as a "half-breed kid" in this memoir that is full of funny stories, but is also "compelling reading." – *Globe and Mail*   *Non-fiction, 6 × 9, 272 pages, hardcover*

KING JOHN OF CANADA *by* Scott Gardiner
This savagely funny political satire foresees a Canada that is falling apart – until the winner of the "Be A Monarch Lottery" takes charge. "A Richlerian skewering." – *Toronto Star*   *Fiction, 6 × 9, 336 pages, hardcover*

THE YEARS OF FIRE *by* Yves Beauchemin, *translated by* Wayne Grady
"Charles the Bold" continues his career in east-end Montreal, through the high-school years when he encounters girls and fights the threat of arson. "One of those 'great books.' No wonder Beauchemin is considered Quebec's Balzac." – Montreal *Gazette*   *Fiction, 6 × 9, 240 pages, hardcover*

STEPHEN HARPER AND THE FUTURE OF CANADA *by* William Johnson
A serious, objective biography taking us right through Stephen Harper's early days in power. "The most important Canadian political book of the year." – *Calgary Herald*   *Biography, 6 × 9, 512 pages, trade paperback*

CHARLES THE BOLD *by* Yves Beauchemin, *translated by* Wayne Grady
An unforgettable coming-of-age story set in 1960s and 1970s east-end
Montreal, from French Canada's most popular novelist. "Truly astonishing . . .
one of the great works of Canadian literature." – Madeleine Thien
Fiction, 6 × 9, 384 pages, hardcover

WHAT IS A CANADIAN? Forty-Three Thought-Provoking Responses
edited by Irvin Studin
Forty-two prominent Canadian "sages," including Roch Carrier, John
Crosbie, Joy Kogawa, and Margaret MacMillan, provide essays beginning "A
Canadian is . . ." The result is an important book for all thinking Canadians.
Non-fiction, 6 × 9, 283 pages, hardcover

THE WAY IT WORKS: Inside Ottawa *by* Eddie Goldenberg
Chrétien's senior policy adviser from 1993 to 2003, Eddie Goldenberg gives
us this "fascinating and sometimes brutally honest look at the way the
federal government really operates." – Montreal *Gazette*
Non-fiction, 6 × 9, 408 pages, illustrations, trade paperback

THE VIEW FROM CASTLE ROCK *by* Alice Munro
The latest collection of short stories by Alice Munro is her most personal yet,
based loosely on her family history. "When reading her work it is difficult to
remember why the novel was ever invented." – *The Times* (U.K.)
Fiction, 6 × 9, 368 pages, hardcover

SAILING AWAY FROM WINTER: A Cruise from Nova Scotia to Florida and
Beyond *by* Silver Donald Cameron
"Silver Donald Cameron is a wonderful chronicler of small-boat sailors," says
Farley Mowat. Armchair travel at its best, this 3,000-mile voyage "offers an
exhilarating experience even to the most sedentary of landlubbers."
Non-fiction, 6 × 9, 376 pages, illustrations, hardcover

RIGHT SIDE UP: The Fall of Paul Martin and the Rise of Stephen Harper's
New Conservatism *by* Paul Wells
Canadian politics were turned upside-down between 2002 and 2006. "Wells
tells both sides of the story in his trademark style – bright, breezy, accessible,
irreverent and insightful." – Montreal *Gazette*
Non-fiction, 6 × 9, 336 pages, hardcover

MAGNA CUM LAUDE: How Frank Stronach Became Canada's Best-Paid
Man *by* Wayne Lilley
An unauthorized biography of Frank Stronach, the controversial man
behind the country's most famous rags to riches story. "Lilley, a versatile
business writer, has produced a judicious, balanced, lively trip through
Frank's balance sheets."– *Globe and Mail*
Biography, 6 × 9, 376 pages, hardcover

YOUNG TRUDEAU: 1919–1944 *by* Max and Monique Nemni, *translated by* William Johnson
A disturbing intellectual biography of Pierre Trudeau that exposes his pro-fascist views until 1944, completely reshaping our understanding of him. "I was extremely shocked." – Lysiane Gagnon, *Globe and Mail*
Biography, 6 × 9, 384 pages, trade paperback

STILL AT THE COTTAGE *by* Charles Gordon
The follow-up to the classic *At the Cottage*, this is an affectionate and hilarious look at cottage living. "Funny, reflective, and always insightful, this is Charles Gordon at the top of his game." – Will Ferguson
Humour, 6 × 9, 176 pages, illustrations, trade paperback

SORRY, I DON'T SPEAK FRENCH: Confronting the Canadian Crisis That Won't Go Away *by* Graham Fraser
The national bestseller that looks at how well official bilingualism is working in Canada. "It's hard to think of any writer better qualified to write about language than Mr. Fraser. . . . He is informed, balanced, judicious and experienced, and a very clear writer." – Jeffrey Simpson, *Globe and Mail*
Non-fiction, 6 × 9, 352 pages, trade paperback

CRAZY ABOUT LILI: A Novel *by* William Weintraub
The author of *City Unique* takes us back to wicked old Montreal in 1948 in this fine, funny novel, where an innocent young McGill student falls for a stripper. "Funny, farcical and thoroughly engaging." – *Globe and Mail*
Fiction, 5½ × 8½, 272 pages, trade paperback

THE QUOTABLE ROBERTSON DAVIES: The Wit and Wisdom of the Master *selected by* James Channing Shaw
More than eight hundred quotable aphorisms, opinions, and general advice for living selected from all of Davies' works. A hypnotic little book.
Non-fiction, 5¼ × 7, 160 pages, hardcover

ALICE MUNRO: Writing Her Lives. A Biography *by* Robert Thacker
The literary biography about one of the world's great authors, which shows how her life and her stories intertwine.
Non-fiction, 6½ × 9⅜, 616 pages plus photographs, hardcover

MITCHELL: The Life of W.O. Mitchell, The Years of Fame 1948–1998 *by* Barbara and Ormond Mitchell
From *Who Has Seen the Wind* on through *Jake and the Kid* and beyond, this is a fine biography of Canada's wildest – and best-loved – literary figure.
Non-fiction, 6½ × 9⅜, 488 pages plus photographs, hardcover

ROLLERCOASTER: My Hectic Years as Jean Chrétien's Diplomatic Adviser 1994–1998 *by* James K. Bartleman
"Frank and uncensored insider tales of the daily grind at the highest reaches of the Canadian government. . . . It gives the reader a front row seat of the performance of Jean Chrétien and his top officials while representing Canada abroad." – Ottawa *Hill Times*
Autobiography, 6 × 9, 376 pages, trade paperback

DAMAGE DONE BY THE STORM *by* Jack Hodgins
The author's passion for narrative glows through this wonderful collection of ten new stories that are both "powerful and challenging." – *Quill & Quire* "A splendid achievement, these stories pulse with humanity." – Alistair MacLeod   *Fiction, 5⅜ × 8⅜, 224 pages, trade paperback*

DISTANCE *by* Jack Hodgins
"Without equivocation, *Distance* is the best novel of the year, an intimate tale of fathers and sons with epic scope and mythic resonances. . . . A masterwork from one of Canada's too-little-appreciated literary giants." – *Vancouver Sun*
Fiction, 5⅜ × 8⅜, 392 pages, trade paperback

ON SIX CONTINENTS: A Life in Canada's Foreign Service 1966-2002 *by* James K. Bartleman
A hilarious, revealing look at what our diplomats actually do, by a master story-teller who is a legend in the service. "Delightful and valuable." – *Globe and Mail*   *Autobiography, 6 × 9, 272 pages, trade paperback*

RUNAWAY *by* Alice Munro
The 2004 Giller Prize–winning collection of short stories by "the best fiction writer now working in North America. . . . *Runaway* is a marvel." – *New York Times Book Review*   *Fiction, 6 × 9, 352 pages, hardcover*

TO EVERY THING THERE IS A SEASON: A Cape Breton Christmas Story *by* Alistair MacLeod, *with illustrations by* Peter Rankin
Almost every page of this beautiful little book is enriched by a perfect illustration, making this touching story of a farm family waiting for Christmas into a classic for every home. A "winsome tale of Yuletide past." – *Toronto Star*
Fiction, illustrations, 4⅝ × 7¼, 48 pages, hardcover

HERE BE DRAGONS: Telling Tales of People, Passion and Power *by* Peter C. Newman
The number one bestseller by the man whose books on politics, business, and history have sold two million copies, *Here Be Dragons* tells the story of his own life, from fleeing the Nazis as a child to editor of *Maclean's*. The *Globe and Mail* calls this autobiography "a work of genius wit and insight."
Non-fiction, 6 × 9, 744 pages plus photographs, trade paperback